THE GLOBAL ENVIRONMENT
AND WORLD POLITICS

International Relations for the Twenty-first Century

Series Editors: R. J. Barry Jones, *University of Reading*, Charles Hauss, *George Mason University*, Mary Durfee, *Michigan Technical University*

Ranging from international political economy to security, migration, human rights and the environment, this series is designed to explore the issues that make International Relations such an exciting, controversial and, at times, confusing field in a world undergoing unprecedented change.

The books are designed as core texts for advanced undergraduate and specialized graduate courses, and each volume follows a standard format. The first section is devoted to general theories and concepts. The second includes carefully selected case studies which students can use to deepen their understanding of the theoretical issues. The books include, as an integral part of the text, addresses of particularly helpful websites, and the series will also have its own website with links to internet-based resources in International Relations.

Please refer to the Continuum Website
<http://www.continuumbooks.com> for further details.

Published titles in the series

International Law and International Relations by J. Craig Barker
International Conflict Resolution by Charles Hauss

Forthcoming titles in the series

The EU Enters the Twenty-first Century by J. Michael Huelshoff
Global Migration by Joanne Van Selm
Peacekeeping: For the Next Generation by David Last

THE GLOBAL ENVIRONMENT AND WORLD POLITICS

ELIZABETH R. DeSOMBRE

continuum
LONDON · NEW YORK

Continuum

The Tower Building, 11 York Road, London, SE1 7NX
370 Lexington Avenue, New York, NY 10017–6503

First published 2002

British Library Cataloguing-in-Publication Data
A catalogue record for this book is available from the British Library.

ISBN 0–8264–5665–0 (hardback)
  0–8264–5666–9 (paperback)

Typeset by YHT Ltd, London
Printed and bound in Great Britain by Biddles Ltd. *www.biddles.co.uk*

CONTENTS

ACKNOWLEDGMENTS

In writing this book I have benefitted from the help of many, including an array of impressive students at Colby College who served as my research assistants over the years I worked on topics related to this book. These students include Kate Litle, Katie Wasik, Stephanie Graber, Carolyn Szum, and Jen Dakin. More importantly, my students at both Colby College and Wellesley College have challenged me constantly to think through how to present information on global environmental politics in a way that is both rigorous and accessible. They have also inspired me to continue working on the issues presented here, and to teach students how to think about the global environment in the hope that they may help to improve it. My colleagues, both at Colby and at Wellesley, are a source of inspiration as well, for demonstrating that excellent teaching and important research can (indeed, must) go hand-in-hand. Others, such as Linda Warwick, Jen Stiles, and Sophie and Molly, rescue me from too much work and help me to remember that a concert or a good game of fetch are necessary in the process of figuring out how to save the world.

Finally, highest thanks are due to Sammy Barkin, who reads and comments on everything I write. My ideas are better for discussing them with him, my examples are more extensive, and errors that might have been in this book are not there because of his help. I could not do what I do without his support, both practical and moral.

INTRODUCTION

Politically, the world is composed of states. International relations at its most traditional examines how states interact with one another in an anarchic world – one that does not have an overarching authority to impose political order on individual sovereign states. Environmentally, the world is made up of ecosystems. The rainforest that forms the watershed of the Amazon River stretches from Brazil to Peru and Ecuador and up through the Guyanas. The ozone layer that circles the stratosphere exists above states; the thinning of this layer over the South Pole affects states like Chile and Australia despite the fact that the main producers of ozone-depleting substances (ODSs) were in the USA and Europe.

This dissociation between ecological and political systems makes addressing environmental issues at the global level both difficult and necessary. The fact that states cannot address many environmental problems successfully on their own impels international cooperation, and there are many situations in which all parties can benefit (in the aggregate, at least) from working together to prevent or solve an environmental problem. States are also pluralistic entities, however, and, within them, some actors will benefit more or be harmed more by action taken to protect the global environment. Even in situations when all states benefit from environmental protection, some may benefit more than others, and most would benefit from taking no action at all and leaving environmental protection to others. Such is a recipe for complete inaction. States must learn – and have learned to a large extent – how to avoid this 'tragedy of the commons.'

Successful mitigation of environmental problems at any level is not easy: the geographic dissociation combines with a temporal dissociation, as politicians respond to electoral cycles that do not include the future generations that would benefit from potentially costly measures taken now to protect resources. If we add to that a multiplicity of states with their own concerns and decision-making structures and a variety of competing domestic interests, then it is indeed impressive that the dumping of the most toxic pollution into the ocean has ceased, that many ozone-depleting substances are no longer used, and that many migratory endangered species are surviving.

This volume examines the process of addressing problems that face the environment internationally. Global environmental politics is a discipline that brings together a wide variety of traditions examining the way states and other actors interact internationally. It draws from traditional international relations theory in addressing the concerns and actions of states, and in reflecting the conflict that takes place over how to protect the global environment. But it also brings in a variety of new perspectives to explain issues that are unique to, or more prominent in, environmental politics than in other international issues.

These issues are explored by considering theoretical concerns and case studies relevant to the politics of the global environment. There is no grand unified theory of global environmental politics. What exists forms something of a patchwork of different theoretical approaches and concerns. This volume explores four of these theoretical issues in depth: the process of international environmental cooperation, the relationship between environment and security, the issue of science, uncertainty and risk, and the role of non-state actors. These are not the only theoretical issues facing those who attempt to respond to global environmental problems, but they are among the most important.

Environmental cooperation is one of the most prominent and innovative forms of international cooperation. The study of this phenomenon can usefully draw from and contribute to the examination of international organization and international cooperation more broadly. Cooperation in addressing issues of the environment gives rise to some issues that are similar to those raised by international cooperation more broadly, such as the role of powerful states and the difficulty of negotiation. But international agreements have evolved a set of practices – most importantly the process of creating framework conventions to which protocols are later added when states are willing to undertake more serious regulation – which help address the issues of uncertainty and the generally multilateral nature of environmental cooperation. Similarly, issues of who has negotiating power, which states need to be brought into an international agreement, and how you determine whether the agreement is effective all take slightly different – and more complicated – forms when addressing environmental issues.

It is important to examine the expanding definition of what constitutes security in this context. Global environmental issues certainly challenge the ability of states to protect their own populations from harm through their own action alone, and also render what may once have seemed to be purely domestic actions potentially threatening to neighboring states. Examining the extent to which security frameworks appropriately describe emerging international relations relating to the environment (and vice versa) is useful for determining which approaches to understanding conflict are relevant to current problems.

What we do not know about the global environment affects political action to address environmental problems in significant ways. Uncertainty and risk pervade discussions of environmental problems and the ways to mitigate them. What we do not know about environmental problems, their consequences, and the costs and effectiveness of mitigating them, affects political willingness to address them. Studies of risk suggest that people, and thus policy-makers, do not approach risk in an economically rational way, and the implication of that observation for environmental policy-making is important. Information and science are essential in this process but are likely to become politicized themselves, as those who are affected by environmental problems attempt to spin the science or represent the uncertainty in ways that best represent their interests.

In this context, where action that causes environmental problems or action to mitigate most frequently comes from those other than states, non-state actors have had a higher degree of influence than in other realms of international politics. The boundaries between what action is taken by international organizations, by states, and by non-governmental actors are particularly porous in this discipline. Most importantly, the way they act on issues of the global environment challenges many of the most state-centric approaches to international relations, and even traditional views of the interaction between domestic politics and international relations.

The proponents of various theoretical perspectives have often focused on different cases or different elements of environmental politics, so it can be difficult to determine where these disparate approaches are compatible or in conflict. It is through the examination of particular issue areas that it is possible to see where various perspectives fit together or clash, and what those experiences contribute to further generation of theory. The cases presented here are chosen to be representative of various types of global environmental issues. They include issues that are primarily addressed by developed countries and those that involve primarily developing countries; issues that take place in the global commons of the atmosphere and the oceans and those that have a directional, non-commons component. There are those that have been addressed by inter-state cooperation and those that have been most effectively addressed by non-governmental actors. There are issues that have been addressed through cost–benefit analysis and those that are debated through ethical arguments. This group of cases provides information about much of the spectrum of global environmental issues.

Climate change and ozone depletion, both issues of the global commons and of long-term ecological processes, have met with varying levels of success in efforts to prevent global environmental damage. They share the similarity that their harm is truly global and not influenced by the location of damaging emissions, but they also present different political problems. Both the science and the economic structure of industry relating to ozone depletion are simpler than is the case in climate change. In particular, the states most concerned about ozone depletion are those most responsible for causing it, and also the most capable of taking action to prevent it. The same cannot be said for climate change, where the industry is varied and dispersed, the effects vary widely and are still uncertain, and many people have not yet been convinced that taking action is politically feasible.

☞ Whaling is among the oldest type of environmental problem: the harvesting of a natural resource that becomes less sustainable when improved technology and increasing population make harvesting more efficient. It also provides an important additional view into the ethical issues of environmental politics: some who want to restrict whaling seek to do so for the reasons that motivated the origins of the International Whaling Commission – the protection of the whaling industry through successfully managing the level of harvesting – but others are concerned about the intrinsic value of whales. The combination of these two approaches allowed the creation of a moratorium on commercial whaling, but they are uneasy bedfellows both in whaling and in other environmental issues. Ethics play a role in addressing the global environment, but there is no clear consensus on who is deserving of consideration or how to act on behalf of non-human entities. The whaling case also demonstrates more mundane but essential political lessons about the ease of cheating on international obligations, and the difficulty of regulating a large number of actors. It also suggests that, even when an industry has a collective interest in protecting the resource upon which it depends, it may fail.

Examining biodiversity, especially in the context of the Amazonian rainforest, suggests the true interconnected nature of environmental resources and their interactions with political structures. The harms to the rainforest come both locally and globally, and from resource harvesting, pollution, and subsistence farming. The loss of biodiversity and harm to Amazonian ecosystems also have both local and global effects, including some that we are unlikely to realize fully until the damage is irreversible. Nevertheless, it is in the area of addressing biodiversity that some of the most innovative strategies have been attempted. Local political action can have global effects in these cases. The fact that the environmental problems happen in physical locations gives political power to the states where biodiversity of concern is located, and suggests that, when properly motivated, they may in fact be able to use their sovereignty to protect resources. Efforts via debt-for-nature swaps, bioprospecting agreements, and ecotourism may not be the panaceas that they were initially believed to be, but they are creative ways to address local concerns with global resources, in a manner that may ultimately protect what some consider to be the common heritage of humankind.

Finally, acid rain presents a traditional problem in some ways: industrial pollution that harms lakes, forests, and the associated resources, as well as destroying cultural artifacts. It followed a traditional path for addressing environmental problems as well, with the discovery of a local environmental problem motivating the search for its cause, and eventual regulation of the activities that caused it. However, acid rain also differs from the model that many intuitively apply to environmental politics in that its effects are directional. How much an area suffers from the problem is determined not only by its natural ecological resistance to acidifying substances but also by its position in windflow. States thus face a quite different situation in negotiations to address acid rain than they do in traditional commons problems like fisheries or ozone depletion, and those that are net importers of pollutants have a greater necessity, but lesser ability, to address the problem. What is notable in this situation is that addressing acid rain in Europe has nevertheless involved even the major polluters in reasonably serious efforts to mitigate the problem. The same is less true in North America, where the USA, which causes more harm than it suffers from acidifying pollutants, was able to resist action for a decade.

Environmental politics poses challenges to a lot of traditional thinking about international relations. At its most basic, environmental politics challenges the idea of sovereignty – states can no longer realistically protect their own territory and populations from harm by actions they take alone. Thinking about the environment expands the sphere of concern of international relations beyond state-centric security-dominated approaches; many recent discussions within international relations theory have their origins in efforts to understand international environmental politics. In examining a number of new paradigms that help explain global environmental politics, however, it is important not to forget the lessons that traditional IR theory can provide. Those who focus on the involvement of non-state actors and the potential for cooperation based on new scientific understanding should not forget that environmental politics can be a realm of conflict, both domestic and international. It should not be assumed, for instance, that all states have the same goals in approaching environmental problems, or even that the issue of relative gains is unimportant. Nevertheless, the challenges to traditional approaches that come from efforts to protect the global environment can be instructive as we work to understand international relations more broadly.

INTERNATIONAL ENVIRONMENTAL COOPERATION

It is through international environmental cooperation that most global environmental problems are mitigated, or at least managed. The amount of cooperation internationally to address environmental issues has grown exponentially in the last century, with much of it reaching maturity in the last 30 years. In addition to an increase in raw numbers of instruments of cooperation, the number of states that participate internationally and the sophistication of international agreements has grown. Certainly there are gains to be made from international cooperation, but that alone is not sufficient to bring it about or to ensure that all actors participate in and comply with international agreements. Moreover, one of the difficult lessons from the last century of international environmental cooperation has been that simply negotiating an agreement, even if all relevant states participate and live up to their obligations, may not be sufficient to address an environmental problem. Despite this difficulty, great strides have been made in understanding and creating international environmental cooperation.

The first essential element to keep in mind in examining international environmental cooperation is that no state can ever be required to join an international agreement or to undertake a particular regulation. The international system is anarchic in that there is no overarching authority (in this case, world government) that can dictate to individual states, or actors within those states, what they must do. And although there are international courts and tribunals, no state can ever be forced to appear before them, or to accept punishment from them. What this structure means is that states must want to make environmental policy on the international level, and that they must be willing to comply with the policies they have made, or submit to dispute resolution procedures to address problems that come up as a result of their actions or inaction. Under what conditions might they be willing to do so?

Theories of international cooperation in a variety of issue areas affect our understanding of international environmental cooperation; more importantly, international environmental cooperation can help support or challenge some of these broader approaches. Cooperation to address environmental issues is clearly a growth field; by the time of the UN Conference on Environment and Development in Rio in 1992 there were more than 900 instruments of international cooperation to address protection of the environment,[1] and the number has grown considerably since then. Examining international efforts to address global environmental issues allows us to apply well-developed theories about international cooperation to the environmental issue area, where it becomes clear that environmental issues provide difficult laboratories that challenge the conventional wisdom not only about what makes cooperation possible, but about how even to study the conditions under which it will come about or succeed.

It is clear that states have turned primarily to international agreements to address global environmental problems, and that sometimes these agreements have been effective at changing state behavior and ultimately affecting the environment in a beneficial way. In other cases, success – either in the creation of international mechanisms, or in their influence on the behavior of states or individuals and ultimately their ability to improve the environmental condition – is less certain. It is through these experiences that we can learn both what may make for effective international environmental cooperation and, more importantly, how to understand why.

RECENT HISTORY OF INTERNATIONAL ENVIRONMENTAL COOPERATION

Despite the difficulty of international environmental cooperation, international action to address environmental policy has developed both depth and breadth since its beginnings. Early environmental cooperation addressed issues pertaining to wildlife; in particular these instruments focused on such things as migratory birds, which would be threatened if not protected in the various areas through which they migrated, and (although it was not called by this name at the time) sustainable hunting of species. One of the most effective early treaties of this sort was the 1911 Fur Seal Convention, which attempted to use biological indicators to make sure that seals were not over-harvested.

Although states have been cooperating to manage natural resources for more than a century, the modern era of international environmental cooperation is generally traced to the UN Conference on the Human Environment, held in 1972 in Stockholm. This international conference

addressed the collective human responsibility for environmental protection on a global scale and put forth the idea that environmental
protection was important for human social and economic development.
More than 100 states participated in the conference, and more than 400
non-governmental and international organizations attended. The main
results of the conference were the Declaration on the Human
Environment and an action plan for the implementation of its principles.
The UN General Assembly, after the conference, accepted a central
recommendation from the action plan and created the UN Environment
Programme (UNEP), which has taken on an important coordinating and
leadership role in international environmental policy since its inception.[2]
The publicity and enthusiasm generated by the Stockholm conference led
to the negotiation of a number of international environmental treaties in
the early 1970s. These treaties addressed such issues as acid rain in
Europe, ocean dumping, the regulation of trade in endangered species
and the protection of wetlands. Although intended to be inclusive, these
treaties primarily reflected the concerns of the developed countries that
initiated their negotiations.

Environmental cooperation in the early 1980s continued and deepened
the focus on international problems of the global commons. What is
notable, however, is a shift in emphasis towards the end of the decade to
some issues that were driven by the concerns of developing countries –
the transboundary movement of hazardous waste, for example. Moreover, developing countries began to recognize their importance to, and
thus negotiating power in, global environmental agreements. Treaties
such as the 1987 Montreal Protocol on Substances That Deplete the
Ozone Layer included measures to help address the development
concerns of non-industrialized countries. At the same time, as evidenced
by the Montreal Protocol, environmental issues began to be seen as even
more clearly global in scope and elusive in character. Issues like ozone
depletion and global climate change could potentially bring environmental disaster, but action to prevent them would have to be taken
before actual damage from human activity became apparent. All
countries, rich or poor, would have to be involved in the prevention of
these problems.

Twenty years after Stockholm, the UN Conference on Environment
and Development, held at Rio de Janeiro in 1992, addressed the
intersection of environment and development issues more explicitly. The
declaration negotiated at that conference included the idea that the
needs of the least developed countries should be given special priority
and that developed countries bore a special responsibility for working
towards sustainable development. Treaties signed in the wake of the Rio

conference addressed issues such as biodiversity, global climate change, and desertification, all of which have significant North-South equity implications. The Rio Declaration on Environment and Development, as well as Agenda 21, the action plan of the conference, reiterated states' rights to sovereignty over their natural resources and to development. These texts also emphasized the 'polluter pays' principle (the idea that those responsible for causing pollution should also be responsible for paying the costs of cleaning it up) and the precautionary principle (the idea that regulations to prevent possible environmental harm should not have to wait until there is full scientific certainty on all aspects of the issue, particularly if the problem would be serious or irreversible).[3] Recent treaties generally consider differential obligations for developed and developing states, and include funding mechanisms or provisions for technology transfer.

INSTRUMENTS OF INTERNATIONAL ENVIRONMENTAL COOPERATION

Any sustained effort at international environmental cooperation can be considered a 'regime' within the international relations literature, generally designated as 'principles, norms, rules, and decisionmaking procedures around which actor expectations converge.'[4] This designation indicates that international cooperation can take place both formally and informally, within and outside of international institutions, and can happen even without high-level state-run negotiations. Nevertheless, it is useful to look at the specific aspects of international regimes that constitute cooperation to address environmental issues.[5]

The main instrument of international environmental policy is international treaties, sometimes bilateral but most often multilateral. These treaties can be regional or global depending on the scope of the environmental problem and the desires of the actors involved. There are different approaches to the making of international environmental treaties, the two main variations of which are, first, treaties in which regulatory authority is delegated to a committee or organization and, second, convention/protocol processes, although in practice many treaties contain aspects of both. In addition, customary international law, legally binding principles that have not been agreed in any specific negotiation, play a role in international environmental cooperation, as do non-binding international declarations.

The regulatory type of treaty involves empowering a treaty organization (composed of representatives of states) to make regular policies, generally through decisions requiring a supermajority of votes (more than 51 percent). These decisions, while they bind the states that are members of the treaty, do not require formal ratification and thus allow policy to respond quickly to environmental conditions. Most fishery treaties and the International Convention for the Regulation of Whaling make annual 'schedules' of catch regulations this way. Similarly, the Convention for the Regulation of International Trade in Endangered Species of Wild Fauna and Flora (CITES) uses this type of procedure for changing the status of, and therefore also the regulations pertaining to, endangered species. As states can never be bound by international law without their consent and this process allows for regulations to be made with which a minority disagrees, states would not join such an agreement without the possibility of opting out of the decisions made by the group. Generally there is a specific procedure, sometimes called an 'objection' or 'reservation' procedure, by which a state can indicate its intention not to be bound by a regulation passed in this manner. Unfortunately, states that benefit most from whatever environmental damage is being regulated may be most likely to opt out of the regulations, thereby free riding on the actions taken by other states. These procedures also allow for other states to opt out of the regulation once an initial state has done so, so that states will not have to put up with free riding if they do not want to. This policy sometimes results in a situation in which none of the relevant actors are bound; for example, there were times when all the states whaling in a certain region opted out of the regulations that would have bound them.[6] Although many complain about opt-out provisions in regulatory treaties, the fact that no state can be bound by international law against its will makes them a necessary evil. Without them few states would agree to regulation created by less than unanimous voting. When states do opt out, it is possible that scientific evidence, domestic pressure, or diplomatic pressure can persuade them to remove their objection to the regulation in question.

The most common approach to recent environmental treaty making is the convention/protocol format, in which an initial convention is first negotiated and then followed by the negotiation of protocols and amendments. Often the initial agreement is what is called a framework convention, because it includes a general approach to the issue without requiring specific obligations to reduce environmental damage. It may call for cooperation on research to increase the understanding of the problem, and may include a plan for negotiating binding controls. These protocols, negotiated later, must be fully accepted by all state representatives and ratified by states, thus making the process more time consuming than the regulatory approach discussed above. However, as these conventions and protocols are fully negotiated they are also generally not subject to opt-out procedures. On the other hand, states may sign or ratify protocols and amendments at different speeds, so a situation can still exist in which different states are held to different standards. Either the recently popular convention/protocol approach or the regulatory process has an advantage, however, over earlier forms of treaties in which a completely new treaty would be negotiated whenever circumstances changed. In international environmental policy, understanding of the environmental problem can change rapidly, so treaties that can adapt to new scientific information or new willingness on the part of states to protect the environment are important.

Customary international law is an often-overlooked form of international regulation because it does not come about by a standard negotiation process. Two things are required for a principle to become customary international law: states must act in a way consistent with the principle (by either undertaking an action or refraining from undertaking an action), and they must do so because they believe they are legally obligated to. Evidence that states have through time acted on and recognized a certain set of obligations can be used in international court cases or dispute-settlement procedures. An example of this type of law is the obligation that states have not to 'use or permit the use of [their] territory in such a manner as to cause injury ... in or to the territory of another.'[7] This principle was deemed customary international law and used to settle a transboundary air pollution dispute between the USA and Canada in 1935; it has been frequently cited as a principle of international law despite not being negotiated into a formal treaty.

Also important in international environmental policy is what is known as 'soft law,'[8] so called because it is not technically legally binding but nevertheless takes on the character of international law. International organizations may adopt 'codes,' such as the International Maritime Dangerous Goods Code, which determines the products that are considered hazardous for shipping and sets up processes for labeling and documenting these goods. Although codes such as this are not obligatory, they are often taken seriously, amended regularly, and lead to a change in the behavior of the states involved. Declarations made by international organizations such as the UN General Assembly can also constitute soft law. For example, UN General Assembly Resolution 44/225 recommended a moratorium on 'all large-scale pelagic driftnet fishing on the high seas by 30 June 1992.' Although this recommendation was not a legal obligation, many states took action to change their own activities to meet this moratorium and encouraged or persuaded others to do the same. Large international conferences such as those in Stockholm and Rio (and many others that received less international attention) also contribute declarations that, while they do not bind states legally, indicate states' intentions. The Rio Declaration on Environment and Development, for example, proclaims a responsibility by states to 'cooperate in a spirit of global partnership to conserve, protect, and restore the health and integrity of the Earth's ecosystem,' but does not assign specific requirements to do so. More importantly, it declares that 'the developed countries acknowledge the responsibility that they bear in the international pursuit of sustainable development in view of the pressures their societies place on the global environment and of the technologies and financial resources they command.'[9] Evidence that these types of resolutions are taken seriously can be found in both the seriousness with which they are negotiated and the activities of states to ensure that their view of what they have agreed to is understood. In this case, the USA released 'interpretive statements' on several of the Rio Declaration principles, including the seventh one, quoted above, indicating that it did not accept any international obligations or liabilities stemming from the declaration.[10] The use of soft law allows states to indicate their intentions to act collectively to address international environmental problems (and sometimes some principles about the way in which they will do so) when they may not yet be ready to accept binding obligations.

NEGOTIATION

The creation of international environmental agreements can be contentious and the outcome uncertain. Nevertheless, a long history of international negotiations has suggested that particular factors are likely to influence the success and outcome of negotiations in potentially predictable ways. Factors examined generally include the interests and power of the actors involved, the number of actors, and characteristics of the problem. This latter one takes on particular importance in the context of environmental negotiations. In addition, there are specific types of tools, such as issue linkage, side payments, and threats, that can be important in the process of negotiations to protect the global environment, and decisions to be made in the process of negotiation in terms of how useful it is to approach the issue broadly and with widespread participation, versus focusing either on a narrower version of the issue or on states that are more likely to be able to agree. Examining the process of negotiation involves both an analytical and a prescriptive discussion: what, empirically, are the effects on negotiations of a variety of factors and, given those effects, how should one approach international environmental negotiations?

Interests of Actors

The interests of the individual states involved with an international problem are likely to have an effect on the extent and type of regulation. These interests collectively can shape both the extent to which a cooperative outcome is likely and the particular form of an agreement that does emerge. Realist international relations theory at its most basic, seeing any international cooperation that does emerge as epiphenominal, would suggest that the interests of the individual states are paramount. This phenomenon is, if anything, more likely in issues relating to the environment. Detlef Sprinz and Tapani Vaahtoranta are among those who see states as rational self-interested actors. They suggest that the worse the state of the environment (in an individual state), 'the greater the incentives to reduce the ecological vulnerability' of the state. Specifically, they expect states that are the victims of pollution to seek international environmental protection, and those that are net contributors to the problem to resist.[11] This formulation still leaves room for a determination of how states define their interests, which may not only be as unitary actors or with unchanging preferences. Certain forms of international cooperation that, for example, demonstrate the severity of a problem, may alter a state's preferences if the state determines it is more harmed by the environmental problem than it believed, or discovers that the cost or effectiveness of abatement measures would be different from its expectations. Similarly, concerns of sub-state actors for or against international cooperation, and their domestic political power, may influence a state's negotiating position. These factors can still fit within the interests framework, but allow the definition of interests to be broadened.

Power of Actors

The power of individual actors involved in international negotiation, especially relative to others, is likely to play a role in the outcomes observed.[12] Some argue that international cooperation is unlikely to take place in the absence of a powerful hegemon whose interests an international agreement serves.[13] Notably, such cooperation would thus be unlikely if it were not in the interests of the hegemonic actor. In addition, international negotiation on issues that require near universal participation to be effective give negotiating power to actors not typically thought of as being powerful in international relations. In particular, large developing countries, not responsible for causing most of the environmental damage in question but capable of causing it in the future, gain negotiating influence due to their 'power to destroy' a resource.[14] They can refuse to participate until an agreement is reached on their terms, and thus demonstrate power that they would not have in many international issues where their participation is less necessary.

Related to this concept is the question of whether cooperation is easier when actors are homogeneous (as is frequently assumed in formal examinations of cooperation theory) or heterogeneous. Conventional international relations theory would hold that heterogeneity of actors makes cooperation more likely, whereas those who study local commons find that homogeneity of actors is more conducive to cooperation.[15] The advantages of a hegemon in international relations may be outweighed by the advantages of actors with similar interests and a shared community in a local commons. What is yet to be determined is which factor weighs more heavily in addressing issues of the international commons.

Number of Actors

The above issues are related to the number of actors involved in a negotiation. The number of actors addressing a collective action problem is thought in general to affect the likelihood and type of cooperation emerging to address it. The effect of different numbers of actors, however, is the subject of some disagreement. Most analysis suggests that collective action is more difficult with larger numbers of actors than with small numbers. The increased difficulty of cooperation with greater numbers of actors comes from increased difficulty of monitoring, ensuring compliance,[16] and increased transaction costs more broadly.[17] Duncan Snidal points out, however, that those who study local common pool resource issues do not tend to find a strong effect from increasing numbers of actors, although even they suggest that cooperation may be easier with smaller groups.[18] It is worth noting, though, that whereas the number of states may be different in different cases, when dealing with environmental issues there may be large numbers of domestic actors who have to change their behavior to address a problem. The overall number of relevant actors may not simply be traceable to the number of states negotiating.[19]

In part because of the role that numbers of actors may play in international negotiations, one aspect that needs to be considered in deciding how to negotiate a treaty is whether to involve all possible states or limit the number to those specifically interested in the issue, or to those willing to take strong regulatory action. International treaties are negotiated in such a way that all involved must agree to their provisions before signing, so they often fall prey to the 'least common denominator' level of regulation that is acceptable to those involved. Some therefore advocate including only those states that are willing to undertake serious commitments, or those that contribute to the problem. Unfortunately two potential problems result from limiting the number of states involved in a treaty negotiation. In one situation, if a state not participating is an important actor in the issue area but unwilling to take serious action, a treaty without that state will have little positive effect on the environment. In the other case, if the states not involved are developing countries or those that may contribute little to the problem or care little about it, the potential for those states to contribute to the problem in the future argues for including them in the negotiations initially. From their perspective it is only fair to have a say in rules they might ultimately be expected to abide by. More importantly, because they cannot be bound without their consent, big developing states that are not included in the negotiating process of an international convention may stay outside the process and refuse to modify their impact on the global environment.

Limiting participation works best when the issue at question is not a global commons problem but is instead geographically bounded; the Mediterranean Action Plan is an example of a regional agreement to protect a variety of aspects of the Mediterranean Sea that involves all the major states in the region. There is no particular reason to involve those outside of the region and doing so would probably have hampered negotiation. Non-environmental cases, such as that of the North Atlantic Treaty Organization (NATO), however, suggest that often the way a problem is defined and the issue of which states to involve are not inherent aspects of an issue but rather constructed socially and simultaneously;[20] it is likely that, even in reasonably clear-cut cases like Mediterranean pollution or European acid rain any decision to keep a negotiation limited comes from consideration of factors other than simple environmental characteristics of the regime. The more we learn about the complexity and reach of environmental problems the more true that statement will become, and the harder it may be to achieve small-scale negotiations.

Problem Characteristics

There are many aspects of any problem for which international cooperation might be appropriate that will affect the ease of negotiations to address it; these issues will probably emerge as well when addressing compliance with and effectiveness of negotiated measures, suggesting the difficulty of successfully analyzing any of these aspects alone, because they are all related. It might be easier to create international agreements to address some types of environmental issues, but it is not clear how to determine whether these are more successful than those that address problems for which it is more difficult to negotiate agreements. Nevertheless, there has been some effort to understand the characteristics of problems that may influence international negotiations, and in what way.

Certain types of problem are structured in ways that make cooperation easier. Early international relations theories on cooperation pointed out the relative ease of addressing coordination problems compared with collaboration problems, largely because of the implications for compliance.[21] Once a solution has been found to a coordination problem (right of way in international airspace, for instance) no one has a reason not to uphold it, whereas in collaboration problems (such as the prisoners' dilemma or the tragedy of the commons) an actor can always improve individual utility by not living up to the agreement. This might appear to be an issue only of compliance, discussed further below, but it is likely that states will be more willing to negotiate agreements when they believe that actors will uphold the deals they make. On the other hand, arriving at the initial agreement may be more difficult in situations structured as coordination games because, although all actors benefit from bringing their behavior into agreement, some may lose more than others from the coordinated arrangement that is reached. So while they will probably live up to it afterwards, they may put up a bigger fight in the actual creation of the standard.

Other characteristics of the problem may be particularly important in environmental issues. Who causes and who suffers from the environmental harm will certainly have implications for how issues are negotiated. This is an aspect of what Oran Young identifies as asymmetries in the environmental issue.[22] While this can refer to any number of differences between actors pertaining to the environmental problem, one major aspect is the difference between true commons problems, in which all parties contribute to the harm and all suffer from it (although outside the game-theoretic world parties rarely do so equally) and directional transboundary problems, in which some states may simply be net polluters and others net recipients of pollution. A true commons problem provides greater incentives for all individuals to be involved in negotiations, because all will benefit from collective regulation that prevents a tragedy. A directional transboundary issue, such as acid rain or river pollution, provides little incentive in and of itself for polluters at the head end of the directional problem to participate. But some of these problems may be overcome by issue linkages, including simple payoff schemes.

Others, as discussed further in the section on effectiveness, come up with additional characteristics on which to classify the differences between environmental issues and how easy or hard they are to address. Some of these include such matters as whether conflicts in the environmental problem are about means, values, or relative or absolute gains.[23] Others focus more on the different preferences of the actors.[24] In any case, it is clear that some environmental problems will lead to easier negotiation than will others.

Issue Linkage

Many international relations theorists see issue linkage as an important tool in international negotiations;[25] states may choose to link their agreement on one issue (within or outside a specific negotiation) to action others take. Given the potential for issue linkage in negotiation on environmental issues, a question that arises is whether it is more beneficial to negotiate a multi-issue treaty or to stick fairly narrowly to one specific issue. The most common example of a multi-issue treaty is the UN Convention on the Law of the Sea, which addresses almost every issue relating to oceans. Multi-issue treaties allow for direct issue linkage within the negotiating process, so that states that might have different priorities can trade off their positions and agree to something they might not want in return for a different regulation that is important to them. In addition, many environmental problems *are* linked to each other, and addressing one aspect without including all can lead to a situation of proliferating regulations that do not take into consideration the effect of their rules outside their narrowly defined issue area. For example, regulations on forestry will have an impact on biodiversity and global climate change and vice versa, and if these issues are addressed separately these links may not be taken into account. On the other hand, the Law of the Sea Convention took eight years to negotiate and ultimately was so politicized that it was not ratified by some of the most important states in the process for decades. At least in part for this reason, narrowly defined environmental treaties are now the most common type.

Environmental Aid and Economic Sanctions

Within the international relations literature, aid, particularly within the context of convincing states to join treaties, can be seen as essentially a side payment, which is also a type of issue linkage. A state's behavior in one area (a treaty) which it may not be particularly concerned about is linked to something else (a type of aid) that is of greater concern. Using side payments is a well-known strategy for encouraging international cooperation. Aid can also been seen within an international relations framework as an effort to change a state's preferences – changing the payoffs, in a game-theoretic structure. If a state's preference ordering is changed from preferring to stay out of a cooperative arrangement to preferring to join, due to aid, cooperation becomes more likely.

Similarly the threat and imposition of economic harm has long been a foreign policy tool used to convince states to change their behavior; as such, the topic has been analyzed within a number of different policy issues. It is also used to change a state's calculation of interest in taking a particular position. Although persuading states to join environmental treaties is likely to meet with far less resistance than some of the other purposes for which sanctions are threatened, sanctions are a controversial tool in international environmental negotiation. They have nevertheless been used to persuade states to negotiate internationally or to agree to measures they might not otherwise have chosen to accept.[26]

Some of the tools used to bring states into international environmental agreements have potential problems. Environmental aid presents the possibility of moral hazard; if states only take a desired action when they receive aid, will they only continue to take that action as long as aid is provided? Will it be possible to convince them of the benefit of undertaking the action in question, or will they simply do it for the payoff? Moreover, paying states to take a beneficial action may have negative long-term effects if states learn that they do not have to take action to protect without aid. It is conceivable that states that might have taken some action on their own will discover that if they hold out they can get side payments, raising the cost of negotiating agreements and the likelihood that they will not be completed. Economic threats, although occasionally effective, can be seen as internationally illegitimate, and may conflict with international obligations or aspirations for free trade. These tools are all used, however, in negotiation of agreements to protect the environment, and may make them possible where they otherwise would not have been.

IMPLEMENTATION, COMPLIANCE, AND ENFORCEMENT

It is obviously not sufficient for states to agree to take action to protect the global environment if they do not then put these regulations into practice. The situation may be worse where states agree to environmental measures but then do not implement them than when they do not agree to cooperate in the first place, because public pressure may decrease if people believe that the issue has been addressed. It is thus important to determine what increases the chances that states will change their behavior in accordance with international environmental agreements they have negotiated, and how to best create agreements that will not only achieve compliance but increase the likelihood that we can detect and address non-compliance. The theoretical connection between issues of negotiation and compliance becomes clear as well. Many of the factors that increase the chances of negotiating an agreement probably relate to the chances that it will be implemented and upheld. While that is useful information for those involved with addressing these problems, it provides more difficulty for those studying them, because the two stages cannot be studied entirely independent of one another.

Aside from possible (and potentially serious) difficulties in determining what states or sub-state actors are doing, compliance with international environmental agreements should be a reasonably simple proposition. In most cases, states will benefit if all states live up to the obligations they have taken on, because environmental conditions will improve. So why should states not comply with international environmental agreements? How much of a concern does that pose, and what can be done about it?

The question of why states might not comply with international environmental agreements takes us back to one of the central articles in environmental studies and the idea of the 'tragedy of the commons.' Garrett Hardin in 1968 observed the difficulty of achieving environmental cooperation, with an analogy to medieval cow herders who all kept their cows on commonly held land. He observed that each herder gains the full positive utility of every new cow put onto the common pasture, but that the negative utility (also seen as environmental externalities) of each new cow is shared by all, with that cow's herder thus only bearing a fraction of the cost of the additional cow. Even if there is a set number of cows the pasture can support, each individual herder, doing a cost-benefit analysis, will always find it advantageous to add another cow. Moreover, this logic remains even if a given cow herder knows that the next cow added to the pasture will push the ecosystem past its carrying capacity and thus ruin the commons for everyone. As long as one herder cannot be sure whether another herder will add the extra cow, the first herder will have an incentive to do so. Practicing restraint can lead to the worst possible outcome if you decide to forego the benefits of adding an extra cow but someone else does not; you have thus not gained the benefits of the extra cow and you still bear the cost of the destroyed ecosystem.[27] While some have pointed to the lack of inevitability in this formulation (and the historical inaccuracy of the analogy),[28] it is nevertheless a useful starting point for understanding the difficulties of cooperation, and the incentives to cheat even on agreements made. This analogy is nearly identical to the game-theoretic formulation of the prisoners' dilemma, used by so many to explain both the difficulties – and nevertheless the advantages – of international cooperation.[29] Work on this subject suggests that international cooperation is, of course, possible, and made more likely under certain conditions, such as when actors can be made to care more about gains in the future than in the present, and when the interaction is likely to be repeated.[30]

When applied particularly to global environmental issues some of these factors change slightly. For instance, the role of free riders takes on increased significance in common pool resource problems. In these situations, in which the environmental good is both non-excludable (people cannot be kept from enjoying its benefits) and subtractable (meaning that the use of the resource by one actor decreases its availability for others), a state that does not comply risks undermining the entire system,[31] as does the cow herder who adds the final cow to the tragic commons. This aspect makes compliance with, and participation in, international environmental agreements more important than in some other situations of international cooperation.

In order to determine when a state is complying with an international environmental agreement, it would seem useful to examine the obligations of the agreement, examine the behavior of states, and determine whether they coincide. While that may certainly constitute evidence of an agreement's influence, it should not immediately be seen as an indication of compliance per se. When state behavior reflects internationally negotiated agreements, there are several possible inter-pretations of the situation. It may be, as is probably the case with Scandinavian states in the Convention on Long-Range Transboundary Air Pollution,[32] that these states are doing what they would have done even in the absence of an international obligation to do so, most likely because their actions have localized benefits, or domestic pressure demands action. It may be that the same action that inspired the regulation independently inspired actors to change their behavior. An example of this relationship may be seen within the USA when information about ozone depletion was publicized in the early 1970s. Laws passed by Congress ending the use of chlorofluorocarbons in non-essential aerosols coincided with a public demand for alternative products; the law and the decreased public consumption can be seen as both deriving from new scientific information, rather than one directly causing the other. They are related, but it is not clear that the law was the primary determinant in the change of behavior. In other words, determining when states change their activities to coincide with international environmental obligations may be difficult. If we want to learn how to make strong international environmental institutions, we need to figure out what it is that makes states change environmentally damaging behavior.

CONDITIONS FOR COMPLIANCE

In his classic observation about international law, Louis Henkin suggests that 'almost all nations observe almost all principles of international law and almost all of their obligations almost all of the time.'[33] Examination of international cooperation generally and cooperation to address environmental issues specifically suggests certain conditions that may increase the likelihood of compliance with international agreements. Characteristics of states – the extent to which a state has control over the actions of its substate actors, for instance, or its general regulatory approach – are likely to make a difference,[34] as are aspects of the international agreement itself, such as monitoring or enforcement provisions or who has to make changes to implement the agreement.

Discussion of how to gain compliance leaves open two important questions. The first is whether we actually need complete compliance, and the second is what general approach is likely to lead to the greatest degree of compliance. To the first question, the answer is a somewhat qualified 'no': most systems of cooperation can survive less than complete compliance by at least some of the members some of the time. The problem with free riders is more serious for commons problems than other types of issues, and certainly full-scale non-compliance by particularly important actors would make a difference, but perfect compliance by all actors is unlikely to be necessary. Moreover, when a state's behavior does not appear to be in complete alignment with international accords, it should not necessarily be taken as an indication that the agreements are not influencing international behavior. As an analogy, think of speed limits on highways. At any given point, a large percentage of cars are going faster than the posted speed, and thus are in technical non-compliance with the regulation. At the same time, the speed of almost all cars on the road is probably influenced by the speed limit. Their behavior, while not living up to the standard exactly, is probably closer to the regulated speed than it would be if there were no limit or if the limit were different. It is thus possible to have rules with a very low level of compliance, strictly defined, that nevertheless have a dramatic influence on behavior. This change in behavior may be sufficient to affect the underlying concern.

The question of what creates the greatest degree of compliance leads to a debate between what have been called the managerial model and the enforcement model of international law. The idea that international cooperation requires enforcement is the more traditional approach, at least from international relations scholars. There is certainly evidence of states or sub-state actors attempting to cheat on their international obligations; usually, if they choose to do so they succeed. As discussed later in this book, the former Soviet Union systematically assisted its whalers in non-compliance with the International Convention for the Regulation of Whaling. Other information that has come to light since the fall of the Soviet Union suggests that the USSR did not comply with other international environmental obligations: the military dumped not only oil waste but also high-level nuclear waste at sea.[35] The enforcement model looks at ways in which states can be made to live up to their international obligations, either by specific penalties for not complying (which may be as diffuse as the increased difficulty of finding cooperation partners in the future if you cheat on your current obligations or as detailed as tit-for-tat retaliation for those who do not do what they have agreed to do) or by 'systems for implementation review' that may point out when states are not living up to their agreements.[36] It is worth noting, however, that, in international environmental agreements, the use, or even inclusion, of formal compliance mechanisms is rare: states, for a variety of reasons, are hesitant to coerce others to follow the rules to which they have agreed. Important exceptions to this observation exist, although many – as the US threats of economic sanctions used to compel action in the case of whaling, discussed later – are frequently about gaining participation rather than compliance.

The managerial approach, while discussed through much of the history of examining international cooperation, gained a higher profile from the work of Abram and Antonia Chayes. This perspective suggests that non-compliance is often unintentional rather than calculated. States may not comply because they are not aware of what sub-state actors are doing or because they do not have effective control over their borders or the funding to put toward environmental priorities. By logical extension, the best way to avoid non-compliance would be through consultation and assistance, rather than by using strict enforcement mechanisms.[37] The 'systems for implementation review' identified by David Victor, Kal Raustiala, and Eugene Skolnikoff most frequently take this form; even when former Eastern bloc states were found to be in non-compliance with their obligations under the Montreal Protocol on Substances That Deplete the Ozone Layer and were required to go through the official non-compliance procedure under the agreement, they were ultimately granted financial assistance and more time to comply.[38] There are certainly potential difficulties with the managerial model. As indicated, states that choose not to comply with international environmental agreements are likely to continue to do so, despite assistance; Soviet whalers who withheld true catch statistics from the International Whaling Commission would not have been deterred by aid or technical assistance, but might have been if an international observer system had been in place to detect their lack of compliance. Most recent work on compliance in international environmental law implicitly approaches the topic with a managerial bias,[39] although there is evidence for the advantages of both approaches under different circumstances.

One link between the two approaches may be action taken by sub-state actors. In some cases states may legitimately want to change their environmental behavior, but have difficulty controlling the action of those whose behavior must actually change for the state to comply with international environmental agreements. Brazil, for instance, has difficulty upholding species and timber regulations in the Amazon rainforest, where it is difficult to monitor what individual actors are doing.[40] Likewise, post-Soviet Russia has much less control over its borders than it did during the era of centralized political authority.[41]

Ronald Mitchell has demonstrated that the point of regulation in an international environmental agreement can have an enormous influence on compliance through regulating actors whose behavior is easier to monitor. He found that regulations on how much oil an individual oil tanker can discharge into the ocean were far less successful than equipment regulations imposed on the far smaller number of shipyards that build oil tankers, primarily because it is much easier to monitor the behavior of a few big actors than many small dispersed ones.[42]

The focus on compliance also raises the possibility that international environmental cooperation can best be achieved through non-binding agreements rather than, as many have assumed, treaties. Victor *et al.* suggest that whereas compliance may be higher with legally binding treaties, implementation – behavior change and thus ultimate effect on the environment – may be more significant in some cases with non-binding measures. Such measures may tend to be more ambitious and therefore have a lower level of compliance, but the actual degree of behavior change under them may be greater. The case that provides the best support for this conclusion is the international regime to regulate trade in pesticides and chemicals through the process of prior informed consent (PIC). Prior to its integration into the Rotterdam Convention on the Prior Informed Consent Procedure for Certain Hazardous Chemicals and Pesticides in International Trade, an informal regime existed. Victor argues that there was no evidence of non-compliance with this regime and that its informal nature allowed it to adapt to changing circumstances and adopt stricter regulations than would have been possible with a binding agreement.[43]

EFFECTIVENESS

Ascertaining effectiveness of international environmental cooperation is difficult for a number of reasons. The first concerns definition: what should be considered as constituting the effectiveness of an international environmental agreement? Until recently, a focus within international relations on issues of compliance led to a bias in favor of examining the influence of an international regime on the actors (both state and sub-state) it was intended to regulate. This aspect is important and should not be overlooked; if international cooperation cannot succeed in changing the behavior of actors whose original behavior has been causing environmental problems, it is reasonable to consider it ineffective. Behavioral effectiveness also has the advantage of being relatively easy to measure. Although there are difficulties in determining what it is that individual actors are doing (and, more importantly, why they are doing it), it is a much more straightforward way to try to determine the impact of a regime than other methods. Many studies simply examine whether actor behavior lines up with that prescribed by the regime.

What most people would really like to know about an international regime's effectiveness, however, is whether it actually has a positive impact on the environment: is the natural environment better because of international regulatory efforts than it would have been otherwise?

Although few large-scale studies have been able to address this issue, due to problems discussed below, the trend in the literature is at least to pay lip service to the idea that what should really be examined is the effect of cooperative efforts on environmental quality. Some progress has been made in determining how effective specific environmental regimes have been at protecting the environment.

The most important difficulty in determining effectiveness is logistical: how would you know whether a regime has succeeded at protecting the environment? On the face of it, evidence that the environmental problem has improved would tend to suggest that the cooperative effort has been effective, and evidence that it has not would suggest otherwise. But it is entirely possible to have improvement in the environment, happening at the same time as international regulation, that is nevertheless not caused by the regulation. The improvement may be a coincidence, or (similarly) due to some natural fluctuation in an environmental resource that has nothing to do with what human action has produced. Fish stocks, some of which go through large cycles that people do not fully understand, may have a beneficial upswing at the same time that international cooperative effects emerge to protect them, or vice versa.[44]

Similarly, a decrease in environmental quality does not necessarily indicate that cooperative efforts are not succeeding. The same natural cycles may – and empirically, often seem to – bring together increased regulatory efforts and natural declines in environmental quality. As the environmental problem gets worse, regulation becomes more likely, and thus international environmental cooperation may begin at a particularly low point for the natural resource. Related is an issue of measurement. If there is a time lag in mitigating the problem, even if it will ultimately improve, at the point at which one measures it there may be increased levels of environmental degradation from when cooperation began. The volume of ozone-depleting substances in the upper atmosphere has not only not dropped but is increasing. The annual thinning of the ozone layer over Antarctica is getting larger every year.[45] Does this mean that human activities to protect the ozone layer are ineffective? Not likely. Some ozone-depleting substances have residence times in the atmosphere of up to a century. Even if the response to the earliest hypothesis in the 1970s about the possible human impact on the ozone layer had resulted in an immediate cessation of all use of ozone-depleting substances, those emitted prior to that point would still be depleting the ozone layer for decades to come. It might be difficult to measure effectiveness and to adjust policies to increase it in a simple regulatory time-frame. These time lags in demonstrated effectiveness make it particularly difficult to gain political action to address a problem that will not improve until after the politicians in question have retired from public office, while any potential costs to changing behavior come in the short term.

In addition, although still probably evidence of ineffective environmental management, one of the reasons the environment may fail to recover even when cooperative efforts have been undertaken may be that these efforts are too late: a point has been reached beyond which recovery is unlikely or much more difficult. Species that have become extinct, or even simply too low in population, are not going to be able to recover. A fundamental shift in the climate system is suggested as one of the possible results of climate change; if that happens, no amount of cooperation to reduce carbon emissions may be able to change the climate back to what it once was. In fact, given the difficulty of gaining political support for cooperation to address issues about which there is uncertainty, we may be chronically predisposed to negotiate agreements at points when the environmental problem has shown sufficient evidence of its seriousness that making the situation better becomes harder.

Most importantly, however, is the fact that a decline in environmental quality coincident with international cooperative efforts can still happen in the face of effective environmental management. What we really need to know is what would have happened to the environment counterfactually – without international cooperation. International regulatory measures may in fact be quite effective at decreasing the amount of damage humans do to the global ecosystem, but may not mitigate them completely, even within a particular issue area. In the case of ozone depletion it is relatively simple to plot the amount of ozone-depleting substances that would have been put into the stratosphere if use of these substances had continued to increase at the rate at which it was already increasing, and infer from that the level of damage to the environment without regulation. Many have shown the presence of a much lower level of stratospheric ozone-depleting substances than would have been likely without regulation.[46]

A final difficulty in evaluating effectiveness of international environmental cooperation is the multiple causes there can be for some environmental problems. On the one hand, it may seem foolish to speak of the effectiveness of a program to address an environmental problem that stops only one source of the problem while others continue to operate and worsen the problem. If the agreements to protect the ozone layer had only regulated chlorofluorocarbons, they could legitimately have been seen as ineffective for leaving out other substances, such as halons, that destroy the ozone layer even more effectively through similar mechanisms. On the other hand, some of the multiple effects on an environmental problem may be diverse and unconnected. Protection of whales from overharvesting has been difficult enough to accomplish effectively, but new evidence has emerged that global climate change may have a serious effect on the well-being of the world's population of whales.[47] In this case, the regime set up to prevent overharvesting of whales from commercial whaling is beginning to consider this possible new cause of harm to whales (although there is probably little it can do in terms of prevention of damage), but it may be unrealistic to expect any single cooperative process to address all potential causes of an environmental problem. At worst, some environmental cooperation may be no better than rearranging deck chairs on the *Titanic*. Such actions can even be counterproductive by suggesting that steps have been taken to address a problem when they have not, thus leading the public to believe that the issue is no longer worthy of attention. As suggested above, however, an effort that may not be effective at completely eliminating a given problem may still mitigate it to an extent greater than if no cooperative solution had been attempted. In some cases that may be far better than nothing.

Conditions for Effectiveness

While we may not be entirely clear about how effectiveness is to be measured, there has nevertheless been some progress in ascertaining the conditions under which environmental agreements may be more or less effective. Certainly the structure of an environmental problem has some impact on how effectively it is addressed. Who causes the problem, who is most harmed by it, how difficult the proposed solutions are to undertake, and a wide range of other factors can influence the ease with which cooperative efforts will succeed at addressing environmental problems.

Peter Haas, Robert Keohane, and Marc Levy suggest that effective regimes are those that build upon existing concern, work with or create capacity, and take place in a reasonable contractual environment.[48] It is easy to understand why these might be important precursors to effective regimes, but far more difficult to ascertain systematically what degree of each of these factors is necessary for success, or whether a large amount of one factor can outweigh the need for another.

A project headed by Oran Young identifies a number of 'causal pathways' by which international environmental regimes can be effective: They can modify the utility of a state by giving it a context (or the information) to care about an environmental issue it might not previously have cared about, or an institutional context that can allow states to avoid collective action problems like the tragedy of the commons. Within this context, cooperation can be effective when it allows for the ratcheting up of obligations. Regimes can also bestow authority, creating rules seen as legitimate and thereby followed by actors who do not necessarily undertake a cost/benefit analysis to determine whether to implement their requirements. They can facilitate learning about the nature of the environmental problems or about ways to mitigate it.[49]

A project led by Edward Miles in Seattle, Arild Underdal in Oslo, and others, also addresses conditions for effectiveness of international environmental regimes, by looking at the role that the structure of the problem plays in effectiveness of environmental regimes. They define effectiveness as both the degree of relative improvement and how far the current situation is from a collective optimum; both difficult-to-measure, but important aspects of the question. Moreover, the major explanatory variables they examine relate to the type of problem (how benign or malign it is, determined by the extent of symmetry of interests, congruity of goals, and extent or nature of cleavages), and characteristics of the regime itself, described as its problem-solving capacity and including organizational structures and political capabilities. Ultimately they conclude that most of the regimes they studied made a difference in actor behavior and environmental conditions, but fell short of providing ideal solutions. Moreover, they find that even malign problems, while scoring lower on both elements of effectiveness, have been improved by the regimes that manage them. Their study supports their hypotheses that problem and regime characteristics influence effectiveness, but they also find that there are pathways to effective environmental regimes they do not account for.[50]

Efforts to explain true environmental effectiveness of international cooperation are of necessity in their infancy, as most of the major international agreements have been around for less than three decades, and the environmental problems they address are long-lived and complex. Attempts to understand what factors make international environmental cooperation more or less effective are likely to be some of the most important aspects of research into the politics of the global environment.

CONCLUSION

Overall, the extent and variety of international environmental cooperation is impressive. States have been willing to undertake potentially costly action to prevent or mitigate environmental problems for which there is initially only theoretical evidence. They have created ways to negotiate international agreements that allow them to respond to changing information and modify obligations accordingly. Early evidence suggests that while not all states uphold their obligations all the time, many have acted collectively in ways that either improve or slow the damage to the global environment.

ENVIRONMENT AND SECURITY

I am persuaded that there is also a new and different threat to our
national security emerging – the destruction of our environment. The
defense establishment has a clear stake in countering this growing threat.
I believe that one of our key national security objectives must be to
reverse the accelerating pace of environmental destruction around the
globe.

Sam Nunn, US Senator[1]

The driving force behind international environmental cooperation comes
from the realization that a degraded environment constitutes a threat to
the wellbeing of people. As such, global environmental issues have
recently been acknowledged as issues of international security. States
cannot protect themselves from environmental harm by controlling only
their own behavior. Cutting down a tree, driving a car, burning a forest,
or operating a factory anywhere in the world has effects that can be felt
outside of the area in which those actions are taken. Most environmental
issues cross borders in one way or another, and in that way impinge on
other states. A concern about the effects of actions of other states gives a
new dimension to consideration of the global environment. States must
be concerned about what others do and may benefit by being able to
influence them. Moreover, environmental issues can become security
issues within individual states in ways that have implications for the
world more broadly. If a state is internally destabilized by environmental
crises, its troubles may create refugees (which in turn can contribute to
the worsening of environmental problems elsewhere), or power
vacuums, or demands that stability be enforced by outside powers.
Environmental issues have changed the way we think about what
constitutes security.

There are two major types of approaches to examining the relationship
between environment and security. One focuses on the prospect that
environmental problems, particularly those relating to shared natural
resources, will cause interstate conflict. The other focuses more locally on

resource scarcity as a cause of local violence or destabilization, which might nevertheless have an international impact as well, through a variety of channels. Although not a clear bifurcation, the first approach focuses mostly on the security of states and the second on the security of individuals. Either way, the idea is that actors are competing in some way over increasingly scarce environmental amenities, and that conflict is a likely result of this competition. To that extent, the debate about environment and security fits into a long tradition, going back to the time of Malthus, of examining the problems that result from scarce resources as well as increasing population growth. That it has come to be seen as a security issue suggests that the understanding of what constitutes security is broader than it once was. From the other direction, that security has been 'redefined' (as the titles of a number of the articles on the subject have it) as involving the environment suggests agreement from both those who focus on national defense and those who focus on pollution and natural resources on the increasing possibility for the intersection of the two realms.

A third, less examined but nonetheless relevant, approach to the environment and security nexus is the argument that, as the old slogan puts it, 'war is not healthy for children and other living things.' In other words, scholars point to the environmental damage created, not only by war itself conducted for non-environmental reasons, but also by the military establishment more broadly. At the same time, many focus on the potentially useful role for the military in helping to address some of the very problems that are seen as sources of national or international insecurity. An effort to ascertain the nature of any environmental threats to security, and the role (positively or negatively) to be played by the military, is an important endeavor in understanding global environmental politics.

ENVIRONMENT AS NATIONAL SECURITY

The idea of environmental problems as a national security threat emerged publicly in the late 1970s and early 1980s. Lester Brown, one of its earliest proponents, began the debate by calling for an environmental perspective to security. He argued that stresses in the relationship between humans and nature can translate into economic stresses, such as inflation, unemployment, capital scarcity, and monetary instability. These ultimately can lead to social unrest and political instability.[2] Richard Ullman picked up this theme, arguing that defining national security in traditional military ways causes states to ignore other, potentially more harmful, threats and thereby make themselves less secure overall.[3] Jessica Tuchman Matthews and Norman Myers furthered the argument, noting that environmental stress and resource problems can be significant threats to national security.[4] Their arguments, coming towards the end of the Cold War when a worldwide change in what constituted threat seemed imminent, captured both academic and political attention.

The timing of the discussion of the connection between environment and security is not coincidental. To some extent this research agenda was spawned as an effort to increase concern about environmental issues – to move them out of the realm of 'low politics' into the central international relations concern about security.[5] This connection could benefit two constituencies at the end of the Cold War. First, those concerned about the environment could gain more attention and funding for their concerns in the wake of a broader re-evaluation of the role of the military. Secondly, and not surprisingly, those concerned with the military – either operating it or studying it – could also benefit from the examination of new emerging threats to security that would justify continued discussion of security issues and maintaining military resources.[6]

The argument is thus made that environmental degradation or scarcity is something that needs to be considered a national security issue, because it is an issue that increases the likelihood of international conflict or decreases the security of the state. There are two basic ways that this can happen. The first is in some ways a reconceptualization of existing security issues. To the extent that access to resources has always provided justification for interstate war, noting the 'environmental' nature of some of those resources (generally non-renewable resources, such as oil, which also can be seen as energy resources) is simply renaming an existing security threat. Doing so, apart from providing potential political benefits to those who want funding from security think tanks to study environmental issues, has the advantage of bringing to bear existing research on resource scarcity and access to the security literature and community.

More useful, though, is the observation of the possibility of conflict over renewable resources. This phenomenon would be relatively new in the purview of security, and it seems likely that a wide array of environmental resource issues provide the fodder for conflict on the international level. The most likely candidate resource as the cause of potential future war is water.[7] Before the breakup of the Soviet Union there were 214 rivers or lakes shared by more than one country.[8] The potential for conflict over shared water resources seems obvious, particularly when one state has the ability to deny access by others to a body of water on which both have previously depended. Such a conflict emerged, for instance, in the 1930s when Belgium diverted water from the Meuse river, which otherwise would have flowed into the Netherlands; in doing so, it decreased the flow of the water on which the Netherlands relied for canals and irrigation. In the disagreement over the Meuse river, the Permanent Court of International Justice decided the issue, helping to codify the important principle that a state can do what it wants in its own territory as long as it does not impinge on the wellbeing of its neighbors.[9] Frequently, however, these disputes over water are not settled by recourse to legal proceedings, or not settled at all.

Whether such conflicts have as yet led to war is more heavily disputed.[10] The most frequently cited locus of actual (rather than potential) international conflict over water resources is the Jordan river. Skirmishes between Israel and Syria took place in the 1950s and 1960s over allocation of water from the river.[11] Israel responded to Syria's attempted diversion of the river in April 1967 by bombing the infrastructure Syria was building for that purpose, two months before full-scale war between the countries broke out.[12] Those who claim this conflict over water contributed to the outbreak of the Six-Day War may be overstating the case,[13] but access to water did in fact result in acts of state-sponsored violence across borders, and likely increased tensions at a time when broader conflict was imminent. The Tigris and Euphrates and Nile rivers are also suggested as locations where conflict may be intensified or brought on in the future for reasons of water scarcity.[14]

Conflict over water is also suggested as a source for increased tension in the Palestinian–Israeli crisis. It is argued that denial by Israel of Palestinian access to water is 'one of the obstacles towards achieving real peace on the West Bank.'[15] Factors traditionally seen as being at the root of resource problems, such as population growth, can contribute to these problems; in this case some argue that the increased water demand by Palestinians because of population growth has not been taken into account in deciding the water allocation.[16] Certainly many such disputes have been managed in a way that reaches at least a *de facto* resolution, even though it may not be one of which all parties approve equally.[17] That in itself may contribute to unfriendly relations across borders.

It is worth noting, however, that the areas in which water resources are most frequently cited as giving rise to interstate conflict are those (such as the Middle East) where tensions are already high. As in the case of the recent Israeli/Palestinian disagreements over water allocation and pricing, the resource conflict may be a tool in a broader animosity, rather than its root cause. Water can also make border conflicts – such as the one between Syria and Israel – more complicated, if the location of a boundary increases or decreases the amount of water to which an arid country has access. But if water suddenly became plentiful in the Middle East the region's political problems would probably not disappear or even lessen. That is not to say that the effect of resource scarcity on interstate conflict should be discounted, but that the broader context is certain to be important. Lowering tensions by other means may be the best route to addressing resource problems in some areas.

Other renewable resources are also suggested as the source of potential crises. In particular, the types of specifically global environmental problems examined in this volume, such as climate change, ozone depletion, acid rain, deforestation or even whaling are suggested as candidate precursors to conflict on the interstate level if sufficient action is not taken to mitigate them.[18] Also important is the ability of these types of environmental problems to exacerbate existing resource issues. The changing climate is already mentioned as one possible cause of worsening tensions over water in the Middle East,[19] as is deforestation for political conflicts in South Asia.[20] Other of these emerging global problems may contribute to interstate conflict on their own.

Acid rain was seen as one of the first environmental challenges to traditional definitions of security, in part due to its magnitude and in part due to its transboundary character.[21] Unlike many of the other international environmental problems discussed generally (but similar to some of the water concerns that underlie discussions of resource scarcity and interstate conflict) acid rain has a directional transboundary characteristic that makes it different from standard commons issues. Not only are states unable to protect themselves from environmental damage simply by undertaking their own environmental protection measures, but states are differentially affected by problems of acid rain, depending on such things as prevailing wind patterns and soil chemistry. This aspect of the problem feeds into discussions of such issues as relative gains, power, and coercion that are elements of the traditional national security debate. If in order to address an international environmental problem states must undertake different levels of obligations and receive different levels of benefits, some states will gain environmental protection with much less effort than others. In the case of acid rain, that may happen simply because of an accident of geography. Concern over relative gains may not be in the forefront of efforts to address environmental problems, but negotiations over acid rain have shown powerful states unwilling to accept greater environmental protection burdens, and having the influence to reshape environmental regimes around their concerns.

It is also interesting that initial efforts to negotiate international cooperation to address acid rain in Europe came less from the perception of an environmental threat than from a military one. As discussed in Chapter 9, the United Nations Economic Commission for Europe decided to focus on an environmental issue as a way to negotiate a cooperative agreement between East and West during the Cold War, and chose acid rain to be that issue. To some extent, then, cooperation on acid rain was made possible both by traditional security threats and by the perception that it was outside them.

On the other hand, acid rain has been cooperatively addressed in a number of regions, and the states involved have been willing to pay for their externalities. The Trail Smelter case before the International Joint Commission (an international tribunal constituted for the purpose of deciding this issue) found that a smelter in British Columbia should be held responsible for sulfur dioxide damage it created across the border in the USA, should cease from creating this pollution, and should pay compensation to those impacted by it.[22] This case helped to further an important principle of customary international law that states are not allowed to use or allow the use of their territory for activity that causes damages in another state. The Convention on Long-Range Transboundary Air Pollution (LRTAP), created out of the UN process, has had an effect in mitigating acid rain. In addition, this cooperative effort has indicated that under some circumstances states may be willing to accept some level of differential obligations depending on the harm they create, even if some of the reasons they create a disproportionate degree of harm have less to do with their own activities than with prevailing wind patterns or particular vulnerabilities of other states to acidifying pollutants. Nevertheless, although such obligations have been agreed to in principle in the LRTAP process, the difficulty of actually creating a system based on them indicates that states may still be concerned about their relative positions, something those in security studies have observed more generally. The issue also illustrates the implications for environmental security of the fact that states cannot be compelled to take on international obligations to which they have not agreed. The acid rain problem in Europe may have been addressed peacefully, but power still played an important role in its resolution.

Biodiversity may present a different type of security threat. Norman Myers argues that states have a security interest in maintaining biodiversity because important sectors of some economies depend on genetic resources.[23] Importantly, though, many of the most useful biodiversity resources remaining are in developing countries, considered traditionally weak internationally. This power disparity points to two possible security concerns: one by those in whose lands the most valuable biodiversity resources lie and who may fear intrusion by those who want access; the other by those who do not have access to biodiversity resources and fear the growing ability of states to exclude others from their resources. The 1992 UN Convention on Biological Diversity was one effort to allay some of the concerns on both sides of the issue, but both sides still face realistic threats to their wellbeing. 'Biopirates' have been able to take and patent resources for their own profit from tropical rainforests. The increasing fear of such activities has led to a strengthening of the international legal principle of sovereignty over natural resources[24] that increases the likelihood that developing countries will be able to prevent access by others to resources on which planetary ecosystems depend.

Global commons issues such as ozone depletion and global climate change are frequently cited as possible threats to national security. Such issues represent in some ways the best claim for the destabilizing effect of global environmental problems. These issues share the characteristic that one state that refuses to cooperate in the mitigation of the problem can undermine the cooperation of the rest. As such, these types of environmental problems represent a type of power resource not traditionally examined in international relations theory but with important implications for the ability of states to control their own wellbeing.

To use ozone depletion as an example, even if all states except China and India (the two major actors who in fact threatened to stay out of cooperative efforts to protect the ozone layer) stopped emitting ozone-depleting substances altogether, if China and India continued and increased their use of ozone-depleting substances they could themselves undermine all the measures taken by the rest of the world and ensure the depletion of the ozone layer. This 'power to destroy' that is present in common pool resources,[25] shifts the locus of power away from those states that have historically been able to impose their will on others. The chances of going to war over India's decisions about methods of refrigeration and fire suppression seem remote, but the USA did consider economic sanctions against states that refused to participate in international arrangements to protect the ozone layer.[26]

Global climate change may provide the greatest opportunity for potential future conflict, particularly in terms of the unevenness of contributions to the problem and effects felt because of it across states. As discussed previously, part of the predicted impact of climate change on national security comes through exacerbation of current environmental problems, such as water shortages, access to strategic fossil fuels, or disruption of agricultural productivity.[27] Some of the impacts of a changing climate will probably be in terms of new or unforeseen environmental stresses, including the possible displacement of large numbers of people and the international instability that can cause. Others argue that the security elements of climate change, particularly the likelihood of applying prisoner's dilemma approaches to climate politics, may make such issues more difficult to negotiate. Marvin Soroos suggests that reactions to climate change share some of the character- istics of arms races, in which states adopt their third best approach (essentially adapting to, rather than abating, climate change) in order to guard against the worst possible outcome, which would be one in which a given state individually used its resources to decrease the amount of greenhouse gases emitted, while other states did not.[28] In this worst case scenario the state would be worse off than if it had done nothing to mitigate the problem, because it would bear costs and not even protect itself. This dynamic is similar to an arms race (the quintessential problem of security) in that states would be more secure if they could agree to limit their arms buildup, but the fact that they cannot guarantee that other states will live up to those obligations (by also refraining from buying weapons, or, in the analogy, emitting large amounts of greenhouse gases) means that everyone in the system will end up with a sub-optimal outcome. That the incentive structure and resulting insecurity from not being able to trust the commitments of other states may be similar across such seemingly different issues is an argument for the use of security perspectives in understanding some global environ- mental issues.

Despite their lower profile in the environment and security literature, fisheries may provide the best examples of the security implications of conflicts over declining commons resources. Fish are the quintessential common-pool resource in that there is (at least on the high seas and to some extent even within the territorial seas of those unable to keep others out) open access to the resource, and it is depletable; if one state, or fisher, takes a fish, it is no longer available to another state or fisher. States have fired shots at each other's vessels over fishery resources: in what came to be known as the 'Anglo-Icelandic cod wars,' Icelandic and British vessels rammed and shot at each other, with damage to vessels and loss of life in a dispute primarily over British access to cod in formerly international waters over which Iceland claimed jurisdiction.[29] In more recent times there have been armed conflagrations, if not actual wars, over fisheries. One example is Canada's willingness to shoot at Spanish fishing vessels in international waters off the Grand Banks, for overfishing in the declining turbot fishery. Another is Namibia's use of helicopters to drop fishing inspectors and soldiers onto Spanish trawlers fishing in its newly declared exclusive economic zone.[30]

An additional pathway through which environmental degradation can

cause threats to national security is through the creation of environmental refugees. The Intergovernmental Panel on Climate Change
suggested the possibility that the effects of climate change could uproot
millions who would then become international migrants.[31] Although
that has yet to happen, more locally derived environmental problems can
cause movement of people across borders in ways that can ultimately be
internationally destabilizing. Evidence suggests this phenomenon is
already under way. An estimate in the early 1990s counted 10 million
environmental refugees;[32] more recent estimates put that number at 25
million and predict an increase of up to 150 million by 2050.[33] Minor
examples of this phenomenon are not hard to come by. Natural disasters
such as hurricanes aggravate problems already caused by slash-and-burn
farming practices destructive of ecosystems. Hurricane Mitch in
Honduras in 1998 is said to have displaced more than 1.2 million
people. The drying up of the Aral sea in Russia and the resulting loss of
fish and contamination of the surrounding cropland is suggested as a
cause for exodus of people from the area.[34] Some even argue that the
impetus for Mexican migration to the USA is frequently 'depleted soils
and declining aquifers' that drive people from their traditional homes.[35]

Refugees from other countries arrive not only with unfamiliar customs
and languages but potentially new diseases or susceptibility to local ones.
They also may in turn be responsible for environmental degradation in
the place to which they flee.[36] Large numbers of refugees moving at one
time (likely in the case of environmental disaster rather than simple
gradual change) are likely to be politically destabilizing, particularly if the
phenomenon is worldwide. Again, as with discussion of security
implications of global environmental problems, most of the discussion
of the effects of environmental refugees on national security is
anticipatory, rather than descriptive of current events.[37] Some even
argue that migration can have a beneficial effect on the environment and
hence increase security, under the right conditions.[38]

There has been a quick and vociferous backlash to the suggestion that
environmental issues be considered an aspect of national security. There
are a number of reasons to doubt that environmental factors will be a
major cause of interstate conflict. As Thomas Homer-Dixon, one of the
major scholars of the impacts of environmental degradation on internal
state conflict has observed, 'there is virtually no evidence that
environmental scarcity causes major interstate war.'[39] Certainly most of
the discussion of the effect of environmental issues on national security is
forward looking and represents efforts to ensure that environmental
issues will not cause interstate war, so the lack of current evidence is not
entirely damning. But others doubt that it is even an issue to focus on

preventing. Daniel Deudney has argued that economic interdependence and technological advancement make war over natural resources unlikely, because using trade or innovation to meet their resource needs will be a more cost-effective strategy for states.[40] One important element, however, on which even some of the critics of the paradigm agree, is that international relations theory traditionally has excluded nature as an important causal concern; the new focus on environmental security has brought it into the mainstream – even realist – discussion.[41]

What would be the response if the environment *is* conceived as a national security risk? Two possibilities seem likely. The first would be an internally focused relative-gains type approach, similar to traditional security concerns. While states may form alliances for the purpose of tackling security problems (the Club of Rome, along these lines, proposed a 'UN Ecological Security Council'),[42] they essentially are competing with each other. As Matthias Finger puts it, 'states derive their security from their perceived relationships with other states; their security is relative not absolute.'[43] In other words, a situation could arise where the overall level of insecurity increases (in this example, via increased environmental destruction), but as long as it is divided equally across states it will not cause national security problems for any of them. But it is more likely that the relative security situation would change, because of the interaction of states on environmental issues. If a state's level of insecurity has increased due to a lack of access to resources on which it depends, and that lack of access comes because of the actions of other states, some sort of coercion (if possible) would be a reasonable response.

Richard Matthew argues that this type of situation might suggest the use of force or economic incentives to persuade other states to address a resource issue cooperatively.[44] As he points out, pure commons issues (such as climate change or ozone depletion) are less likely to be amenable to these types of solutions than are directional transboundary issues such as acid rain or access to fresh water.[45] On the one hand, he is right that a state whose water is held hostage upstream is in the most difficult situation, because the upstream state gains nothing from cooperatively allocating the resource, and may itself benefit from not doing so. To the extent that individual states are hurt by their failure to protect a commons resource (such as the ozone layer or the global climate system) on which they depend, their threat not to participate in cooperative ventures may be less persuasive than the threat of an exporter of sulfur dioxide to continue its acidifying activities. The difference is that there are many more potential free riders in a global commons issue, any number of whom could by their actions increase the environmental damage to all other states in the system. So the opportunity to costlessly not participate in addressing a resource problem may be smaller in a global commons issue, but there are many more opportunities to do so.

This element of self-reliance is where environmental security differs from traditional conceptions of national security. Although military security may to some extent be relative and it is certainly socially constructed (in that states are not threatening only because of their capabilities but also because of their intentions and their relationships), states can individually or collectively increase their capabilities in ways that make them less vulnerable to attack from abroad. States cannot protect themselves from global environmental problems alone, however, and may not even be able to do so within alliances. Some argue, in fact, that environmental problems help to create a 'global community of interests'[46] suggesting (although not simplifying the process of) greater international cooperation to address the problems. Whether or not this makes natural resources an important aspect of, or a challenge to, traditional security concerns may matter less than how capable states are at cooperating to overcome natural resource problems.

ENVIRONMENT AND INTERNAL CONFLICT

The other well-developed thread of the environment and security debate examines the possibility that resource scarcity can have a destabilizing effect on domestic politics. Ultimately this effect may well result in international conflict as well (or may be made worse by existing international political or environmental problems), if it fails to be resolved. The major effort to understand this phenomenon has been carried about by Thomas Homer-Dixon in the Peace and Conflict Studies project at the University of Toronto. This project begins by identifying pathways through which internal instability could result from resource scarcity, and then goes on to examine a number of cases of conflicts within (or occasionally across) states to determine whether resource scarcity played a role.

Such a research design is not ideal, because of selection on the dependent variable. Looking at a set of places where there are wars or violence and examining them for resource scarcity is likely to be biased in favor of the hypothesis; after all how frequently do you find a society (particularly in the developing world, where most of the research on this topic has been done) where there are no scarce natural resources? Determining causality is particularly difficult because, as Shin-wha Lee argues, even a conflict that begins for purely political reasons can be changed or intensified by environmental degradation.[47] In trying to examine whether there is a link between violence and environmental degradation it would be preferable to examine levels of scarcity of resources across countries and try to determine whether those with the highest level of scarcity (or scarcity in certain types of resources) are more prone to social instability.[48]

To the credit of Homer-Dixon and others working on this issue, they are aware of some of the methodological difficulties. In the first place, they do not argue that resource scarcity will cause wars; only that it can.[49] There are some places where essential natural resources are not all that scarce, or where sufficient wealth exists to gain access to resources that are lacking. More importantly, the project aims for more than simple correlation: it is not sufficient that there exist both resource scarcity and war; researchers attempt to ascertain whether there is a causal link between the two. This causal link, however, is difficult to demonstrate, because there is often some kind of resource scarcity in the conflicts they examine, and it is not hard to derive a set of pathways through which it might matter. Counterfactual analysis, difficult under the best of circumstances, can be particularly difficult when one tries to imagine what would have happened if a certain resource had not been scarce. Researchers do admit when it is difficult to find a causal link. For instance, in the case of South Africa, while Homer-Dixon and Valerie Percival argue that environmental scarcity could have contributed to pre-election violence in South Africa's transition away from apartheid, they admit that they cannot establish the counterfactual argument that the violence would not have occurred in the absence of resource scarcity.[50]

More frequently, however, they do see the scarcity of certain natural resources as playing a role in the conflicts they observe. Homer-Dixon and others see a causal role for resource scarcity in conflicts that have erupted in Mexico, the Himalayas, the Sahel, Central America, Brazil, Rajasthan, and Indonesia, among others.[51] There are a number of pathways through which natural resources can play a role in social conflict within societies, however, and they are rarely direct. First, Homer-Dixon sees three sources for environmental scarcity: degradation, increased consumption of, and unequal distribution of, resources.[52] The scarcity in turn has social impacts in a number of different ways. Groups within society may use power they already have to 'shift in their favor the regime governing resources access.'[53] Moreover, some sectors of society may be pushed onto more and more marginal land, which can create greater environmental degradation and in turn lead to greater social unrest.

The likelihood of violence comes from the population movement, economic decline and weakened states that can result from the ways societies respond (or fail to respond) to resource scarcity. In particular, there is evidence that environmental scarcity causes large population movements, which can lead to conflict based on group identity.[54] The second major pathway through which environmental scarcity may cause conflict is through the creation or intensification of poverty, which can itself provoke conflict.[55] Finally, all these impacts would likely happen through the weakening of a state that results from the combination of factors.[56] One impression that emerges when examining the literature on this topic is that determining the causal direction of relationships that exist is complicated and perhaps impossible.

Hypotheses have emerged from this research, however, about some of the conditions under which we might expect resource degradation to most likely lead to violent conflict, or the ways in which environmental scarcity can have an impact on a society. As such, although most of these are predictions for the future (some of them rather distant in the future, making them even harder to examine empirically), the research agenda has generated testable hypotheses. Homer-Dixon, for instance, expects more environmentally derived conflicts to arise in the developing rather than developed world, because wealthier countries will have a greater capacity to adapt to resource scarcity.[57] Unlike some scholars discussed above, he also expects degradation of resources such as agricultural lands, forests, water, and fisheries to be more likely to lead to conflict than will global issues like climate change.[58] He also suggests that environmental conditions can lead to what he calls 'hard' (praetorian) regimes, those likely to be corrupt and non-democratic, when environmental scarcity coincides with a history of military strength.[59] Brazil, Nigeria, and Indonesia would be candidates for such regimes. He thus argues that recent moves towards democracy in some such countries may ultimately be overwhelmed by environmental factors that lead them back to traditional approaches to conflict.[60]

Importantly, one of the things that is demonstrated by these research projects is the complexity of causation of conflicts. Instead of a direct path between resource scarcity and violent conflict, we see overpopulation, migration, hunger and other resource-based issues playing a role in intensifying political instability and ethnic tensions. They may not cause, but instead trigger or accelerate conflicts.[61] In terms of research, however, this shift only complicates research into causality. Add to that the complexity of potential causes for resource problems (some of which are social, some the result of complex natural phenomena and some a combination of both) and untangling the relationships becomes even more difficult.

Some theorists go so far as to suggest that these resource conflicts can lead to complete social collapse (and, potentially, interstate war as in the national security version of the issue). Robert Kaplan argues that 'environmental scarcity will inflame existing hatreds and affect power relationships,' that will presage broader destruction. Such collapse, in an extreme, could lead to the destruction of states.[62] Others predict genocide or mass death in 'the coming age of scarcity.'[63]

But what do we mean by 'scarcity'? An important issue for understanding the role of environmental degradation in internal conflict, as well as the broader relationship between environment and security, as Marc Levy points out, is how we define 'environment.'[64] The term has been used remarkably imprecisely in many of the discussions of the role that environmental factors play in creating conflict. Many of the most notable factors leading, for instance, to what are known as 'environmental refugees,' as discussed above, tend to be natural disasters. Those may be made more likely or more severe by the way humans have interacted with the environment, but surely these types of environmental issues are not new. Homer-Dixon acknowledges that environmental aspects to conflict have been examined since classical Greece, and points to discussions of food-scarcity-induced political unrest in fifteenth-century Spain.[65] Theorists since Thomas Malthus in the eighteenth century have suggested the dangers of population growth outstripping food supply, and population growth or demographic shifts have probably been important factors in civil unrest throughout history. The danger is that if all natural phenomena, or all resource issues, are considered environmental, the category will become so broad as to become meaningless. Moreover, as the long history of awareness of this phenomenon suggests, complete social collapse has not yet come about as a result of environmental scarcity. Societies, while impacted dramatically by the natural environment in which they find themselves, can also be remarkably resilient, depending on other circumstances. And conflict can be due – even primarily – to a wide variety of factors other than natural resource degradation. What is likely is that environmental factors, however defined, have probably often played a role in local conflict. That role may be increasing. Moreover, though we do not currently have a good understanding of the conditions under which scarcity will play a deciding role in local conflict, or the types of scarcity that are likely to matter, we do now have a set of hypotheses to examine to gain a clearer sense of the relationship between natural resource issues and conflict.

What would be the implications of viewing internal conflict as motivated or accelerated by environmental scarcity? Certainly this perspective gives alternative approaches to preventing or halting local or regional conflict. If local violence erupts only from political factors or historical or ethnic hatreds, there is little that can be done, aside from mediation. It may, however, be possible to identify problems of resource scarcity before they can lead to violence. If an ongoing conflict is likely underpinned by environmental problems, addressing those problems, or ensuring adequate natural resources to various sides in a dispute, can be an alternate avenue for dispute resolution. Moreover, addressing issues of natural resource degradation as an effort to prevent or mitigate conflict has the potential advantage of being a 'win-win' solution, in the terms of negotiators, to local problems. While we may not be certain that focusing on improving environmental problems will prevent intrastate violence, doing so can be advantageous and beneficial in its own right. If it can also decrease the likelihood that other political animosities will turn violent, so much the better.

One implicit advantage of this approach to the environment and security nexus is that it moves past the state centrism of the national security debate. Although neither approach truly focuses on security as a concept that applies to individuals, the Homer-Dixon *et al.* approach does implicitly discuss effects on individuals of environmental degradation. While states remain important actors in international relations and ultimately the ones likely to have to act to prevent large-scale environmental degradation, the environmental effects themselves (as well as the changes of behavior that must be undertaken to address these problems) will be felt at a local, and sometimes individual level. A focus on the role that environmental degradation or resource overconsumption plays in the lives of individuals is thus an important aspect of international environmental politics to keep in mind.

THE MILITARY AND THE ENVIRONMENT

One of the major arguments put forth against linking the issues of environmental degradation and national security is that the institutions that each engages are 'mismatched.'[66] Some go as far as to argue that the mechanisms on which the national security apparatus relies (state sovereignty, at the broad end of the spectrum; military force at the narrow end) are the ultimate causes of environmental decline. If a focus on protecting a state from threats from abroad, and the use of the military to do so, are at best ineffective and at worst counterproductive, the idea of merging the two concepts may be misguided. It is thus important to ascertain the role the military can or does play in either protecting or degrading the natural environment.

Certainly war is likely to be damaging to the environment. As the states present at the UN Conference on Environment and Development in Rio in 1992 felt compelled to include in the Rio Declaration, 'Warfare is inherently destructive of sustainable development.' The principle goes on to suggest that 'States shall therefore respect international law providing protection for the environment in times of armed conflict.'[67]

Some of this environmental degradation is intentionally inflicted in the service of warfare; witness the defoliation (and additional damage done because of the toxicity of the defoliant used) in Vietnam.[68] Efforts have even been made to disrupt the weather as a practice of war.[69] Iraq's intentional spilling of oil into the Persian Gulf and burning of the oil wells as it was forced out of Kuwait may have served little military purpose, but were certainly intended as a message in the course of war, and caused widespread environmental damage as well as the destruction of a non-renewable resource. In addition, discussion of the possible military uses of environmental degradation have gone far beyond what has been carried out in practice.[70]

Environmental damage inflicted as an externality of warfare, if not an intentional tool in its arsenal, is also commonplace. Endangered species in central Africa fared poorly in the fighting that broke out in Rwanda, Burundi and the country formerly known as Zaire: the civil war in the Democratic Republic of Congo is cited as the 'most acute problem' facing primate species in the region, largely because of habitat destruction and displacement.[71] Richard Carroll, the Director of the World Wildlife Fund's program for Central Africa points out the role that civil wars play in increasing the diffusion of guns across the population and the opportunities that result for wildlife poaching.[72] The fighting in the former Yugoslavia has also had devastating environmental impacts. For example, NATO bombing in Serbia in April 1999 destroyed fertilizer plants and oil refineries located on a tributary of the Danube river, resulting in fires and the release of petroleum byproducts and other carcinogens into the water. Additional bombs that month released large amounts of PCBs and liquid mercury into other Danube tributaries, both posing severe danger to human life.[73] In neither of these examples was environmental destruction intended, but it certainly resulted.

Moreover, militarism, even in the absence of active conflict, has severe environmental effects, through consumption and pollution. Market forces, never ideal at addressing environmental externalities, are all but absent in creating military budgets. Consumption of resources for defense of national interests is vast, and the privileged position of the military within most states makes resource conservation in this sector unlikely. The armed forces of the USA alone account for between three and four percent of the direct US oil demand; more if indirect use is taken into account. The military worldwide consumes more than a quarter of all jet fuel used.[74]

The military also creates a disproportionate amount of waste and pollutants during its non-wartime operations. Creating and testing weapons systems produces pollutants. In the USA the military 'is quite likely the largest generator of hazardous waste.'[75] Almost all the high-level radioactive waste and the vast majority of low-level waste produced in the USA has come from reactors used for the military; moreover, accurate information on how much and what type of hazardous pollutants are created by the US military is generally unavailable. Examples of this pollution abound, however. For instance, pollutants from training activities at military bases on Cape Cod in Massachusetts have entered the groundwater, threatening the Cape's only drinking-water supply. Pollution from unexploded ordnance from military testing is blamed for dangers to coral reefs and suspected in increases in leukemia in children.[76] A US General Accounting Office study in 1988 found that federal facilities (including, centrally, the Department of Defense) were twice as likely as private industry not to comply with water-pollution regulations.[77] Secrecy about military operations is commonplace, so even the regulations supposed to bind the military can be difficult to monitor and hard to enforce. United States' and European military bases, closed in the post-Cold War downsizing, are rarely decontaminated before their inhabitants depart, leaving behind toxic pollutants.

The recent evidence of Eastern bloc environmental destruction from its military efforts during the Cold War is even more frightening, and demonstrates the role that secrecy can play in allowing actors to avoid protection of the environment. Certainly much of the Soviet nuclear weapons program was conducted without regard to human or environmental health, and the Soviet military disposed of nuclear waste in the ocean in contravention of the London Dumping Convention.[78] Waste from the extraction of plutonium was dumped in local lakes and rivers and nuclear-powered vessels were sunk at sea, leaking fuel.[79]

Additionally, because of national security concerns, the military is often exempted from international and even national regulations to protect the environment. For example, the 1973 International Convention for the Prevention of Pollution from Ships indicates that it 'shall not apply to any warship, naval auxiliary or other ship owned or operated by a State and used, for the time being only on government non-commercial service.'[80] Likewise, the 1992 Convention on the Protection of the Marine Environment of the Baltic Sea Area does not apply 'to any warship, naval auxiliary, military aircraft or other ship and aircraft owned or operated by a State and used, for the time being, only on government non-commercial service.'[81] Although not noted in the text of the Kyoto Protocol, the Conference of the Parties agreed to partially exempt military fuels used in support of UN operations from the obligations of the Protocol.[82] The military is also given a privileged position in some international agreements with respect to reporting requirements. The 1997 UN Convention on the Law of the Non-Navigational Uses of International Watercourses exempts states from providing 'data or information vital to its national defense or security.'[83]

Even in the USA, where much (though not all) environmental regulation is binding on the military operating within the country, military bases and operations abroad are not required to uphold these standards.[84] Moreover, for reasons of 'national security' the military or military contractors can be granted exemptions from the environmental rules to which they are otherwise subject. Finger argues that 'the more important the military-industrial complex is within a country, the more likely it is that that nation state will act as a protector of its military rather than as a protector of the biosphere.'[85]

On the other hand, the military, particularly in the post-Cold War world, may have technological capabilities that can be helpful in detecting or preventing environmental destruction. Technologies such as the global positioning system (GPS), sonar, and radar that were first developed for military applications have already been used for environmental monitoring. (They have also been used, however, as they have become available to civilians, for increasing the ability of people to harvest resources more efficiently, thus contributing to their depletion. Fishers have used this technology, for instance, to be able to locate and catch fish more efficiently.) Satellite imagery, from technology developed and deployed by the military, has been used to gain an understanding of the extent and pattern of deforestation.[86] More recent efforts have been focused on monitoring desertification, cloud cover, and coastlines, issues likely affected by global climate change.[87] Spy technology could be used to monitor compliance with various environmental agreements. The US began a Strategic Environmental Research and Development Program, intended to put the resources of such actors as the Department of Defense and the intelligence community to use against the 'massive environmental problems facing our nation and the world today.'[88] In addition, the US Department of Defense has given millions of dollars in funding in support of biodiversity protection in developing countries.[89]

The use of former military technology for environmental monitoring pleases two quite different sets of constituents: environmentalists, faced with a need for information and lacking resources, and the military, in search of a new mission in the post-Cold War world.[90] Some of these processes use actual military equipment. Others use technology developed in a military context, but now run by civilian agencies. The US National Aeronautics and Space Administration (NASA) satellite program called the 'Earth Observing System' monitors atmospheric conditions, pollution, vegetation cover, and a variety of other environmental indicators.[91]

There is disagreement about how valuable this participation of the military in environmental endeavors can be. Kent Butts argues that the military will inevitably play an environmental role, often because the environment plays a role in military objectives.[92] It is therefore to the advantage of the military to collect information on the state of the environment. Moreover, particularly in developing countries, the military may be 'better organized, trained and technologically-sophisticated' than other actors in society, and may be present throughout the country[93] in ways other parts of national bureaucracies may not. The military may thus be able to enforce environmental regulations, such as the protection of endangered species, better than underfunded conservation agencies.

Others are less sanguine about the involvement of the military in environmental protection. In an argument akin to his broader concern about the concept of environmental security, Deudney expresses a concern about the potential 'militarization' of the environment. He points to important differences between standard military threats and the types of environmental threats with which the military may be called upon to deal under a new environmental security paradigm. In particular, the military is most successful at addressing problems with short-term solutions, not a generally accurate or useful characterization of environmental problems.[94] Deudney observes that organizations that provide national security through military means tend to be 'secretive, extremely hierarchical, and centralized' and use advanced technologies.[95] Those characteristics are precisely the ones many see as elements of the creation of environmental degradation. Certainly increasing levels of technology have allowed increasing degrees of pollution and resource consumption. Moreover, he argues that in addressing environmental problems all people must be involved, because a whole range of human activities are implicated in causing, or are affected by, environmental degradation. Hierarchical centralized approaches would at best be ineffective, if not counterproductive.[96] In addition, the secrecy that has allowed military operations to pollute without detection may similarly allow nefarious uses of nominally

environmental activities; for those concerned (as are many environmental activists) with creating greater transparency, the military seems a
dubious path to that goal.

Others argue further, although somewhat unspecifically, that it is the
whole approach to security in the first place that has created the types of
ecological problems the world faces. Cited are variously the division of
the world into nation states,[97] the focus on wealth as an element of
security,[98] and a division of 'high' from 'low' politics that gives security a
pride of place in approaches to policy.[99] While any of these factors can
surely be considered contributors to environmental degradation, the
broad brush with which 'security' is painted as an inherent villain in
environmental problems is probably not the most useful way to approach
the topic. It is exactly this linking together of all issues as either about
security or environmental degradation, and then drawing connections
between any of the elements under either umbrella that leads to the
'muddled thinking' on the topic Deudney observes, and to some degree
participates in.[100] At best, he argues, these two paradigms are
mismatched. More importantly, he believes that adding a security focus
to environmental problems will result in nationalistic rather than global
thinking,[101] with the latter necessary to truly address international
environmental problems.

Others propose different ways out of this dilemma. Hugh Dyer argues
in favor of viewing environmental security as a norm rather than
an interest. Doing so would recognize the socially constructed nature
of security, and focus on the value of ensuring freedom from
environmental harm.[102] The constructivist trend within international
relations theory[103] is perhaps nowhere as appropriate as when
examining issues of security as traditionally defined. States with similar
capabilities may be seen to be a greater or lesser threat depending on the
social relations among those states, whether they be traditional allies,
enemies, or unconnected to each other, which depends, of course, on
how the other state views your state as well. Thinking of security as
something no longer objectively determined but socially constructed
suggests new ways to examine the impact of environmental problems.
This conception also calls into focus the socially constructed nature
of states themselves. With environmental issues not contiguous with
state boundaries, people may be best able to be safe from environmental
harm when 'the image of the state as a referent object for security
fades.'[104]

One of the important aspects of examining the relationship between
the military and the environment is that it represents a point of tension in
the discussion of environment and security. If the argument prevails for a

focus on environmental quality as an aspect of national security as conventionally conceived, then the military is at least likely to be part of the solution to the problem. This would be the case either if environmental degradation led to conventional warfare, in which case the military would be involved in preventing or defending against it, or if military capability or technology were used to support environmental protection.[105]

We certainly have seen efforts to protect shared natural resources that rely on military or quasi-military action. From Israeli bombing of river diversion projects in the Middle East to fisheries disputes in the North Atlantic or off Namibia, military force has shown itself capable of playing a role in preventing the overexploitation of natural resources. More recent examples of the use of military apparatus for monitoring environmental quality are evidence that the military has the capability and will to be involved in environmental issues. If the military itself, however, is implicated in the destruction of the environment, perhaps the focus on environmental elements to national security would, at best, require a reconceptualization of how to respond to such threats.

CONCLUSIONS

There are no neat ways to tie up the loose ends in the debate about the interaction between environment and security. Certainly in terms of a colloquial definition of security, people are less safe because of global environmental problems. There is evidence that these problems have contributed to, and in rare cases perhaps even caused, violent conflict on the local level. Resource degradation has not on its own caused actual interstate wars, but it has been the cause of military posturing, skirmishes, and even death, and it has certainly increased tensions in already difficult interstate relations. Moreover, evidence suggests that the increasing degradation likely with major global environmental changes will exacerbate and possibly create new types of resource conflicts. Whether to call this phenomenon an issue of national security or not is to some extent an issue of semantics. Whether to make use of the apparatus of national security or to refocus efforts on creating a globally cooperative process to manage environmental problems is a more existential question. Both perspectives have merit. Will environmentalists co-opt the military, or the other way around?

Certainly a redefinition of what it means to be 'secure' will need to look beyond traditional issues of military threats from abroad. Conversely, examination of civil unrest within countries will have to start taking more seriously the complex role that resource degradation can play, either as a cause or result of domestic violence. What we call these redefinitions is less important than that we do them.

SCIENCE, UNCERTAINTY, AND RISK

Uncertainty – of what other states will do, of how serious a threat is – underlies international relations broadly, but is nowhere more important than in the area of the global environment. The causes of many environmental problems are uncertain, as are the effects of a wide variety of proposed solutions. Environmental problems are often addressed as uncertainties, although in some types of cases resolving uncertainty may make international cooperation more difficult. International agreements are often designed to elicit information and research that will help gather the understanding needed for continued regulation. The designing of international regulation to allow for changes as uncertainties are resolved is a hallmark of international environmental policy-making. And scientific cooperation may in some cases drive political cooperation, to an extent often not present (or at least not examined) in other international issue areas.

Related, but important to distinguish, is the concept of risk. Risk relates to the probability of the occurrence of an undesirable event. In some cases (the chance that a flipped coin will come up heads, for example), probability is easy to determine. The reason that risk and uncertainty are so frequently confused stems from the fact that determining probabilities for many environmental, or political, events is fraught with uncertainty. Risk may therefore be a statement about likelihood, but in most cases relevant to this topic the likelihood is fundamentally uncertain. They are thus separate but intertwined issues. Examining risk demonstrates primarily that people, and politicians, do not evaluate risk in the same way that economists or risk assessors do. That leads both to a certain predictability about the concerns that will generate the greatest public pressure and to a concern that the public does not value risk correctly, and thus that attention and resources are not allocated in the best possible way.

The role of science and scientists within this framework is essential, but complicated. A view of science as an objective search for truth must be balanced against an examination of science as politics – what we think we know may depend on who asks what questions. Scientists themselves play political roles intentionally or not; international agreement may be more likely when there is a community of scholars who share similar approaches and agree on the basic components of a problem. It is within the study of environmental politics that an objective role for science has been most effectively questioned, but also within global environmental issues that such a role appears inescapable.

UNCERTAINTY

Uncertainty is most frequently referred to as incomplete information or disagreement between information sources. It occurs in any discipline and is certainly important in any aspect of international relations; policymakers want to know what other actors will do in order to be able to decide what *they* should do. The issue becomes more complicated in environmental politics, however, as political uncertainty intersects with scientific uncertainty. It is suggested that 'in environmental regulatory affairs we are confronted with data for which neither the level of precision nor the level of accuracy is particularly high.'[1]

Scientific uncertainty is given as an underlying cause for the failure to reach prompt international agreements, particularly with respect to environmental issues. Oran Young suggests that science may play a role in influencing the success or failure of the creation of international regimes.[2] The role of science and uncertainty of this sort is essentially functionalist, in that science is seen as a non-political, objective activity that generates additional information that can be used by the policy-making arena to generate cooperative outcomes.[3] This type of uncertainty is almost always seen to be detrimental to international cooperation and within international environmental politics there are a number of examples of agreements that have become possible once uncertainty has been resolved. The history of the Montreal Protocol on Substances That Deplete the Ozone Layer is a good example, as increased understanding of the damage caused to the ozone layer, of the increasing numbers of substances that could be held responsible for it, and the effects of this damage, caused states to agree to stricter controls over time. Likewise, learning that acidifying substances could travel long distances in the air, and the discovery during national assessments of damage that had not previously been noticed, made some states more willing to undertake substantial changes in their emissions of the pollutants that contribute to acid rain.

There are circumstances, however, in which uncertainty may be beneficial. If resolution of uncertainty about the costs and benefits to actors considering cooperation to address a problem meant that certain states would know that they do not suffer net harm from a pollutant, they might be less willing to negotiate mitigation measures. Lawrence Susskind argues that this type of phenomenon was at work in negotiations for the Antarctic Treaty. The fact that states were unaware of the existence or extent of mineral wealth in Antarctica helped facilitate the negotiation of a minerals regime; if it were demonstrated that valuable minerals were present states would have had a harder time bargaining over their regulation or division.[4] Seong-lin Na and Hyun Song Shin suggest that coalitions to address international environmental problems are easier to form before the resolution of some uncertainties. They argue that information about an environmental issue can help policymakers make more informed decisions, but nevertheless find that 'cooperation is more difficult to achieve when the likely winners and losers are known when negotiation takes place.' They demonstrate, in a game theoretic framework, that outcomes achieved with more information are less beneficial overall than are those made under uncertainty.[5] In other words, if we assume that states negotiate strategically to try to get the best deal for themselves, they will be willing only to undertake the minimum action required to benefit. If they do not know, however, exactly how they will be affected, they are closer to a Rawlsian veil of ignorance in which they will agree to outcomes that make the entire group better off.[6]

The extent to which uncertainty helps or hinders negotiation on international agreement has yet to be systematically empirically investigated, and there are different types of matters about which actors can be uncertain, some of which clearly benefit from being resolved. There is, for instance, a big difference between not understanding the mechanism by which an environmental effect occurs (or even if actual problems will result from hypothesized effects), and not understanding the costs of abatement measures or which actors will contribute most to or suffer most from the environmental problem.

Additionally, evidence abounds of the ability to use uncertainty for political ends. Industries most likely to be harmed by regulations to mitigate a suspected environmental problem are likely to play up the existing uncertainties and fund scientific studies to attempt to call the environmental problem into question. The role of the media in many advanced industrialized countries plays into this strategy, by focusing on disagreement or giving equal time to opposing viewpoints.

International environmental agreements often address legitimate underlying uncertainties by the format of the regulation. Many recent global or regional environmental agreements begin with framework conventions to which protocols are later added as the cause and magnitude of the harm become clearer and more widely accepted, and the costs of regulation more clearly understood. More importantly, these initial framework conventions often contain specific processes for scientific cooperation generally, and for gathering information on the environmental issue and state actions. Parties to the Vienna Convention on the Protection of the Ozone Layer agree to cooperate in a wide range of activities relating to investigation of the nature and extent of the problem of ozone depletion.[7] Parties to the Convention on Long-Range Transboundary Air Pollution agree to 'initiate and cooperate in the conduct of research' relating to development of technologies for abatement and measurement of pollutants, models for understanding the transmission of air pollutants, and the effects of air pollutants on human health and the environment, and to implement the 'Cooperative Programme for the monitoring and evaluation of the long-range transmission of air pollutants in Europe.'[8]

Likewise, one of the most important but easily overlooked aspects of uncertainty that generally needs to be resolved is the actual behavior of states with respect to an environmental issue: most states in the international system (even before the fall of communism in Eastern Europe) are not so economically centralized that they know exactly how much carbon dioxide or CFCs the state as a whole emits. Before any abatement measures can be undertaken, states need to know their contribution to the problem, both to gain a greater understanding of the scope of the environmental problem and because obligations (for pollutants at least) are frequently given as a reduction of a certain percentage of emissions from a certain year. That requires that states find out how much they are contributing to the environmental problem, and continually monitor their behavior afterwards. To this end, for example, parties to the Framework Convention on Climate Change agree to 'develop ... and make available ... national inventories of anthropogenic emissions by sources and removals by sinks of all greenhouse gases.'[9]

Precautionary Principle

One of the important international efforts to address environmental decision-making under conditions of uncertainty is the precautionary principle, first elaborated in environmental policy in Europe in the 1970s.[10] The principle suggests that uncertainty should not prevent action to mitigate environmental problems. The most widely quoted version appears as Principle 15 of the 1992 Rio Declaration on Environment and Development: 'Where there are threats of serious or irreversible damage, lack of full scientific certainty shall not be used as a reason for postponing cost-effective measures to prevent environmental degradation.' As the Rio version suggests, the principle is generally taken to be most applicable to cases where environmental damage, if it occurred, would be impossible or difficult to reverse. In addition, most recent versions of the principle focus to some extent on the cost of the action; not requiring every possible action to be taken, but rather suggesting that scientific uncertainty should not be used as an excuse for not taking any action until the uncertainty has been resolved. Stronger forms of the principle suggest not using any new technology (such as genetically modified organisms) until proven safe. This is a more controversial and less widely accepted formulation.

This precautionary principle has become enshrined in international environmental law, most prominently as the basis for European environmental law under the Treaty on European Union.[11] It is included in various forms in a wide variety of international environmental instruments, from the non-legally binding 1984 Declarations of the International Conferences on the Protection of the North Sea[12] to its first treaty appearance in the 1985 Vienna Convention on the Protection of the Ozone Layer,[13] to the 1992 Transboundary Watercourses Convention, and the 1992 Framework Convention on Climate Change, among others. Apart from its use, generally in a permissive sense (allowing states to take action despite uncertainty), within treaties or in a variety of non-binding international declarations, the precautionary principle has not quite reached the status of customary international law. More recent statements of the principle (such as in the Rio Declaration) do suggest, however, that states are coming to see it as a standard international legal principle. It is also an important corrective to the traditional delaying tactic of requiring more research before taking any action on environmental problems that politicians would rather not endure costs for beginning to address.

It is one that is difficult to apply in practice, however. Daniel Bodansky suggests that it is 'too vague to serve as a regulatory standard.'[14] As it currently stands, the principle is open to interpretation. One study found fourteen different versions of the principle in treaties and multilateral declarations,[15] suggesting at minimum that there is not an international consensus on what it entails. Bodansky, moreover, suggests the real question left unanswered is 'what types of precautionary actions are warranted and at what price?'[16] The principle does not suggest whether actions should be taken under conditions of uncertainty to prevent all possible risk of harm, or simply to decrease the risk, nor does it give a clear indication about how to decide how much uncertainty is enough to prevent action.

Others critique the principle on philosophical, rather than practical, grounds. Some see it as damaging the role of science by moving away from the requirement of demonstrating cause and effect before taking regulatory action.[17] It is also worth noting the inevitable trade-offs: in working to mitigate one uncertain risk, say global climate change, we will inevitably take on other uncertain risks, such as potentially lost jobs or wealth. It is for this latter reason that recent statements of the precautionary principle focus more on the cost-effectiveness of the measures taken.

RISK

The evaluation of risk, and the process of making decisions about how best to prioritize the mitigation of risk, is essential in the process of understanding how to respond to environmental problems globally or locally. Addressing risk is also essential in international relations, and the intersection of the ways different sets of scholars have conceptualized and applied the idea of risk is illuminating in determining what role it plays, or should play, in decisions about global environmental problems. It is clear that political decision-makers, led by the individuals who elect them, systematically value risk in ways that appear to be economically irrational. It is less clear how to address these seeming irrationalities, or whether they in fact are irrational at all.

Much discussion of the difficulties of evaluating risk comes from psychology. Cognitive psychologists Paul Slovic, Sarah Lichtenstein and Baruch Fischhoff and others provided the empirical foundation of risk perception beginning in the 1970s. Their findings suggested that people are generally not adept at judging the likelihood of hazards.[18] Early such experiments asked people to assess the lethality of 41 different causes of death, and suggested that we tend to underestimate the likelihood of death due to high-frequency causes (like asthma) and conversely overestimate the likelihood of death due to low-frequency causes (like tornadoes).[19] Such research also indicates that experts tend to be more accurate assessors of risk than are laypeople.[20]

Some of these incorrect assessments of risks can be traced back to uncertainty. In most social or scientific situations worth evaluating there is insufficient information to allow people to assess the likelihood of an outcome, so they apply certain heuristics to help them approach the process of assessing risk. Scholars have identified some of the frames that people use to assess probability. These heuristics have systematic biases that can be anticipated. The 'representativeness' frame is the belief that events have similar probabilities because of other similarities they share. Rose McDermott gives as an example of this phenomenon attendance at an arms-control lecture in which it is known that three-quarters of the audience are academics and one-quarter artists. When attempting to guess the profession of a questioner from the audience, dressed in black, with an earring and a beret, people simply playing the odds should guess that the questioner is an academic, since three in four audience members are. But since the person up for analysis resembles other people we have perceived to be artists, people are more likely to guess 'artist' for that person's profession.[21] Daniel Kahneman and Amos Tversky suggest that 'people appear to believe in a hologram-like model of personality in which any fragment of behavior represents the actor's true character.'[22] In the political realm, people often use historical analogies for current policy events.[23] They may also see international environmental problems as similar (ozone depletion and climate change, for instance) when they share some similar characteristics but are in other ways fundamentally different.

A second systematic bias is what several people have termed 'availability.' Tversky and Kahneman find that availability of information about an uncertain risk makes people overvalue it. That suggests that events with a small chance of occurring, such as shark attacks, appear more likely when the film *Jaws* is shown, or when there is news coverage of shark attacks. Similarly, we believe that homicide happens more frequently than suicide, because there are more reports about the former, when really the latter is the more common.[24] People may be more concerned about environmental risks that are widely discussed than those (persistent organic pollutants, for example) that are probably more serious but have not received media attention.

A third risk heuristic commonly found is the idea of 'anchoring.' People tend to stick to their original assessments of probability even when new information would allow them to update their information and make better predictions. Experimental psychology has shown that people even use these anchors in entirely unrelated issues. When people have been told a number and are then told it has nothing to do with the question that they are about to be asked (estimating the number of hospitals in the USA, for instance), they are nevertheless likely to come up with an answer that makes use of this unrelated number.[25] This phenomenon suggests that people accept outdated information on environmental problems (including such things as the level of uncertainty of human impacts on the global climate), even when that information has changed.

People also demonstrate overconfidence, being 'more confident in their judgments than is warranted by the facts.'[26] One piece of evidence suggested for this phenomenon is the propensity by people to begin small businesses despite the knowledge that two-thirds of small businesses fail in the first four years. Dale Griffin and Amos Tversky found evidence for overconfidence in a wide range of professions. They note, however, that overconfidence is not universal; as suggested by Slovic *et al.* in 1973, there are particular circumstances in which people are likely to be underconfident in their assessments. Griffin and Tversky find that overconfidence happens when the strength of the evidence is high and sample size is small. For example, in determining whether a tossed coin is biased, the percentage of heads is likely to be given far larger weight than the number of coin tosses. Conversely, under-confidence occurs when the strength of the evidence is high and sample size is large.[27] Probability gives us a systematic way to assess these two factors but robust evidence from psychology suggests that people do not follow the rules of probability in determining risk.

People also have a desire for certainty that leads them to insist that uncertainty does not exist, even when evidence suggests that it does. People who live in areas where a disaster has just happened are quick to state that it could never happen again.[28] This is a central tenet of prospect theory, discussed below. What is important about this particular frame is to note that denial of risk often provokes anger at risk assessors or policy-makers who insist on presenting risk assessments in probabilities, rather simply stating whether something is safe or dangerous.[29]

Apart from, but often confused with, the question of our ability to understand how risky various activities are, is the issue of which risks people tend to care most about preventing. In general, it has been found, people tend to be most concerned about risks that are imposed rather than voluntarily undertaken, risks that are shared unfairly, and human-created risks, including those from exotic technologies, rather than those that are natural.[30]

The discussion of how to prioritize decisions based on risk comes from economics, but it is clear that even apart from people's inaccurate risk assessments, they way they value risk is also not reducible to simple economics. Economically rational behavior suggests that a dollar is worth a dollar no matter the circumstances, and assumes that gains and losses are identical. Evidence suggests that people do not behave this way.

Evaluating risk is thus also about loss; something is considered to be a greater risk not only when it is more likely to happen, but when the value of the loss is greater. Thus risk assessment needs to consider both the likelihood of outcomes and a judgment about their relative subjective utility.[31] One of the first theories to assess risk was the idea of 'expected value'; this approach suggests that the expected value of an outcome is equal to its payoff multiplied by its probability. Problems with this approach were first noted by Daniel Bernoulli in 1738 when he observed that assuming a direct relationship between expected value and payoff did not accurately predict behavior, because people may have different individual values that they attach to a particular payoff.[32]

The modification suggested initially by Bernoulli adds a utility function to the idea of expected value, acknowledging that outcomes have different utilities to people in different situations, and in particular 'increments of utility decrease with increasing wealth.' As McDermott suggests, $1 is a lot of money if that is all you have, and you would be unlikely to take a risk of losing the dollar; if you have $101, you would not value that dollar as highly and might be more willing to accept a risk of losing it.[33] This model thus produces a concave risk function (because increments of utility should become less valuable with increases in wealth) and assumes risk aversion. The next major modification of the approach to valuing risk came from John von Neumann and Oskar Morgenstern, who approached the issue from the opposite direction to Bernoulli. They used utility to derive preferences. The only rules they applied were that a person's utility must show transitivity, dominance, and invariance. The first assumes that if a person prefers A to B and B to C then that person prefers A to C. Second, if an option is better in one way, and at least equal in other ways, it will be preferred to other options. Third, a person's preferences will not change based on the way in which the options are posed, as long as they are the same options. This allowed for individual utility functions within certain sets of assumed rules, rather than uniform ones across all people. In this model people act to maximize their subjective utility, even though they may not share the same views of utility.[34] But it turns out that even these sets of assumptions do not accurately describe how people approach risk.

Prospect Theory

The most important new set of insights into decision-making under risk came originally from Kahneman and Tversky's revision of expected utility theory that they termed prospect theory. Their initial article on the topic pointed out several types of situations in which people systematically violate the assumptions of expected utility theory. One is the idea of certainty, discussed above. People will take a smaller certain gain over even a high probability of a bigger gain. A second observation suggests that when a gain is likely, people will choose an option with the higher probability but lower payoff, whereas when gains are highly unlikely they will choose the option with the higher payoff but lower probability. Most importantly, when the idea of gains is replaced by losses, their choices in the above situations completely reverse: people will choose even a high chance of a larger loss over the certainty of a small loss; when losses are probable they will choose to take a smaller risk of a higher loss, and when losses are unlikely they will choose to take a higher chance of a smaller loss. An additional observation Kahneman and Tversky make is that people are more willing to endure higher costs to reduce the probability of a negative outcome to zero than they are to undertake small costs to reduce, but not eliminate, a risk. Finally, they identify what they call 'the isolation effect;' the propensity of people to irrationally simplify decision problems by focusing on what distinguishes the sets of decisions from each other, rather than by looking at the entire set of decisions.[35]

To put it more generally, they suggest that people tend to be risk averse when there is a situation of gains, and risk acceptant when there is a situation of losses. This approach returns to the idea of decision curves that are identical for all people; they are simply not identical in all situations. In their new approach they create a system that assigns value to gains and losses rather than to assets, and 'decision weights' replace probability. They also describe different value functions for these situations: for gains (as consistent with Bernoulli's observations) the value function is concave, for losses it is convex, and it is steeper for losses than for gains. Similarly, what they term 'decision weights' differ from actual probabilities; people particularly misapprehend probability at the extreme ends of the spectrum, considering very unlikely events to be impossible and very likely events to be certain. Moreover, these extreme ends take on more psychological importance. People are willing to pay a lot more to reduce a low risk (0.01) to zero than to reduce a slightly higher risk by exactly the same amount (0.02 to 0.01). Consistent with this weighting of decisions is that somewhat low-probability events are seen as more likely than they really are, and medium- and high-probability events seen as less likely[36]

Prospect theory has a number of implications for political decision-making generally, and for global environmental politics more specifically. First it suggests that decision-making at the extremes will seem economically irrational. People will be more likely to try to reduce a risk to zero even when doing so is costly, than to simply reduce risk by a large amount. It also means that states are more willing to take chances when it means that they might be able to avoid losses than when they are trying to create gains. In essence, entering into a negotiation is a form of risk, because it is not clear what the outcome will be, so negotiation may be easier if it involves preventing a loss.[37] That should be good news for the likelihood of environmental agreements, but other aspects of prospect theory suggest a bias towards the status quo in politics. Because of a preference to avoid losses, people are particularly attached to the status quo; Robert Jervis suggests, for instance, that wars are more likely when each side believes it is trying to defend the status quo.[38] In addition, how people identify whether something is a gain or a loss depends on their reference point,[39] and in political interactions the existing situation is usually the reference point.[40] It is also possible, however, for expectations to take on the role of reference point,[41] which suggests that what the public expects to accomplish out of a negotiation may then come to mean that anything less is seen as a loss.

These factors can help explain such things as the willingness of politicians to persevere in deteriorating situations, such as US President Lyndon Johnson's escalation in Vietnam or Richard Nixon's decision to try to cover up the Watergate break in.[42] Similarly McDermott argues that the willingness of the USA to attempt to rescue the Iranian hostages despite the high risk can be explained by assuming that the USA perceived itself in a situation of loss, and was therefore more willing to undertake risky action.[43]

There are few outright disavowals of prospect theory, but its usefulness for political situations (because it takes psychological observations about individual decision-making and applies them to situations where people act in groups) can be questioned. In addition, calculation of probability or even of decision weights in political situations is much more difficult than simply assigning numerical values and must rely on an interpretation of what people say and do;[44] doing so is easier *post hoc*, which can make its use in predictive social science problematic. It is interesting to note that most of the political applications of this theory so far focus on single case studies, rather than drawing broad conclusions about international negotiations. Some also challenge the validity of prospect theory outside the laboratory, and note that even in experimental settings it fails to predict the actions of up to one-third of the individuals involved.[45] Nevertheless, it is clear that prospect theory helps to systematically describe some of the ways that people value risk, and accounts for many of the differences between what concerns average people and what concerns experts.

If people do not assess risk correctly, even if their misassessments can be predicted, the next question is what should be done about the situation. Even if prospect theory may help us better to anticipate the ways in which people are likely to perceive risk, would it not be better if policy could be made to avoid the greatest risks at the lowest costs, rather than spending resources on something that concerns the public but is likely to cause less harm than other problems? Stephen Breyer points out that states do not have unlimited resources to devote to issues of human health or environmental protection and suggests that if we do not allocate funding based on accurate risk assessment, the money 'will not be there to spend, at least not if we want to address more serious environmental or social problems.'[46]

There are two main suggestions about political approaches to dealing with the public's misevaluation of risk. These two approaches could be termed efficiency and democracy, and they differ based on their view of the role of science in decision-making. A third option is the argument that people's assessment of risk is not as irrational as it may seem, and that even though it may differ from that of professional risk assessors (or perhaps, even, because it does) it can be seen as valid in its own right.

Breyer, now a US Supreme Court Justice, sees as the solution to the public's misvaluing of risk the creation of a politically insulated, technically sophisticated, and well-respected bureaucratic elite that would allocate resources to health and environmental problems in a more rational manner.[47] Because politicians have to act on people's concerns or run the risk of not being re-elected, Breyer suggests that the prioritization of risk should be left to experts who cannot be voted out of office. There are certainly logistical questions about how such a risk-assessing body could be created (and it is not clear whether it would be harder or easier on the international level than on the domestic level), and whether it could truly insulate itself from political pressures. The main criticism of this approach, which Breyer acknowledges but considers less important than the advantages it conveys,[48] is that it is anti-democratic.

A second approach moves in the other direction; it would involve greater citizen participation in policy-making processes, because citizens' groups often work through organizations and experts.[49] Sylvia Tesh argues that environmentalists have emphasized science over unfounded perceptions of risk since the beginning of the environmental movement. The literature on risk (and particularly on inaccurate perceptions) misunderstands the conflict about the dangers of environmental pollution because it ignores environmental organizations, which reason in the same ways that professional risk assessors do. In her view, then, the answer is not to cut the people out of the political process as Breyer suggests, but to involve them more directly.[50] A similar view is the call for more 'grass-roots science,' particularly as a way to avoid the capture of risk assessment in the other direction: by industries who have an incentive to skew risk assessment to reflect their interests.[51]

An altogether different response to the issue of different valuation of risk by the public and risk assessors shifts the blame and suggests an alternative to 'rational' risk prioritization that has profound implications for policy analysis. Although it does not address some of the concerns raised by prospect theory, this approach suggests that there are good reasons why people value risk they way they do. Part of the reason for this difference between laypeople and experts is that most people bring a number of subjective characteristics into their assessments of risks.[52] For instance, most professional assessments of risk evaluate an activity based on the likelihood of dying. While that is certainly one of the worst outcomes possible, it is not clear that an activity in which three people die suddenly is worse than one in which no one dies but hundreds become horribly sick for years. Moreover, when you take these additional human harms into consideration, regulations that those like Breyer present as prohibitively costly (such as his argument that the US Environmental Protection Agency's ban on asbestos containing products would have cost between $200 and $300 million to save only seven or eight lives otherwise lost to cancer over thirteen years)[53] seem quite inexpensive. One estimate of the illnesses and non-cancer deaths from asbestos, along with cancer deaths (which the EPA estimated at a higher 202) suggests that this regulation would thus cost only fourteen cents per US citizen to prevent a wide variety of harms not limited to death from cancer.[54] This estimate does not even consider the advantages beyond the thirteen-year period under consideration.

For those concerned about environmental issues in particular, the focus on human mortality is even more limiting; there are ecological values that are excluded when risk is identified only as risk to human life.[55] Even for those concerned primarily with human wellbeing, there are a variety of environmental damages that may contribute eventually to a lower quality of life for humans and are not taken into consideration in most risk assessments. The burning of forests may cause few direct human deaths, but it may lead to soil erosion that makes agriculture more difficult and runoff that decreases water quality; it may contribute particulate air pollution that has health implications and greenhouse gases that affect the climate in ways that could have much broader effects. Moreover, for those who believe that ecosystems or non-human species have value apart from their benefit to humans, it can be important to prevent (for example) an oil spill simply because of the harm caused to nature, not because any loss of human life will result.

There are also distributional issues worth considering. The environmental justice movement suggests that environmental hazards, such as the siting of toxic waste dumps, is more likely to happen in low-income or minority neighborhoods. Even if the risk of loss of human life from these activities is low, or even in the unlikely event it is lower in these locations than in other possible locations, is it acceptable to impose risks upon generally disenfranchised people? Removing asbestos from schools may cause more risk to the asbestos removal workers than it prevents in exposure by schoolchildren, but the asbestos workers knowingly take on the task, wear protective clothing, and receive higher pay than do other workers who incur less risk, whereas children are required to show up for school without regard for the health risks they may encounter. In cases where the relative degree of harm from an environmental problem is determined by natural conditions rather than political decisions, the issue of equity persists. Some low-lying countries may simply cease to exist after the sea-level rise predicted to occur with global climate change, despite their infinitesimal contribution of greenhouse gases to the atmosphere. The Association of Small Island States (AOSIS) has had a greater degree of influence in international negotiations on climate change than might otherwise be predicted, largely because people recognize the inherent unfairness of the situation these states face. Being more concerned about risk that occurs to those who did not choose it and cannot control it may not be economically rational, but may be ethically valuable.

Similarly, some of the harshest critics of the public's valuation of risk fail to differentiate based on who is causing the risk. Focusing simply on the amount of risk avoided per unit of cost avoids holding those most responsible for creating risks also the most responsible for preventing, mitigating, or paying for them. There may be advantages in requiring industries to internalize externalities – in other words, to bear the full environmental, health, and safety costs of their activities, even if the risks of disaster are small. If industries knew they could be held responsible for any potential environmental damage their activities caused, would they be more risk averse?

Victor Flatt also points out the advantage of being able to make our own decisions, on which it is difficult to put a price. Is it actually irrational to be more concerned with those risks that are imposed on us than those that are voluntarily undertaken? People may choose to value having control more than they value reducing risk, per se. Studies suggest that people are willing to undertake voluntary risks over involuntary risks by a factor of up to 1000.[56] The suffering that is caused by being exposed to risks not voluntarily undertaken may be greater (though, again, in a calculus that considers more than human mortality) than from those risks we choose.

It is also possible that there is a basis for people's seemingly irrational fears of non-natural phenomena. Breyer suggests that regulating to prevent ingestion of small amounts of carcinogens from newly created chemicals is irrational in a situation in which people are subjected to similar levels of cancer-causing substances occurring naturally in such substances as peanut butter or mushrooms. As Lisa Heinzerling points out, these comparisons overlook the fact that many foods that contain potential carcinogens also contain cancer-preventing substances.[57] Moreover, people have evolved alongside these naturally occurring substances and may have evolved defenses to them that do not exist for newly created chemicals. While both of these potential explanations are subject to a high degree of uncertainty, they do at least suggest rational explanations for otherwise irrational fears.

It is also the case that risk assessors focus on a limited number of factors (although the number is increasing with improving technology) in determining risk; people may in fact be able to include additional factors in their analysis without being aware of it. To return to McDermott's example of the beret-wearing questioner at an arms control lecture, it may be true that if you reduce the audience simply to number of academics versus artists the person is more likely to be an academic. But how many of us honestly believe that the questioner is not an artist? We take a variety of factors, many of which we may not even be able to quantify, into consideration when making those judgments. We may not be wrong.

Certainly, as Mary Douglas and Aaron Wildavsky point out, risks are social constructs and there is no objective way to say that one risk judgment is better or worse than another.[58] Whatever one's perspective on how to correctly value risk, it is likely that communication about risk can be improved. Better information about risk is crucial in allowing people to participate more effectively in the political process.[59]

POLITICS OF SCIENCE

Given the role of risk and uncertainty in decisions pertaining to the global environment, it should not be surprising that scientists are important throughout the process of addressing these issues. Scientists are often the ones who first notice that environmental damage is taking place, or theorize that certain substances may be harmful even before damage has become evident. So the process of addressing international, and domestic, environmental issues may begin with scientists. They become even more important in international issues, however, because states must collectively be convinced that there is an environmental problem and that it has anthropogenic causes before they are willing to take costly action. Transboundary scientific investigation contributes to the raising of concern and resolving of uncertainty about environmental problems.

Epistemic Communities

The school of analysis within international relations that examines the role of scientists and other related actors as an explanation for international outcomes was elaborated by Peter Haas under the term 'epistemic communities'. These are 'knowledge-based networks of specialists who share beliefs in cause-effect relations, validity tests, and underlying principled values and pursue common goals.'[60] Although they are not limited to scientists, or even to environmental issues, it is argued that these communities have a profound impact on international cooperation, and most discussion of them occurs in the context of addressing uncertainty in international environmental issues. The theoretical approach suggests that the existence of such communities allows those within them to affect decision-makers and policy in the face of uncertainty. A wide collection of anecdotal evidence suggests that collections of actors organized around providing knowledge have influenced outcomes in particular environmental issues; examples most frequently given are the protection of the Mediterranean, the protection of the ozone layer and, more controversially, climate change. The influence of such communities may depend on a variety of factors, including the number and importance of states a given community can persuade on the issue in question, which may relate to the interest of states.[61] (Certainly what seems to be a strong epistemic community on climate change has failed to persuade politicians in the United States.) Uncertainty is given as a reason why policy-makers would turn to such communities for advice,[62] and their transnational character can give them added influence on international issues.

Others are less sanguine about the influence of epistemic communities. Martin List and Volker Rittberger acknowledge that 'shared knowledge may be a necessary condition of regime formation,' but doubt that epistemic communities are alone responsible for creating international regimes, and may in some cases help delay international cooperation.[63] Jutta Brunee and Stephen Toope suggest that political officials will often not take the advice of scientific and policy experts, partly out of an interest in maintaining control.[64] Jonathan Wiener suggests as an example that negotiations on climate change are not influenced primarily by epistemic communities,[65] although his example of the Intergovernmental Panel on Climate Change as controlled by governments undermines his own logic; most see this group both as an epistemic community, and one that is willing to act against the wishes of the governments that appoint the scientists. It certainly has been influential (although perhaps not the determining factor) in international cooperation to address climate change. Ozone depletion is a case about which there is considerable disagreement, as well, about the role of an epistemic community. Some, like Karen Liftin, are critical of the idea of objective science and find 'discursive practices' a more useful explanation of the ozone case.[66] Others see economic and political interests as the most important factors in producing agreement on protecting the ozone layer.[67] It is clear, nevertheless, that communities of experts play some kind of role in policymaking on global environmental issues; whether it is the primary role in reaching international cooperation remains to be seen.

Science is rarely entirely disconnected from politics and it is important to note the difference between scientific uncertainty and political uncertainty.[68] The approaches that different states take to operating under conditions of uncertainty, or the different institutional mechanisms for interpreting science within the political process, can lead to differences in policies. This approach to the relationship between science and politics sees the differences of interpretation of science as arising unintentionally from institutional constraints. Sheila Jasanoff has compared the different ways states approach risk, noting, for instance, that in Europe the policy process is more cautious about accepting risk than is true in the USA; strangely, these initial early approaches also have allowed the USA to slow down international cooperation with claims of uncertainty.[69]

It is also possible for science to be used in an explicitly political way. Ronald Brickman, Sheila Jasanoff, and Thomas Ilgen illustrate that scientific uncertainty can 'make it possible for proponents and opponents of regulation to interpret the scientific basis for ... risk assessment in ways that advance their particular policy objectives.'[70] Interested parties or groups, notes Young, 'manipulate scientific findings ... in their efforts to promote their preferences' in the creation of new regimes or the operation of existing ones.[71] Liftin's work on science allows for either the intentional or unintentional use of science for political ends.[72] Susskind argues that the USA uses scientific evidence to argue in favor of the courses of action it prefers but 'when we prefer to take a different political course we attack the available data as insufficient, regardless of the strength of the worldwide scientific consensus.'[73]

The prevailing view of science's role in diminishing uncertainty would suggest simply doing more science (making climate models more detailed and including more information in them, for instance). Others disagree. A different perspective on the same issue is the observation that science is socially constructed; what experts give is 'varying interpretations of uncertainty shaped by their own and their informants' local contexts and locally colored world views.'[74] Dale Jamieson concurs, suggesting that what we take to be uncertain depends on what questions we are asking. He gives as an example his process of selling a bicycle to a friend. Both he and the friend are likely to believe that he owns the bicycle, and thus do not act as though there is any uncertainty about that part of the transaction. But there could be a different situation in which he either suffers from amnesia or kleptomania; if his friend knows this, the friend is likely to require proof of ownership before buying the bicycle. In other words, social context influences the things whose certainty people stop to consider.[75]

Jamieson also points to the importance of reference points in a similar way to that explored in prospect theory but even more fundamental. When people discuss an increase in global mean temperature, it matters what their frame of reference is (compared to the last decade, century, millennium?), where their measurements are taken, or even that they examine global mean temperature rather than average temperature.[76] The broader point to take from all of this is that uncertainty is not simply an objective value that can be reduced by more scientific inquiry; social priorities for what issues to value and what questions to ask influence how we make policy about environmental risks under conditions of uncertainty.

The level of uncertainty about the role of science, risk, and uncertainty in addressing global environmental problems thus remains high. As soon as one moves past a simple cost-benefit assessment of risk and a belief that more scientific inquiry will make environmental problems easier to address, it becomes clear both that we do not fully understand how the global environment functions on its own or intersects with political or economic systems, and that we are not even clear about how best to study these phenomena.

THE ROLE OF NON-GOVERNMENTAL ACTORS

NGOs appear to be key actors in moving societies away from current trends in environmental degradation and toward sustainable economies.[1]

The environment is not going to be saved by environmentalists. Environmentalists do not hold the levers of economic power.[2]

Maurice Strong, UNCED Secretary General

International relations tends to be a state-centric endeavor; even the name of the field suggests that it is about relations among 'nations.' To the extent that non-governmental actors play a role, it is generally assumed that this role is subsumed within the actions of states, constituting, perhaps, the interests and actions of the states, but still fundamentally part of creating the process by which states interact with each other.[3] There are important advantages to examining international relations in this manner: much of the major action undertaken, even in international environmental politics, is done by, or mediated through, states. States, in governing themselves, affect the international system. States are the actors that, through their representatives and political processes, negotiate international environmental agreements and then work domestically to implement them. Certainly they are central actors in examining what happens to the global environment.

Although it is states that actually agree to undertake environmental commitments, there are a number of ways in which non-state actors influence this process, even within the state-centric view. Scientists (discussed further in Chapter 4), international organizations, environmental non-governmental organizations (NGOs), and industry actors all contribute to the making and implementation of international environmental policy. Without their concern, often expressed first on the domestic level, international environmental policy would rarely be made, because one or more states must be interested enough in an environmental issue to attempt to create international cooperation to address it.

Environmental NGOs work to raise concern about environmental problems, both domestically and by sharing information across borders. Within one country, they can raise public awareness about the presence of an environmental problem. They can also lobby governmental actors to take action on international environmental policy issues, or lead consumer boycotts of products deemed harmful to the environment. Once an international organization exists to address a global environmental issue, NGOs may be invited to participate as observers, and may be allowed to participate in other ways.

Industry actors are also important players in environmental regulation on the international level. Often it is industrial activity of some sort that is implicated in the creation of a global environmental problem in the first place. So sometimes industry actors are active in resisting any costly regulations on their activities, and may call into question the scientific justification for acting. But occasionally it can be in the interests of industries to themselves undertake environmental regulations, and there are conditions under which businesses can benefit, comparatively at least, from international regulations. Industry actors within a state can sometimes be found, therefore, pushing for the creation of international environmental policy, or at least not hindering it.

From a theoretical perspective, however, it is also important to pay attention to the role that non-state actors play outside of the traditional view of state-centered politics. Examination of action by non-state actors, particularly within the literature on environmental policy, suggests that they help to create change in ways that subvert the traditional state-oriented approach to political analysis. Raised awareness may lead to citizen action to undertake environmentalist action with international consequences, even without national requirements to do so. Non-governmental organizations from within one country may work directly to influence citizens of another country to pressure their own governments, rather than doing so by influencing governments to negotiate with governments. Multinational corporations may bring higher environmental standards than required to their foreign subsidiaries because of advantages to themselves in doing so, not because states have decreed that certain policies must be followed. Or industries may pick up and move their operations to states with lower environmental regulations, influencing both global environmental quality and the likelihood that states will resist higher standards for fear of losing revenue. Moreover, environmentalist and industry non-state actors may end up working together to influence the shape of international environmental policy, despite the general perception that the two groups are inherently at odds. To understand global environmental politics it is thus essential to examine the multiple pathways through which non-state actors influence behavior that affects the natural environment.

ENVIRONMENTAL NGOS

The growth of environmental organizations addressing international problems has been dramatic over the last 30 years. Although they are different in some ways from other non-governmental organizations, they share a number of characteristics with such organizations, and it is useful to examine what is known generally about the role of non-governmental organizations addressing international issues. An initial question is what accounts for the development of citizen organizations, particularly transnationally? Have they become more prevalent on the international scene, and, if so, why? More importantly, what types of effects do they have? To what extent do they challenge, or support the roles of states?

Non-governmental actors, even those with a great deal of influence, have been around and even acting internationally for more than a century-and-a-half, with religious and labor organizations among the first citizen groups to work for international goals.[4] One study suggests that conventional international NGOs numbered at about 1000 in the 1950s, 2000 by the 1970s, and had risen to nearly 5000 by the mid-1990s.[5] The Economist estimates an increase in international NGOs from 6000 to 26,000 during the 1990s.[6] Estimates that include local NGOs (which may nevertheless have international interests) put that number far higher,[7] and one of the important phenomena of the past 30 years is the growth in internationally interested indigenous non-governmental organizations in the developing world.[8] Environmental NGOs specifically have increased in number and have begun to focus more directly on international elements of the environment. The first domestic environmental NGOs were created at the end of the nineteenth century in the USA and Britain, and although these organizations began communicating across state borders early in their existence it was not really until the second half of the twentieth century that environmental issues were perceived as international in scope, so few organizations existed to address them in that form.[9] By the time of the UN Convention on the Human Environment in Stockholm in 1972 the parallel NGO meeting drew the participation of nearly 400 NGOs; the 1992 United Nations Conference on Environment and Development in Rio counted 7000 participating NGOs.[10]

The phenomenon of NGO activity overall has thus grown, and

certainly the presence of environmental activists, sometimes with different agendas and strategies from those in traditional NGOs, has been an important and growing phenomenon in the last half century. There are a variety of explanations for the growth of environmental NGOs, suggesting that there may be different contexts that lead to the formation or influence of different types of NGOs. Social movement theory, developed to explain activist organizations within national political systems, would seem an obvious place to look for explanations. Theories, such as those by Alain Touraine, suggest a cyclical process by which movements of underrepresented populations organize, fight for acceptance, and ultimately are co-opted into the system.[11] Traditionally these approaches would expect collective action to be triggered by some combination of relative deprivation, common interests, and economic or political conflicts. Matthias Finger supports the conventional wisdom that NGO participation is a political response to a lack of previous individual participation.[12] Related is the idea that it is the inability of states to provide for their citizens that creates a global civil society.[13] Others see NGO responses to the ineffectiveness of states as a positive element, viewing social movements as efforts to politicize activity to help national political systems adapt, evolve, and learn.[14]

Certainly one explanation for the greater role of NGO involvement in international affairs is, as Peter Spiro calls it, the 'dramatically heightened permeability of national borders' and the accompanying improvement in communications. It is simply easier for activists in dispersed locations to work together for a common goal than it used to be.[15] Increasing worldwide democratization contributes to this trend.[16] Paul Wapner suggests that NGOs, particularly those that have transnational impacts, emerge as part of a broader growth of 'international civil society.' He sees civil society, the realm in which 'people engage in spontaneous, customary, and nonlegalistic forms of association' for common goals as apart from, but interacting with, the state system.[17] The growth of the opportunity for people to work for common goals internationally both reflects and allows the growth of NGOs.

Additional external factors may account for the increasing prevalence of international NGOs more broadly. In particular, the end of the Cold War has changed the international arena in ways that may be conducive to creation or influence of NGOs. To the extent that a lowered sense of security concerns (at least vis-à-vis other states) allows for a lessening of the central importance of national allegiances, coordinated action by people across borders may be more possible.[18] Taking a longer view, Steve Charnovitz argues that the influence of NGOs internationally coincides with periods of peace.[19] Similarly, those who study the growth in human rights regimes, often seen as parallel to environmental organizations, suggest that the lessening of tensions between the former Eastern and Western blocs has allowed for an international consensus to develop in favor of humanitarian action.[20] A related phenomenon is the lessening attention paid to developing countries that previously were courted with aid to keep them solidly in one bloc or another; with less funding from traditional donor states there is more unmet need.[21] This explanation fits into the privation explanation above, but with a post-Cold War twist: there is more non-governmental activity happening, because the major powers no longer see the political advantage in meeting the needs of people in developing countries. NGOs arise, both domestically and internationally, to meet these needs.

The level of uncertainty present in environmental issues in particular is suggested as an additional reason that non-governmental actors are so involved in environmental policy-making.[22] Margaret Keck and Kathryn Sikkink note that what they call 'transnational advocacy networks' arise most frequently in issues with high 'informational uncertainty.'[23] Barbara Bramble and Gareth Porter point to the rise in organizations during the 1970s and 1980s that collect and disseminate data and analysis.[24] Non-governmental actors may be particularly well placed to address transnational issues, which are less likely to be the focus of states, whose constituents are domestic.[25] While this kind of non-governmental actor exists within a number of different issue areas, there are numerous matters about which there is uncertainty (as discussed in chapter 4) in environmental issue areas, and non-governmental actors can help fill the information void.

It is also important to examine how it is that environmentalist organizations work to achieve their goals within global environmental policy. The types of tasks they perform could be divided into almost infinite categories, but it can be useful to think of them as fulfilling functions either within the state process or outside of it. Part of the reason this distinction can matter is that recent NGO activity, particularly by environmental organizations, challenges the traditional view of how non-state actors influence policy. Occasionally it can be difficult to categorize NGO actions even this simply; the variety of types of activities they undertake and pathways through which they attempt to influence the human impact on the natural environment are many. As Wapner points out, transnational NGOs are unconstrained by the idea of territoriality; 'they focus and pursue aims free from the tasks of preserving and enhancing the welfare of a given, geographically situated population.'[26]

The traditional view of how non-state actors influence international environmental politics generally begins with organizations that raise awareness of an environmental problem. They may be responsible for helping to create the awareness of the environmental problems in the first place, or the will to do something to address them. This is the role for which they are generally known, but it is by no means the only role they play. They also work within the legislative process inside states, either by working to elect candidates who are likely to support environmental causes, or lobbying the legislature to pass environmental laws. On international issues, they can likewise work to put pressure on a state to adopt policies domestically that will ultimately help address international environmental problems, and they can put pressure on state actors to participate in, and take certain positions during, international environmental negotiations. They can be particularly effective within a political context in part because they do not share the time horizons of the politicians, thinking only of the next election; as Karen Liftin points out, 'most environmental problems will outlast the policymakers charged with addressing them.'[27] Similarly, transnational activists have a potentially global constituency whereas politicians are elected locally or nationally. On the one hand both these factors make the work of activists more difficult; on the other hand, both make their work more necessary.

There are a number of ways NGOs can influence environmental action that do not involve lobbying their own state to take particular action. Certainly the increased number of organizations with membership or chapters in multiple countries creates opportunities for influence across state lines. A useful way to categorize these less traditional forms of avenues for non-state actor influence is to look at those acting within the state system but not through states, and those acting internationally in ways that circumvent the state system.

Environmental organizations can act within the state system without acting within states per se. Doing so may be as simple as working to raise awareness in a different state of an environmental issue in a way that inspires people to take action to get their own state to address the issue internationally. Moreover, during the process of negotiation of international agreements NGOs have come to play roles as critics or informants in the negotiation itself. More and more frequently NGOs are allowed, if not to participate in, at least to observe, international negotiations. They are often allowed to speak in meetings when recognized by the chair, and interact with delegates in the hallways and during coffee breaks where some of the most important details of an impending agreement are discussed. Sometimes they help draft elements of what eventually becomes the treaty. In the negotiation, for instance, of the Basel

Convention on the Control of Transboundary Movements of Hazardous Wastes and Their Disposal, both Greenpeace and the Center for Science and the Environment drafted some of the language that ultimately ended up in the text of the treaty.[28]

While the participation of environmental organizations in the delegations of national representatives to international organizations may be considered part of the conventional activity of NGOs, in some contexts environmental activists have taken this approach one step further, by essentially representing states in international fora. One clear example of this phenomenon is in the International Whaling Commission, where non-governmental organizations have brought a number of states into the agreement, by taking over the tasks normally required of a state in an international organization. The former IWC Secretary tells the story of the commissioner of an unnamed member state who simply signed over the check from an environmental organization to pay its dues. Similarly, a representative from a recently joined non-whaling state showed up late for a meeting and had to ask directions to the non-governmental organization section to get his briefing book from the organization that had prepared it for him.[29] A former Greenpeace consultant tells of a plan that added at least six new anti-whaling members in the period from 1978 to 1982 through the paying of annual dues, drafting of membership documents, and naming of commissioners to represent these countries, at an annual cost of more than $150,000.[30] Japan's representatives at the 47th IWC annual meeting in 1995 pointed out that 'some individuals are listed as government delegates attending the preliminary meetings of working groups and sub-committees but registered as NGO observers in the plenary week.'[31]

Non-governmental organizations can play an essential role in monitoring compliance and reporting on other elements of state behavior on the international level after an environmental agreement is in place. While this role is often played informally, there are circumstances in which some NGOs are formally involved in the process of monitoring structured into the agreement itself. For instance, the International Bureau for Whaling Statistics in Norway has been the organization to which catch statistics are transmitted during the whaling season when commercial whaling is allowed; this organization is empowered to determine when overall quotas have been met and to end the whaling season.[32] The World Conservation Union (IUCN), which is an organization with both governmental and non-governmental members, acts as the secretariat for the Convention on International Trade in Endangered Species of Wild Fauna and Flora (CITES).[33] Even when NGOs are not formally involved in monitoring, they can play an invaluable role. The organization TRAFFIC tracks wildlife trade world-wide and has provided important evidence of smuggling of endangered species. Greenpeace has done an impressive job of publicizing the whaling activities of IWC members (even when those activities may be within the letter of the law), in a way that makes the general public more aware of state behavior than would otherwise be the case. The same is true for organizations such as Ozone Action, which first addressed issues of ozone depletion and has now moved on to address global warming, reporting especially on the behavior of member states relative to their obligations under international agreements. Non-governmental organizations may also participate in the treaty implementation process by using advocacy or litigation to support international legal processes.[34]

Non-governmental organizations may also act internationally in a way that essentially subverts, rather than participates in, the state system, in a practice Wapner calls engaging in 'world civic politics.'[35] This type of action challenges most directly the traditional view of how non-governmental actors matter in international relations. It is discussed most directly with respect to activist environmental organizations but there are also parallels within the discussion of industry influence on the global environment.

One way organizations can work around the state system is simply by attempting to change the actions of individuals, rather than working to change the regulations facing individuals. Greenpeace uses this tactic when its members place themselves between whales and whalers' harpoons. If whalers cease that particular whale hunt, it is not because environmental organizations have changed the law, or even changed their minds, but because the whalers have calculated that it would be damaging to their interests to harpoon Greenpeace members, as they would be portrayed in the international media.

At the same time, the international perception is created that these activists care so much for whales that they are willing to put their lives on the line, which is intended to influence public opinion worldwide. This is a second method of working around the state rather than through it. Wapner calls this strategy 'bearing witness.' This strategy is the most important one that organizations like Greenpeace employ. While blockading the shipment of ozone-depleting CFCs from a DuPont plant by placing people literally on the railroad tracks by which the chemicals were shipped out, the organization made no noticeable dent in CFC production, but it did managed to raise awareness worldwide of the problem of ozone depletion and DuPont's role in it.[36]

There are other ways that non-state actors can work to change individual behavior, or lead to conservation, without working within a state regulatory structure. Organizations such as Conservation International literally buy tracts of land that they preserve,[37] rather than waiting for state or international agreements to provide protection. The non-governmental organizations involved in debt-for-nature swaps (discussed further in Chapter 8) spend their own money to purchase from banks the commercial debt of highly indebted countries with rich biodiversity resources, and work out agreements to retire the debt in return for conservation activity on the part of the indebted states. More directly, organizations like the World Wide Fund for Nature (WWF; still called the 'World Wildlife Fund' within the USA) work with local people in environmentally sensitive areas to help create a situation where they can protect their own local environment, whether required to by law or not.[38]

Collette Ridgeway calls this phenomenon 'free-market environmentalism,' and argues that it is a more effective method of protecting wilderness than state action provides.[39] It bears a resemblance to voluntary corporate environmentalism, discussed in the following section, in that individuals and organizations undertake to provide environmental protection, or raise awareness of environmental issues, when not compelled to by domestic or international regulation, and often without even the goal of creating such regulation. This type of activity, combined with the more 'direct action' approaches of Greenpeace or Earth First!, suggests that much of what happens to influence the condition of the global environment happens outside of the standard framework of the state, and suggests that non-governmental actors play a far more complex and nuanced role than traditional social movement theory would expect.

Assuming that NGOs have at least some effect on activity relating to the global environment, what determines how effective environmental NGOs will be at achieving their goals? There is some degree of uncertainty about the extent to which NGOs play a beneficial function in particular environmental issue areas,[40] but certainly there are conditions under which they are more or less likely to influence action on issues with which they are concerned. Although this question does not easily lend itself to categorization, the major factors examined here include choices of strategy (with whom one chooses to ally, whether to work within or against the system), and the context in which activist organizations are operating.

In terms of strategic choices that environmental organizations make (many discussed above), primary among them is whether to work within a system or challenge it. Alan Thomas concludes that, at least in African NGOs, outright opposition may be more likely to be successful than working on activities complementary to those of the state.[41]

The question of international collaboration among NGOs is also an important strategic question. While some, such as Wapner, Princen and Finger, and Keck and Sikkink, point to examples of successful transnational collaboration, others suggest that when organizations from developed and developing countries work together the resulting power struggles and conflicts over ideals decrease the effectiveness of the organizations within the developing countries.[42] This could happen when the interests of northern NGOs are sufficiently threatening to governments in developing countries that they curtail NGO access to the policy process in the wake of collaboration with developed country NGOs. Additionally the added outside attention can cause developing country governments to put a gloss of 'scenic and figurative environmentalism' on existing policies,[43] making true change less likely because progress appears to have been made. Nevertheless, most agree that collaboration between organizations from developed and developing countries on environmental issues does lead to additional information, financial resources and expertise that might otherwise not have been present.[44]

On the issue of context, one question is the role that democracy plays in determining the effectiveness of non-governmental actors in global environmental politics. Though democratization may have led to an increase in NGOs overall, it is unclear whether NGOs hoping to influence policy in, or from within, a democracy have a greater degree of success than those working on issues in non-democratic regimes. Conventional wisdom might expect greater success from NGOs acting within democracies because of more points of access into the political process, and because there are likely to be more non-governmental actors in general. Thomas' study, discussed above, supports this hypothesis broadly.[45] But there is at least some evidence that this expectation does not necessarily hold. One study comparing NGO success with policies on tropical deforestation within democratic India and non-democratic Indonesia did not find the expected relationship.[46] It is also possible for NGO participation through democratic (or, more likely, democratizing) governments to create a backlash against the very openness that allowed participation. Thomas points out, however, that even when governments try to restrict previous NGO access to policy-making, they may nevertheless pluralize the political process by including additional institutions in the making of decisions.[47]

Related issues include other elements of state structure, including the extent to which the state NGOs are trying to influence is 'state' or 'society' dominated. Ideas, as Thomas Risse-Kappan points out in an effort to persuade us to examine domestic structures, 'do not float freely,'[48] but instead need to have a receptive state structure, for transnational organizations pushing them to be successful. Roger Payne examines this model in the context of environmental NGO influence, and concludes that both the openness, or 'society-dominated' nature of a state, and the centralization of that state, leave it more vulnerable to influence by non-governmental actors.[49]

Another element of context that must be considered, although difficult to quantify, is the difficulty of the issue faced. As discussed in Chapter 2, the difficulty of changing action depends on many factors unrelated to NGOs, including some about how difficult the goal they are pursuing is. Related is the issue of what other actors in the process desire. Although the logic seems somewhat tautological, some suggest that NGOs have the greatest influence internationally when their issues are backed by powerful countries.[50] In this logic, NGOs do not necessarily supplant or replace states, but become another way through which powerful states exert pressure.

That view is perhaps overly pessimistic of the ability of environmental organizations to have an influence on international environmental politics, but it does suggest that, while their role in working around or challenging the state is essential to remember and an important corrective to much of international relations theory, the role that they play acting within states, or that states play acting in concert with them, is also essential.

INDUSTRY ACTORS

Businesses, whether local or international, can be some of the most important players in influencing global environmental policy. It is often actions, directly or indirectly, by industry actors that help create environmental problems in the first place. In a number of circumstances, however, businesses are finding that it can pay to be 'green,' and are undertaking environmental measures not required of them. It is essential to ascertain the conditions under which such corporate environmental-ism is likely to be undertaken, or is likely to benefit the environment, when trying to understand the impact of industry on the global environment. It is also important to examine the power of industry actors, particularly multinational corporations, relative to the state. To what extent can big polluters or those industries that rely on resource extraction influence policies of states, or be influenced by them? Related is the question of whether states lower their environmental policies to attract businesses that do not want to pay the added cost of environmental protection, or whether increasing globalization instead results in higher industry standards worldwide. Finally, does increased environmental regulation increase or decrease the incentive for industry environmentalism?

All else being equal, there are costs, at least in the short run, to operating an environmentally friendly industry. Pollution is a problem precisely because it is an externality; it is an unintended and generally unpriced consequence of industrial activity whose effects are felt by those who do not create it. When environmental resources are not regulated by the government, a polluting factory shares with everyone the cost of decreased quality of the air or water, but alone bears the benefit of not having to clean its emissions. It therefore has little economic incentive to behave in an environmentally responsible manner.

Why, then (or, perhaps more usefully, under what conditions), do we see voluntary acts of corporate environmentalism? There certainly are instances in which running an environmentally friendly business can be economically advantageous: 3M's slogan that 'pollution prevention pays' can be true under certain conditions. Livio DeSimone and Frank Popoff of the World Business Council for Sustainable Development suggest many of the reasons that it may advantage industry to undertake environmental action. First, doing so may reduce current costs, under some circumstances. Second, future costs – or the possibility of future liability – may be reduced. Third, a 'green image' may affect the company's worth – to investors, consumers, or potential employees. Fourth, research into environmental alternatives or technology can open new markets for substitutes for environmentally harmful substances or technologies. Finally (and related), adopting environmentalism before being forced to by national or international regulation can lead to a long-term competitive advantage, despite potential short-term cost.[51]

The idea that pollution prevention actually does 'pay,' in its own terms, has spawned the field of industrial ecology. One definition of the concept notes that it is 'a systems view, which seeks to optimize the total materials cycle from virgin material, to finished material, to component, to product, to obsolete product, and to ultimate disposal.'[52] By taking this overall view of their operations, industries may be able to reduce costs by taking environmentally beneficial actions. Redesigning equipment can allow steam generated from one process to be used in another. Recovered waste products can be used as raw materials that would otherwise have to be purchased (or that can be sold to other manufacturers who need them). For example, 3M discovered that by making re-usable shipping containers the company could simultaneously reduce the amount of waste generated and decrease the costs of procuring new shipping containers, with a yearly saving of more than $4 million. Industrias Fronterizas, a Mexican company that makes car engine manifolds, discovered that installing a filtration unit that separates waste products from clean water used in manufacturing saved the company more than $1 million annually by reducing overall waste and machine downtime.[53]

Pollution prevention, or environmentalism more generally, will not be equally beneficial to all industry actors. Stuart Hart and Gautam Ahuja, for instance, find that the economic advantage of environmentalism is greatest for slower, more inefficient firms they call 'high polluters.'[54] Not surprisingly, these are the ones for which making environmental improvements are the least costly; the closer a firm comes to zero pollution, the greater are the costs of innovating more environmentally sound production techniques.

It is essential to note, however, that the idea of national or international regulation is often lurking in the background, unacknowledged, in discussions of whether voluntary environmental action by industries will be economically beneficial. As Frances Cairncross notes, 'Most companies will only be as green as governments make them.'[55] It is thus important to examine the intersection between voluntary and mandatory environmental protection by industries. First, one of the reasons that pollution prevention may pay comes when governments or consumers force industries to internalize the costs of externalities. It pays to diminish the waste stream in manufacturing when regulations prohibit dumping waste into the water, or when local dumps charge more for accepting waste or limit the amount or types of waste they will accept. The use of substitutes for environmentally damaging substances may become cost effective only when the harmful chemicals they replace become more costly. Non-renewable natural resources (such as oil) provide that incentive on their own; as they become depleted they become more costly and it pays to develop ways to use them more efficiently or to find substitutes. However, the same incentive can be created by governmental regulation.

Second, the anticipation of regulation, and the hope to prevent it through environmental good citizenship, is often behind the actions of firms to address environmental problems. A study by the World Resources Institute in the 1980s suggests that self-regulation by industry could stall the imposition of national or international environmental rules.[56] Similarly, Bruce Smart emphasizes the advantages to industries of working to increase environmentalism on the local level, where they can find compromises with people whose economic lives are tied to the industry, before the need to regulate at the national or international level becomes an issue.[57] This incentive operates similarly for firms hoping to avoid liability; they may adopt environmental practices not specifically required by law because they operate in a system in which they can be held responsible for accidents or other environmental problems.[58]

In addition, the advantage gained through making the technology used in environmental clean-ups, or substitutes for environmentally damaging substances, comes primarily when other industries undertake environmental action, most frequently because they are required to domestically or internationally. The 'first mover' advantage is only advantageous if others move eventually as well, and technology made to counter pollution or clean up environmental damage is only valuable if states have decided to do so.

There are also, surprisingly enough, situations in which industries may *want* to be regulated, either nationally or internationally. This phenomenon comes despite the possibility of costs to an industry due to environmental regulation, either from increased costs for pollution abatement or higher prices for more environmentally friendly inputs. Several studies of pollution regulation in the USA suggest that they do decrease industry productivity,[59] certainly in the short run. Why, then, would industries push for environmental regulation? There are a number of circumstances under which regulation may be advantageous to industries.

First, and perhaps least convincing, is the argument that environmental regulation on its own actually helps industries compete. Counterarguments to the studies mentioned above, by those such as Michael Porter, suggest that 'tough standards trigger innovation and upgrading.' Moreover, Porter argues that states with the strictest environmental requirements generally are leaders in exports, even of the regulated product.[60] While there are certainly alternative explanations for such a correlation – the possibility, perhaps, that states with higher wealth from competitive industries are concurrently likely to have a greater degree of environmental regulation – at the very least it suggests that regulation will not be harmful for the economy as a whole, and may not even harm individual industries in the long run. This would be particularly true if environmental regulations result in the use of resource-efficient advanced technologies that could lead to lower production costs.[61] There are reasons to be dubious of this logic – after all, if new technology would lead to cost savings, could it not be adopted without regulations? Nevertheless, the existence of standard operating procedures, and the investment of time required to develop potential new ways of doing business, may hinder useful innovation unless required by regulation.

Second, regulation, particularly at the international level, can help standardize obligations that industries must meet when operating across countries. A World Resources Institute study suggests that MNCs 'can thrive in a planned and regulated climate if the rules are explicit and predictable,' and that consistent national and international regulation actually facilitates corporate planning.[62] Participation in such processes as ISO14000 from the International Organization for Standardization is one way that industries attempt to replicate this process on a voluntary level.

Similarly, industry can play an important role in moving international environmental regulation forward, in several different ways. If a state that is a leader in environmental protection domestically has already regulated its industries, these industries may prefer international regulation. This preference can come from several different sources. Perhaps the industry fears that future domestic regulation is likely to be more severe than international regulation. More importantly, since environmental regulation generally bears a cost, if the regulated industry competes internationally with industry in another state that is not regulated, the regulated industry will suffer a competitive disadvantage because its production process will be more costly. It would therefore prefer, if it is going to be regulated anyway, that these regulations apply worldwide. Second, if a certain industry has developed substitute products or processes to address the environmental problem in question, it would prefer that as many actors as possible be bound by regulations on this issue, so that the market for its substitutes will increase.

The question of whether or how to regulate industry leads to a broader and prior discussion of the influence of industry on the creation of policy, particularly the role of multinational (or transnational) corporations vis-à-vis the state. Industry in general tends to have a disproportionate level of influence within politics, for several understandable reasons. Building on Mancur Olson's 'logic of collective action,' many theorists have pointed out that public or collective goods tend to be underprovided,[63] because of the problem of free riders. David Vogel, for instance, points out that groups with diffuse interests, such as those desiring environmental protection, can be less successful than industry actors at having their interests represented in the political process.[64] This phenomenon occurs because a given industry fighting environmental regulation cares most intensely about this particular issue and gains specific benefits from avoiding a regulation. For the population at large it may be one of many issues people care about and those who care are more likely to be geographically and ideologically dispersed and therefore harder to organize to work for a specific goal.

Does it matter? One concern on the international level is that, if there are different levels of environmental regulation, industries are likely to want to locate in areas where they have the lowest regulatory burden. That would be of concern for states that lose economic advantages because they have chosen to impose tough environmental standards. The logical extension of this hypothesis is the concern that some states will decide to competitively de-regulate, creating what have come to be known as 'pollution havens' in order to attract industry.

H. Jeffrey Leonard suggests, in support of the pollution haven hypothesis, that there is more to the question of location of industry than naturally existing comparative advantage and that, in particular, 'artificial factor endowments [such as low levels of regulation] created by governments have become at least as important as natural factor endowments' for states that want to attract industries.[65] On the whole the evidence for the existence of individual states lowering environmental standards to attract industry is mixed. Leonard's study showed that Ireland, Spain, Mexico and Romania in the 1970s all took steps consistent with the pollution haven hypothesis. The states that Leonard examined, however, all eventually reversed or moderated some of their laxity.[66]

Some argue that empirically the evidence is in, and that 'the literature as a whole presents fairly compelling evidence across a broad range of industries, time-periods, and econometric specifications, that regulations do not matter to site choice.'[67] There are several reasons why, even if competitive lowering (or avoidance) of environmental standards existed, firms might not move to take advantage of them. One would be if the firm has already adapted to the regulatory costs. Particularly in the case of environmental controls that require investing in equipment or altering production processes, there is little to be gained from going back to a form of production that does not control pollution. When the cost of relocating and the other disadvantages (such as a lower quality labor force) that may accompany a move to a pollution haven are added in, there may be little incentive for an industry to take advantage of low regulations in a new location.

Yet evidence, both anecdotal and statistical, suggests that industries will sometimes move to take advantage of low environmental regulations. An examination of level of environmental regulation and industry location choices in OECD states does find a relationship between environmental regulations and level and patterns of exports.[68] The jury appears to be out on the extent to which pollution havens will come to exist and to draw industry to them.

Moreover, there is evidence that even industries that make initial decisions based on trying to avoid regulatory standards may ultimately be able to be held to them regardless of their decision about where to locate. A good example is the phenomenon of 'flags of convenience.' Some states have, as the pollution haven hypothesis would suggest, tried to attract ship registrations by removing the traditional rules by which ship owners need to abide in order to register a ship in a given location. These rules have generally included restrictions on the nationality of the crew (so that a large percentage would need to be from the state in which the ship is registered), and certain environmental, safety, and labor requirements, both national and international. Ship owners have increasingly chosen to register their ships in flag-of-convenience states, in order to circumvent these restrictions. Since 1993, more ships have been registered in Panama, as measured both by number of ships and by gross tonnage, than anywhere else in the world. Second in both categories is Liberia.[69]

Recent trends in international environmental standards as they pertain to ocean vessels, however, suggest that while the phenomenon of flag-of-convenience registration is growing, its ability to reduce international environmental standards is less clear. That these open registries exist as pollution havens is clear. That they have forced a lowering of overall global standards is less so. More importantly, there is evidence that ships flying flags of convenience have been persuaded themselves to undertake higher standards than would be required by their flag states, and have sometimes been able to convince their flag states to join international agreements or require higher levels of environmental regulation than they initially did.[70]

There are also circumstances under which industries operating across borders may export environmentalism[71] such that subsidiary or related plants take on higher environmental standards than they would otherwise be required to do. Ronie Garcia-Johnson concludes that multinational chemical firms operating in Brazil and Mexico took on greater environmental protection measures than they would have had they not been pressured by US parent companies. Even so, a variety of factors influenced the degree to which corporations were willing to upgrade their environmental practices when pressured. In particular, a high level of dependence on trade with the USA, previous adoption of neo-liberal policies by the government, nationalist sentiment, and economic uncertainty all increase the likelihood that industries within a state will import the environmentalism of their parent companies.[72] Moreover, she provides evidence that this process can, under these conditions, lead to greater adoption of environmental standards than domestic or international regulation would induce, and to square the circle of industry influence presented here, that adoption of these higher standards can pay off in terms of competitive advantage.[73]

Certainly there is evidence of corporate 'Greenwash' in which industries disguise business as usual as environmental,[74] and certainly it is not true that industry action will always raise environmental standards. However, it is clear that industry is an influential non-state actor that needs to be considered when examining global environmental policy. In addition, once policy has been created on the international level, industry actors often remain involved, as advisors, consultants, and in industry organizations present at international meetings to ensure that their interests are considered. It is, after all, those who have created a particular manufacturing process that may best know how to retrofit it with new technology, and the manufacturer of substitute chemicals knows in what circumstances they can be used. While the presence of industry actors within the international system can lead to a situation of chemical solutions to chemical problems rather than a complete rethinking of the way industrial activities are carried out, it is hard to imagine, given their influence within states, a realistic system on the international level that would not include industry actors as important players.

CONCLUSIONS

The discussion of the role of non-state actors in international environmental politics leads to important conclusions about the roles of industry actors and environmental organizations separately, but also some broader observations about the types of roles that actors who are not governments can play in a realm that otherwise appears to be dominated by states. Certainly few expect the state-based international system to disappear any time in the near future, but many attribute the rise in importance of all types of non-state actors to a dissatisfaction with the institutions of state-run civil society. The extent to which, and ways by which, these types of actors challenge the state system is an important question more broadly. It is also essential to examine the means by which they gain influence in ways that contribute to addressing international environmental issues, either directly, or mitigated through or across states. Finally, both types of groups present concerns about accountability. On the one hand, non-governmental actors tend to undertake action because of a concern that their interests, whatever they may be, are not adequately represented by the state apparatus, and NGOs in particular are often applauded for the grassroots support they represent. But a reasonable argument can be made that they are fundamentally as undemocratic as industry organizations. Finally, the relationship among these groups is important to examine, particularly in light of how it relates to the other themes.

Certainly the dominant view of the role of non-governmental actors is that they challenge the state-centric view, either for better or for worse, in terms of their effect on the environment. Non-governmental actors may increase environmental destruction by escaping the regulatory confines of state structures, or may improve the ability of the world to address environmental problems that states would otherwise overlook or not be able to mitigate. Concerns about the abilities of multinational corporations to circumvent or prevent the creation of national or international environmental regulations abound.[75] Similar stories about the ability of international industries to bring environmentalism to areas where states have failed to do so, or of environmental activists to fulfill roles that states cannot, suggest that non-state actors have supplanted some of the functions of states in addressing the global environment. Charnovitz notes that 'participation by NGOs does not mesh well with a state-centric view of global governance.'[76]

Many, however, argue that these actors actually reinforce the role of states, or are (or should be) at least subsidiary to them. States are certainly susceptible to the influence of both environmental organizations and business actors, but that may serve to make them more effective. Wapner's view of NGOs as challenging the state nevertheless implies that there is a necessary and desirable role for the state overall.[77] Charnovitz, despite his comments on the incompatibility of state-centric approaches and NGO activities, suggests that NGO participation is directly related to the needs of the government, with NGOs stepping in to take over certain roles when states lack capacity.[78] Helmut Breitmeier and Volker Rittberger suggest that the international activities of environmental NGOs have the effect of preserving the power relationship between the state and civil society, rather than weakening the state.[79] The role that states play in actually negotiating and signing international agreements ensures their continuing centrality, even when NGOs may influence the process.[80] Kal Raustiala even argues that NGO participation enhances the ability of states to regulate through the treaty process, as evidenced by the greater roles states grant to these organizations over time.[81] Others go so far as to suggest that non-state actors are 'unlikely to become central to world politics in the short or medium term.'[82]

This debate is particularly strong in discussion of the role of industry, especially trans- or multi-national corporations (MNCs). Much of the concern about these actors has been in the power they wield, particularly vis-à-vis impoverished developing countries. Many point to the ability of these transnational corporations to replace the role of states in making – or preventing – regulatory decisions. It has been noted that the bargaining power of MNCs engaged in extracting natural resources, relative to their host countries, shifts over time in favor of host-country control, as part of an obsolescing bargain. But Steven Kobrin finds that this transfer of bargaining power is less true in manufacturing sectors,[83] and thus pollution-producing industries do not lose their influence on policy matters in their host countries. Matthias Finger and James Kilcoyne argue that MNCs have used the guise of sustainable development and their influence over governments to 'subvert the efforts by the United Nations to prevent the further degradation of the natural environment.'[84] Jennifer Clapp points out that voluntary environmentalism on the part of multinational corporations may result in decreased state oversight when it is not yet clear that industry will choose the most environmentally beneficial options for its activity.[85]

Others, however, note that, even with respect to industries operating across borders, the state either does retain ultimate control or should. These are quite different arguments; the first empirical and the second exhortatory. Those who argue the latter make the point that voluntary corporate environmentalism can only accomplish certain things, and even those most frequently within the context of a governmental regulatory structure.[86] Others, however, make the case that despite the importance of companies as international actors, they are vulnerable to state regulation, particularly when combined with the ability of non-governmental organizations to influence state behavior. Moreover, industries rely on states and the state system more broadly to create the framework within which they do business.[87] Nazli Choucri points out that international environmental agreements force MNCs to evaluate the environmental impacts of their actions in order to stay competitive.[88]

How do non-state actors gain the influence they seem to have? In part by their ability to frame issues. Both industry actors and non-governmental organizations seek to gain leverage by framing issues into a form that appeals to the desires of a society that is increasingly concerned with environmental degradation. Business actors are particularly astute at framing their efforts. The World Business Council on Sustainable Development supports free trade and business growth as a solution to the problem of environmental degradation, arguing that ending poverty will improve the state of the environment.[89] Voluntary corporate environmentalism, and the public relations campaigns that usually accompany it, are certainly aimed at gaining the support of consumers and often leverage in specific debates about form, content, or existence of regulation. In some instances the frame may be all there is;

examples include industry organizations that give themselves 'environmental'-sounding names in order to work against environmental regulations. The Information Council on the Environment (with the chilly acronym ICE) was the creation of a group of utility and coal companies that embarked on a public relations campaign to call climate change into question.[90] The Global Climate Coalition, comprised of major coal, oil, and automobile companies (some of which have now left), was created to cast doubt on the idea that human activity, particularly the burning of fossil fuels, causes global warming.[91]

Non-governmental organizations frame their appeals as well; organizations concerned about protecting biodiversity more broadly frame their appeals with posters of endangered elephants and giant pandas, charismatic megafauna that will move the general public to contribute, even if the goals of the organizations may be broader and the resources used to protect species that don't look as cute on calendars. Non-governmental organizations may present their work as relevant to a wide range of interests, such as sustainable development, indigenous rights and multiple specific environmental problems, as a way to appeal to a wide variety of interests and sources of funding.[92] Keck and Sikkink argue that successfully framing an issue is central to the activities of transnational activists, suggesting that they can 'transform the terms and nature of the debate.' Such framing of issues can help intended audiences understand the message, or fit the issues to the mandate of the institutional structures within which they are working.[93] Keck and Sikkink see this as a particularly important role in addressing environmental issues, which have less of an immediate emotional pull than issues like human rights, and cannot rely on existing 'rights.' They point to the creation of the issue of 'tropical deforestation' as an important way in which environmental organizations chose to frame issues such as land conflict, development, or indigenous people.[94] The way organizations choose to frame issues can have important effects later on activity in that issue area, as certain issues, such as tropical deforestation, come to have resonance with the public and others are successfully fitted within the frames already created. The use of symbolism is also closely related.

Non-governmental actors also gain greater effectiveness by the alliances they make. Groups of ideologically opposed NGOs working together on a particular issue may have a greater influence because of their increased constituencies.[95] Often alliances are made internationally, with organizations (business or environmental) working elsewhere for similar goals. In the wake of Montreal Protocol-mandated reduction in the use of ozone-depleting substances, producer industries across countries cooperated to test toxicity of substitute chemicals, and to jointly run recycling processes.[96] The greatest concerns of NGOs are expressed about industry organizations, multinational corporations in particular.[97]

Importantly, some of these alliances may be across different types of organizations, with industry and environmentalist actors working either explicitly together or at the same time for compatible goals. Kenneth Oye and James Maxwell note that 'general environmental concerns are often advanced through the particularistic pursuit of rents or subsidies,' and argue that environmental regulations are most successful when they benefit those actors that are regulated. They argue that when a coalition of self-interested rent-seekers and environmentalists joins together in favor of rent-generating environmental regulation, the coalition is more likely to achieve its goals than either coalition partner acting alone.[98] Insights from the study of public policy more broadly support these observations. Randall Ripley and Grace Franklin report that industry actors may accept inevitable regulation but 'pursue other options designed to make the regulation as light as possible or to acquire governmentally conferred benefits simultaneously as a form of compensation for being regulated;'[99] working with those that are the source of the regulation is one option for doing so. Other observations have been made that states are most likely to push domestic environmental regulations internationally when supported by both industry and environmentalist actors.[100]

The issue of accountability is important. Certainly, non-governmental actors can bring people into the process of global environmental politics whose voices would never have been heard without the activities of such groups. Wapner argues that NGOs are a positive challenge to statism in that they increase accountability vis-à-vis under-represented sectors of society; moreover, they help increase accountability outside of their borders.[101] Per Lindstrom argues that 'NGOs can be the voice of the people when [g]overnments prevent the people from speaking.'[102] Some go as far as to suggest that NGOs are essential aspects of the development of a political democracy. In particular, they can represent minority aspects of a society, whereas a democratically elected legislature may only represent majority interests.[103] A study in former Soviet bloc countries suggests that environmental NGOs can be the vehicle through which people express views they would otherwise be afraid to express to officials in authority, resulting in both greater public participation and a better environmental outcome.[104] While this study specifically examined post-communist governments, the representational aspect of NGO participation would probably be even more true in non-democratic societies. Ultimately, then, many see NGOs as bringing the voices of the otherwise under-represented into the political process.

But NGOs are not representative in the sense that most people mean when they think about representative democracy. This lack of representativeness can happen along a number of axes. One is simply the fact that NGOs are in essence self-appointed political actors who are not generally elected to represent specific interests. When they are then given consultative status in international organizations or negotiations it may give the impression that they speak for the population, but there is no guarantee that they do. As Marie Price points out, NGOs 'are accountable only to their supporters. It is therefore difficult to know how well these organizations represent popular concerns.'[105] John Clark points to this lack of accountability as a reason that NGOs are so easy to form.[106] They are really special interest groups influencing elected governments; should they be considered as any more accountable to society at large than any other special interest group? Moreover, they may become even less responsive to the needs of those they arose to serve as they grow in size and influence.[107] A second element comes into play particularly when NGOs operate across borders. Organizations operating internationally may be out of touch with the people whose interests they supposedly represent. For instance, Rusli bin Mohd and Jan Laarman argue that in the case of forestry policy, US-based NGOs rarely consult with the forest-dwellers in the countries whose forests they aim to protect.[108] Third, there may not be accountability across groups of NGOs working jointly on issues, even apart from the issue of whether these groups adequately represent the broader population. Jonathan Fox and David Brown point out that many NGOs working on international issues are intermediary organizations, that may not always fully represent the interests of the grassroots organizations with whom they are supposed to be in coalition.[109] Philosophical differences between environmental organizations in industrialized countries and those in the developing world may prevent one from adequately representing the interests of the other,[110] and some have called relations between the two 'emerging colonialism.'[111]

Non-governmental organizations may face difficulties of representation in other ways as well; many operate on a shoestring budget and can thus become beholden to their donors.[112] Others point out that as NGOs become more integrated into the state or international decision-making process they may lose some of their representational advantages, becoming part of the system rather than bringing otherwise unheard voices to the table.[113]

Regardless, it is clear that the policies and practices pertaining to the global environment are not made by states alone, nor even by non-state actors acting solely within state borders. Action taken by industry actors and by non-governmental environmental organizations influences the existence, character, and success of international environmental regulation in ways that challenge the state-centric view of international relations.

OZONE DEPLETION AND CLIMATE CHANGE

It is fitting to begin an examination of cases in international environmental policy with an examination of problems of the atmosphere, among the most global of problems. This chapter examines one of the true success stories in international environmental cooperation, and one seemingly similar case that has met with much greater resistance.

Ozone depletion and climate change (also known as global warming) are different environmental problems that share important structural similarities that have influenced the way they have been addressed. Both are true problems of the global commons: emissions of harmful substances from anywhere in the world have an equal impact on the atmosphere. It is thus essential to involve all states engaged in activities that produce the substances responsible for these threats in efforts to address them if the environmental problems are to be prevented or mitigated. Both ozone depletion and climate change involved initially highly uncertain science and international processes that responded to potential future threats to the global atmosphere before the impacts of these problems were manifest. Regulation on both of these issues was likely to have significant impacts on industrial processes, and the preferences of industrial actors (along with environmental non-governmental organizations) strongly influenced the process of international negotiations to address the problems. Moreover, precedents set in the earlier negotiations to protect the ozone layer have carried over to influence the negotiations on climate change.

There are nevertheless important differences between the two issues. The types of activities that cause the harm to the ozone layer are almost entirely the result of industrial processes, and, at the time the potential problem was discovered, carried out primarily by the industrialized world. It was also the industrialized world that cared most about the potential problem. While it is certainly also true that developed countries bear the greatest responsibility for the increase in greenhouse gases over the course of history, many of the types of activities responsible for the emission of greenhouse gases take place in developing countries as well. There are many more types of activities that contribute to the level of emissions of greenhouse gases, some relating to industrialization, but some from land use and agriculture. Likewise, the impact of the environmental damage caused by these global problems is differently distributed in these two issues. While there are a few states near the Antarctic ozone hole that have thus far felt the greatest impact from harm to the ozone layer, and there are others that depend more on activities likely to be disrupted by ozone depletion, the harm in general is likely to be globally dispersed. The variation across states in terms of the likely harm to result from climate change is much broader, and in particular does not fit neatly into 'developed versus developing states'.

To make things even more complicated, while the environmental issues themselves are largely unconnected, there are some substances (chlorofluorocarbons, for instance) which contribute to both environmental problems. And the regulatory processes, almost entirely separate, have some impacts on each other, apart from the precedents adopted. For example, some of the substitute chemicals used in place of those that deplete the ozone layer are themselves greenhouse gases, contributing to climate change. These points of connection raise the broader question within regulation of global environmental issues of whether the regulations of different environmental issues by different treaties and organizations is an appropriate way to address environmental issues that turn out to connect to each other in various ways.

OZONE DEPLETION

Ozone depletion is caused by the interaction of various industrial chemicals with ozone molecules in the stratosphere. The chemicals in question (the most common of which are chlorofluorocarbons and halons) have been used primarily for refrigeration and air conditioning, cleaning of electronic parts, as propellants, and in fire suppression.[1] These substances are stable and therefore do not decompose until they reach the upper atmosphere, where in the presence of sunlight they break down into chlorine or bromine free radicals that attach themselves to ozone molecules, causing a chain reaction that destroys large numbers of ozone molecules at a time. A depleted ozone layer allows increased levels of ultraviolet radiation to get through to earth. The potential effects of depletion of the ozone layer include increases in skin cancer, immune disorders and cataracts in humans, crop damage, and similar harm to other species.[2] Although there was uncertainty about this process when first hypothesized (and when early negotiations to address it were taking place) there is now strong scientific evidence that these substances cause ozone depletion and that such depletion has already occurred. Early evidence of effects from the damaged ozone layer is becoming apparent.

CLIMATE CHANGE

Climate change, more commonly known as global warming, is caused by increasing levels of greenhouse gases in the atmosphere. These gases include carbon dioxide, methane, chlorofluorocarbons, ozone, and nitrous oxides. These substances are primarily naturally occurring, but are produced by human activities in larger quantities than occurred before industrialization. The activities most responsible for production of greenhouse gases include fossil fuel burning, agriculture (particularly cattle ranching and rice cultivation), deforestation, and other industrial processes. The increased greenhouse gases in the atmosphere essentially absorb radiation from the sun that would otherwise be released, increasing the average global temperature. More important than the possibility that the average temperature will become higher are the associated weather effects; storms are expected to increase in frequency and severity, rainfall patterns in general will probably change, polar ice caps are expected to melt, and sea level is expected to rise.[3]

INTERNATIONAL COOPERATION

International cooperation to address ozone depletion and climate change has followed a number of similar patterns. Surprisingly, international scientific efforts to begin cooperation on research with an eye towards building a regulatory regime began for both issues in the 1970s, with the climate discussions beginning somewhat earlier, even though international regulations were created much more quickly and, so far, effectively, to address ozone depletion. They both began under conditions of great uncertainty, and the process and form of international cooperation reflect that.

Ozone Depletion

The science of ozone depletion began in the early 1970s. Two US scientists – F. Sherwood Rowland and Mario Molina – hypothesized in

1974 that chlorofluorocarbons (CFCs) could, because of their stability, last long enough to reach the stratosphere where interaction with sunlight would cause them eventually to break down into chlorine free radicals which could destroy ozone.[4] It was quickly realized that international scientific efforts would be needed to determine whether this hypothesized reaction was taking place, and what impact it would have on the earth's environment.

International cooperation started with a conference of experts from 32 countries, convened by the UN Environment Programme (UNEP) in 1977. This conference adopted a World Plan of Action and established a Coordinating Committee to continue to address the issue. By May 1981 the UNEP Governing Council authorized negotiations to attempt to create a binding treaty on measures to protect the ozone layer. This negotiation process resulted in 1985 in the Vienna Convention for the Protection of the Ozone Layer. This treaty created a framework in which states agreed to take 'appropriate' (but unspecified) measures to protect the ozone layer, cooperate in scientific research and exchange information.[5] The 1985 Convention was followed by the negotiation in 1987 of the Montreal Protocol on Substances That Deplete the Ozone Layer, which required specific abatement measures for ozone-depleting substances. As laid out in the Vienna Convention, amendments to the Protocol can be made with a 2/3 majority vote and are then subject to ratification by the parties.[6] Only those that ratify the amendments are bound by them, although states that ratify the Protocol are bound by any amendments in force at the time of ratification. Amendments have so far been agreed in London in 1990, Copenhagen in 1992, Montreal in 1997, and Beijing in 1999.

The Convention/Protocol process resulted in a more robust agreement, at an earlier point, than would have occurred if negotiations had only begun once serious abatement measures could have been agreed upon. The Protocol added specific abatement measures and the amendments added new regulated substances and new regulatory processes. The London amendments added regulations for carbon tetrachloride, methyl chloroform, and fully halogenated CFCs, as well as introducing the funding mechanism to provide assistance to developing countries.[7] The Copenhagen amendments added HCFCs, hydrobromide fluorocarbons, and methyl bromide to the list of controlled substances, and made the funding mechanism permanent.[8] The Montreal amendments adjusted the timetable for phaseout of some substances, and modified trade restrictions, including the creation of a licensing system to attempt to decrease the black market in ozone depleting substances,[9] and the Beijing amendments also set and advanced timelines for control of various ozone-depleting substances. An agreement that would have addressed all these issues could certainly not have been negotiated in 1985 or even 1987, and it can be argued that it was only because of the incremental action that further regulations were made possible within an existing framework.

In addition, the Montreal Protocol makes use of a system of adjustments that sets it apart from both major approaches to creation of environmental law.[10] It neither empowers a commission to make rules that states are allowed to opt out of, nor requires that all changes be ratified by all parties before they take effect. Unusual among treaties that follow the convention/protocol approach, the Montreal Protocol allows for adjustments within the agreement. Adjustments require the consent of two-thirds of the Parties, representing a majority of both developed and developing countries (the latter part an addition of the London amendments). They become binding on all Parties six months after they are formally notified about them – even those states that did not vote in favor of them.[11]

Adjustments have taken place at meetings of the parties and other negotiations and have addressed such issues as faster phaseout of certain chemicals. Many of the most dramatic changes in the phaseout schedule for various ozone-depleting substances have come through adjustments rather than amendments.[12] For example, the original Montreal Protocol called for a freeze at 1986 levels for the main halons by 1993 for developed countries. That was first adjusted in 1990 to a freeze in 1992 and a complete phaseout by 2000. In 1992 it was adjusted to consumption by 1994 at 25 percent of 1989 levels and a complete phaseout by 1996. Similarly, the initial Montreal Protocol requirement that developed countries cut their use of the major CFCs to 50 percent of 1986 levels by 1999 was ultimately adjusted to a complete phaseout by 1996. Similar adjustments were made for developing country parties.

Climate Change

Scientific exploration into the climate has taken place for centuries, but modern climate science can be traced to Jean Baptiste Joseph Fourier who, in 1827, postulated that the atmosphere influenced the temperature of the earth's surface and described what is now known as the greenhouse effect, by which certain gases of the atmosphere trap the sun's radiation from escaping and keep the earth warmer than it would otherwise be. Throughout the nineteenth and the beginning of the twentieth centuries this understanding was further refined, and international scientific cooperation undertaken to monitor the atmosphere. Swedish scientist Svante Arrhenius even explored, at the turn of the twentieth century, the idea that a doubling of carbon in the atmosphere, made possible by human activities, would increase the temperature of the earth. These observations, however, went largely unexplored until after World War II, when interest in meteorological data increased, due to better technology and to air travel.[13] The UN designation of the International Geophysical Year (IGY) from 1957 to 1958 increased the focus on the relationship between carbon and climate, and resulted in the first permanent station to monitor CO_2 emissions. Regular measurements taken initially at this station indicated that emissions of CO_2 are not all absorbed by the ocean, as was previously believed, but are also taken up in the atmosphere.[14] After the IGY even more scientific cooperation emerged on issues of climate and weather, including the creation of the World Weather Watch and the Global Atmospheric Research Programme.[15]

International cooperation on climate science thus has a long history, and it is difficult to pinpoint when international efforts to address human effects on the climate began. An important early step to integrate scientific study with political concern came in 1971, with an international meeting of scientists in Wijk, Sweden, to discuss issues of long-term climate change. The Stockholm Conference in 1972 also helped raise the profile of the climate issue, although no specific steps were taken there. The World Meteorological Organization (WMO) sponsored a symposium on the topic in 1975, at the same time that the US National Association of Sciences published a report suggesting the need to improve climate science. The WMO convened the First World Climate Conference in Geneva in 1979, with a number of other international conferences following in the subsequent years.[16] One of the most significant developments nearly a decade later was the creation, by WMO and UNEP, of the Intergovernmental Panel on Climate Change (IPCC) in 1988. This group, consisting of the world's most eminent climatologists and other relevant researchers, appointed by their own governments, was not a standard international organization in that the scientists did not represent their states but rather were charged with investigating climate science and issuing a report on the status of the science and recommending options. It consists of three working groups that investigate the scientific, socioeconomic, and mitigation aspects of climate change.[17] In this same year, an international conference in Toronto called for 20 percent cuts in emissions of CO_2 by 2005, and the United Nations General Assembly passed a resolution calling for 'protection of the global climate for present and future generations.' In

1989, the UNEP Governing Council requested that UNEP and WMO begin negotiations for a framework convention to address issues of climate change; the first IPCC report the following year, as well as the Second World Climate Conference, agreed on the necessity for negotiation for a global climate treaty.

These negotiations led to the first international agreement to address issues of climate change: the UN Framework Convention on Climate Change (FCCC), signed in 1992 at Rio. As suggested by its title, it is a framework convention, requiring no actual abatement measures but instead committing states to working to achieve 'stabilization of greenhouse gas concentrations in the atmosphere at a level that would prevent dangerous anthropogenic interference with the climate system.' Parties commit themselves to undertake national inventories of greenhouse gas emissions and to cooperate in the process of studying and controlling greenhouse gas emissions, among other important, but quite general, obligations.[18]

The Kyoto Protocol to the FCCC, signed at the end of 1997, requires actual reductions in emissions of greenhouse gases of varying amounts for developed countries, with an average of a 5 percent reduction from 1990 emissions by the period 2008 to 2012. The Protocol includes three instruments to introduce flexibility into how states meet their goals: emissions trading among states with reduction obligations is allowed, a clean development mechanism permits developed country states to get emissions reductions credits for projects undertaken to reduce carbon emissions in developing countries (which do not have emissions reductions obligations initially under the Protocol), and what has come to be known as joint implementation, which allows the developed country parties to get credit for projects done in other developed country parties. In addition, the agreement allows the removal of carbon from the atmosphere by sinks (such as forests) to count towards states' goals.[19] All these measures have been controversial and subject to negotiation on how they will be implemented. At the time of writing a major stumbling block is the refusal of the US Senate to ratify the treaty unless developing countries are given obligations, something that was never seriously considered during the Kyoto negotiations or since, for the initial implementation of the Protocol. Not only is the USA the largest emitter of greenhouse gases and therefore an essential part of any agreement to address the global climate but the dynamics of negotiations over the Protocol change without its participation. Article 25 requires that 55 states, representing 55 percent of developed country emissions of greenhouse gases as of 1990, ratify the protocol before it enters into force. Since the USA accounted for more than 36 percent of 1990 GHG emissions by the group of regulated states,[20] participation by almost all other developed country parties is essential for the agreement to enter into force. That role gave states such as Japan and Canada a much greater degree of influence in negotiations in the fall of 2001 over how to implement the agreement, because without the USA their role was essential.

THE ROLE OF SCIENCE

Both ozone depletion and global climate change challenged the conventional approach to the role of science in regulation of international environmental agreements in several ways. In the first place, unlike an issue like transboundary acid rain in which an effect was first noticed and a search undertaken for the cause, regulation began for ozone depletion (and, to a lesser extent, climate change) when there was no clear evidence of an actual environmental problem.

The Vienna Convention on the Protection of the Ozone Layer (or, more realistically, the Montreal Protocol, which required actual abatement measures) is seen as the first global environmental treaty to address an environmental problem that was still only theoretical at the time it was negotiated. The idea that halogenated compounds could destroy ozone had been demonstrated in the laboratory, and Roland and Molina had theorized that human-created CFCs could migrate into the stratosphere where the ozone layer protected the earth from harmful ultraviolet rays. But no one had seen the destruction of the ozone layer by these chemicals and, more importantly, no one had witnessed actual environmental damage resulting from this potential problem. Even initial evidence of a season thinning (known as the ozone 'hole') over Antarctica was initially disregarded by scientific instruments designed to discard information so far from expected measurements.[21] Once this hole had been observed in 1986, there was no immediate evidence linking it clearly to human activities.[22] Conclusive evidence was offered by the NASA-sponsored Ozone Trends Panel, which reported in 1988 (after the Montreal Protocol had already been negotiated) that ozone depletion was occurring and that it had human-induced causes.[23] The timing suggests, as Karen Liftin points out, that scientific knowledge was necessary but not sufficient in the process of negotiating the Montreal Protocol, and that the combination of politics with science is essential in understanding the willingness of states to agree to change their behavior before the mechanisms or extent of ozone depletion were clearly understood.[24]

The Montreal Protocol process made scientific inquiry an integral part of the regulatory process. Some of this happened outside the treaty organization but in response to it; the WMO/NASA Assessment from 1986 that helped provide the basis for the Montreal Protocol was an explicit response to the call under the Vienna Convention for international cooperation to provide a better understanding of ozone depletion.[25] The Conference of the Parties to the Protocol created assessment panels shortly after the negotiation of the Protocol: a panel on science, one on technology, one on environmental effects, and one on economics.[26] As discussed above, findings and recommendations from these panels and other research brought about by the existence of the international agreement were essential in the amendments and adjustments to obligations under the agreement.

Science in international negotiations to prevent climate change has likewise been uncertain and controversial and, unlike with ozone depletion, new research has tended to create as many new uncertainties as it resolves. On the one hand, there is now a strong consensus from the international scientific community that humans have had an effect on the global climate system. The latest IPCC assessment indicates that 'there is new and stronger evidence that most of the warming observed over the last 50 years is attributable to human activities.'[27] The IPCC in 2001 also indicated its increasing confidence in climate models to predict climate in the future.[28] However, there is a lot that is still not known about climate science, and this uncertainty has been used for political ends by those who would prefer not to take action to mitigate global climate change.

Initial international scientific cooperation to understand climate change is discussed above. One interesting difference between the case of ozone depletion and climate change was the existence of a broadly international scientific body, the IPCC, before the climate negotiations. In 1990 its first report indicated that 'emissions resulting from human activities are substantially increasing the concentration of greenhouse gases' and that these 'increases will enhance the greenhouse effect, resulting on average in an additional warming of the Earth's surface.'[29] So while the Framework Convention on Climate Change required cataloging of greenhouse gas emissions by states and called for international scientific cooperation, most of it has been carried out through the IPCC, a group independent from the agreement, as well as the pre-existing WMO. Findings from the second IPCC Assessment Report in 1995, augmenting its 1990 report, were influential in the willingness of states to negotiate the Kyoto Protocol.

Much remains uncertain about climate change, however. Estimates of the magnitude of expected average temperature change have varied over even the last decade, with IPCC estimates of the amount of average warming increasing (from a 1995 estimate of a 3.5 degrees Celsius increase by 2100 to a predicted 5.8 degree increase in the 2001 assessment) but the range of uncertainty increasing as well, particularly in describing the extent of warming that has already taken place.[30] The role of other factors in climate change brings new uncertainties. Aerosols, which come from burning of all sorts (including of fossil fuels) play some sort of role in atmospheric response to solar radiation, but in a way that is unclear. They may, if bright, reflect energy back to space, which would moderate the effects of greenhouse gases, or they may, if dark, absorb even more energy and increase the greenhouse effect. As climate modeler Jeffrey Kiehl of the National Center for Atmospheric Research explains, 'the more we learn [about aerosols], the less we know.'[31] Clouds, which may be more abundant with increasing water vapor likely from higher temperatures (as well as independently from aerosols), are subject to similar uncertainties. Clouds could increase from warming, but then in turn block solar radiation from entering the atmosphere leading to cooling, or clouds may decrease or form in a different part of the atmosphere, and thus increase warming.[32] The role played by oceans is also complicated and not sufficiently understood. Climate research from a century ago already demonstrated that much of the human-created carbon dioxide is taken up by the oceans, but what it will do there, or how the warming of the oceans affects broader climatic patterns, is still unknown.[33]

Potential mechanisms for abatement of anthropogenic carbon are also untested, and new large-scale ideas, if attempted, could have a big effect on how much carbon is released into the atmosphere. Recent suggestions have included seeding the ocean with iron or nitrogen to increase the growth of plankton or other aquatic plants that would serve as a carbon sink, or burying CO_2 in oil wells or at the bottom of the ocean.[34] Any such schemes could have a huge impact on human ability to mitigate climate change, but they create even greater uncertainties about long-run effects of these types of policies.

The biggest uncertainty is, as Dale Jamieson suggests in other contexts, social.[35] Jerry Mahlman, who recently retired from the directorship of the US National Oceanic and Atmospheric Administration's Geophysic Fluid Dynamics Laboratory, agrees that social uncertainty is both important and difficult to resolve: 'we don't have a clue how people are going to react 30 years from now.'[36] There are too many types of activities, practiced by too many sectors of very different countries, to realistically predict human behavior with respect to greenhouse gas emission or abatement in the near future. This level of uncertainty, both scientific and social, cannot help but affect the ability to make political decisions about how to address climate change.

NON-GOVERNMENTAL ACTORS

Industry

In both the issue areas industry actors have played a significant role, though a somewhat different one. In particular, the industry involved in ozone depletion is much smaller and more uniform than in the case of climate change, and while important to industrial development the substances that deplete the ozone layer are less integrated throughout the fabric of daily life than are those activities that contribute to climate change. Industry's action on ozone depletion was thus much more unified than has been the case with climate change. It is also important to note the relationship between industry action and domestic and international regulation. In both cases, industry resisted initial attempts at regulation. In ozone depletion consumer demand combined with US regulation gave ozone-depleting substance (ODS) manufacturers an incentive to create the substitutes that would be used for their products, push for international regulation, and thus benefit from being among the first to change their behavior. The experience with ozone depletion may suggest some of the reasons that industry has been much more successful in resisting regulation in climate change; lack of consumer demand and little domestic regulation has given industries a weaker incentive to change their behavior in the absence of international regulation. This creates a Catch-22 situation in which states resist regulating their industries because the industries resist regulation, yet they will see few advantages to changing their behavior until regulated. Fortunately, some consumer pressure combined with an acceptance of the inevitability of action on climate change is convincing multinational industries in particular to begin changing their activities, even before they are required to do so.

Industry's main role in addressing ozone depletion was the eventual creation of substitute chemicals to use as international regulations required the phaseout of ozone-depleting substances. It is often mistakenly assumed that there were readily available substitutes for ozone-depleting substances at the time of the Montreal Protocol, and that the existence of these substitutes made the negotiation process simpler.[37] That perception is incorrect. DuPont, the primary manufacturer of CFCs, after introducing non-CFC propellants for use in aerosol spray cans due to US consumer pressure in the 1970s, had ceased research into other CFC substitutes at the beginning of the 1980s. It began research again in 1986, only after the Vienna Convention was signed and negotiations for the Montreal Protocol were under way.[38] The realization that international regulation was likely (and, in the USA, that domestic regulation was inevitable), jump-started the search for alternatives.

In the intervening years, in an effort to stave off regulations, industry downplayed the possibility that substitutes or recycling would be cost effective or viable. The Alliance for Responsible CFC Policy, an industry organization, indicated that 'all promising compounds identified have one or more limitations ... consequently, we conclude that fully satisfactory fluorocarbon alternatives will not become available in the foreseeable future.'[39]

It is all the more remarkable to note, then, how quickly substitutes became available and widely adopted after the negotiation of the Protocol. In 1988 several traditional CFC producers such as AT&T and DuPont announced the availability of competitively priced CFC substitutes for use in electronics, food packaging and other applications.[40] Other substitutes followed in the early 1990s. Ultimately most OECD countries phased out their use of ozone-depleting substances faster than was required under the Protocol.[41] While meeting obligations ahead of time could be seen as evidence that the obligations were not onerous or were not due to the treaty process,[42] in this case the fundamental shift in industrial processes is evident and would have been inconceivable without international regulation. Several factors, both from the Protocol itself, and from the ways that individual states chose to implement it, contributed to this profound industrial transformation.

The mere existence of the Vienna Convention, which promised abatement measures, followed by the negotiation of the Montreal Protocol, which required them, put industry on notice that it would not be able to continue profiting from ozone-depleting substances to the extent it previously had. In the same way that DuPont found substitute propellants for aerosol spray cans in anticipation of certain US regulation (and with the support of consumer demand), the ODS industry responded to the inevitability of international regulations.

More importantly, the same industries that several years previously had reasonably concluded that substitutes would not be cost effective had reason to change their calculations. As well as adding the element of necessity, international regulations provided further incentives for the creation of viable substitutes for ozone-depleting substances. Alan Miller argues that 'the competitive incentive brought forth by a recognition that those companies who develop the best alternatives will capture a multi-billion dollar world market' created a sufficient incentive for innovation.[43] Investment in research could pay off with the promise of a huge set of potential consumers required to use non-ozone depleting chemicals[44] in a way that it might not for a purely domestic market.

The other major hurdle for the development of substitutes, their probable cost, was surmounted both by the existence of the Protocol itself and by the way states chose to regulate under it. Many substitutes were projected to, and in fact did, sell for five to ten times the price of the CFCs they would replace. Only the presence of an assured market of consumers who would be required to use them, despite the increased cost, would make it reasonable to develop them.[45]

For instance, when substitute chemicals were first introduced by DuPont and AT&T for ozone-depleting substances they were prohibitively expensive. It was only the US implementation of an excise tax on ozone-depleting substances, adopted in the context of the Montreal Protocol on Substances that Deplete the Ozone Layer, that made them increasingly expensive relative to their substitutes. Substitute chemicals that might have been more expensive than them before the Montreal Protocol and domestic regulation suddenly became the most cost-effective option. Even when industries were still allowed to use ozone-depleting substances, they chose the more environmentally friendly option of not doing so, because it was more cost effective. It was therefore a regulatory tool that made taking the environmentally beneficial action cost effective. The excise tax in Europe was smaller, but still significant enough to lower the relative cost of alternatives. Some, in fact, attribute the success in phaseout of ozone-depleting substances overall more to the tax than to the regulations themselves,[46] although of course domestic taxes, particularly in the USA, would have been unlikely to exist had it not been for the international regulations.

Other ways in which industry has been involved in the Montreal Protocol process have added to its willingness to work within the regulatory system. For example, much of the funding from the Multilateral Fund, discussed below, goes to purchase equipment, chemicals, or expertise from industries in developed countries, thereby disseminating technology and increasing the advantages to the main ODS industries of the overall regulatory process. Moreover, the role of industry actors within the committees discussed above may also contribute to the implementation of regulations. Owen Greene suggests that the participation of industry actors on the Technology and Economic Assessments Panels increases the likelihood that new ozone-friendly technologies are adopted within the industries represented. He gives the example of oil and gas industry representatives who, after serving on panels discussing the options for phasing out the use of halons, were able to change the way fire fighting was conducted within their own companies and then in the industry as a whole.[47] In short, the Montreal Protocol process has found a way to give industry actors incentives to create and use the substitute chemicals and processes required to implement the agreement.

Industry's role in climate change has been as varied as the industries and countries involved in creating greenhouse gases. Traditionally, the economic health of a country has been attributable largely to its reliance on fossil fuels. Ian Rowlands suggests that the willingness of a state to take action on climate change can be ascertained from the extent to which it has been able to de-link its gross domestic product from pollution-generating industries.[48]

In the USA, the largest emitter of greenhouse gases and the most resistant participant in international measures to mitigate climate change, the fossil fuel industry has been particularly active in leading the opposition to global (or national) action. A group of utility and coal companies created an industry group, The Information Council on the Environment, and in the runup to the FCCC negotiations hired a public relations firm to increase publicity to 'reposition global warming as theory rather than fact' and increase the visibility of scientists skeptical of some of the hypotheses about climate change.[49]

The international industry organization, with the intentionally misleading name of The Global Climate Coalition, initially included the major fossil fuel industries worldwide, and lobbied strongly against the Kyoto Protocol, out of concern that reduced greenhouse gas emissions would hurt their profitability. More recently many of the main companies involved, including Royal Dutch/Shell, BP Amoco, Dow Chemical, Ford, and Texaco have withdrawn from membership. Moreover, the group has recently toned down its message, questioning the magnitude of climate change rather than its existence or causes.[50] Additionally, former members of the coalition have been moving into alternative energy operations: Texaco, for instance, bought a large stake in an energy conversion company whose main focus is energy from hydrogen.[51]

The sector that has taken the lead in pushing for regulation on greenhouse gases has been the insurance industry. Insurers face the biggest potential for losses from dramatic weather events and rising sea level predicted from climate change, and they have been involved in addressing the situation, both privately and in urging international action. In 1995 fourteen of the world's largest insurance firms signed a Statement of Environmental Commitment pledging to incorporate climate considerations into their future assessments; the first US insurer signed on the following year.[52] Other industries, including those involved with the use of fossil fuels, are themselves taking out insurance to hedge against the possibility that their profits will go down if people consume less greenhouse-gas producing substances.[53]

What is particularly interesting is that, whereas many industry groups have publicly opposed any action on climate change, most are preparing for what they see as approaching obligations. This is particularly true of automobile manufacturers, which are working towards increased fuel efficiency and towards alternatives to the internal combustion engine. Other companies in fossil-fuel-intensive industries, such as Royal Dutch/ Shell, which has just announced its intention to spend up to a billion dollars over the next five years on renewable energy programs,[54] realize the inevitability, even if some of their governments do not, of international regulation to restrict greenhouse gas emissions.

Other Non-State Actors

Environmental and consumer groups created pressure for behavior change on both ozone depletion and climate change long before government action was taken; it is their pressure, in combination with increased understanding of these global problems, that influenced industry actors to change their behavior even before being required to do so by national or international regulation. In the USA, the first country to restrict use of ozone-depleting substances, consumer pressure created markets for goods made without ozone-depleting substances.

In addition to activists lying down across rail distribution lines for ozone-depleting substances or occupying what they thought was a US oil platform to protest the USA's unwillingness to work within the Kyoto framework,[55] traditional methods for gaining media attention, organizations have started to gain influence at other levels in addressing these two issues. Non-governmental organizations have been increasingly active participants in pushing for negotiations on both these issues and have generally been present at the negotiations and at subsequent meetings of the parties.

An interesting strategy used by environmental activists on both these issues involved getting commitments from sub-state governmental (or quasi-governmental) entities to address the environmental problems, either acting sooner or more thoroughly than states or international organizations have been willing to. In the case of ozone depletion, Berkeley, California, declared itself to be 'styrofoam free,' as a way of indicating its support for protection of the ozone layer. The environ-mental organization Friends of the Earth convinced twenty-four other cities to undertake similar pledges, going further in the immediate wake of the Montreal Protocol than they were required to do.[56] The more explicitly international 'Cities for Climate Protection' project, led by the International Council for Local Environmental Initiatives, has done the same for climate change policies, with nearly 400 participant cities worldwide by 2000,[57] agreeing to undertake climate protection greater than that legally required. A similar initiative operates on the university level. The organization Clean Air-Cool Planet attempts to persuade universities to undertake pledges to reduce their contribution to climate change. Tufts University, for instance, has pledged to meet Kyoto obligations on its own, although obviously not required to do so.[58] This organization also works to obtain voluntary commitments from businesses and cities to take action to reduce their greenhouse gas emissions.

This type of action, sometimes intended to have a demonstration effect, may in fact show governments both the concern of the population and the feasibility of climate-protection measures. On the other hand, it presents an irony, to the extent that it is largely the unwillingness of people in developed countries to undertake lifestyle changes that precludes serious governmental action to address the issue.

PARTICIPATION, COMPLIANCE AND EFFECTIVENESS

Both of these issues are problems of the global commons, so participation of all major states is required for cooperation to have a meaningful impact. Negotiators for both agreements chose to address the issue of participation by giving developing countries aid to meet any obligations they undertake, and by giving them extra time before they would have to meet any emissions reductions deadlines taken on by developed countries. In the case of the Kyoto Protocol to the Framework Convention on Climate Change differentiation in abatement obligations was even made among developed countries (and developing countries were given no abatement obligations at all) in order to induce them to join; notably, former communist countries with economies in transition were given a choice of base year from which to calculate reductions.

It is much simpler to address the success of mechanisms for participation in and compliance with the Montreal Protocol and its ultimate effectiveness, because the process of cooperation has been much more complete. Nearly all states have joined the agreement. Developed countries have entirely phased out their use of the initially regulated ODSs and decreased their use of newly regulated ones; developing countries have begun the process of freezing and then lowering their consumption of regulated substances. The ozone layer has not yet recovered and will not for some time, but a process has been started that, if it continues, will eventually fully address the problem. There is evidence of non-compliance both on the state level and in a thriving black market in regulated substances, but both these aspects are minor and temporary compared to the overall accomplishments of the treaty and its probable eventual effectiveness.

In the case of climate change, it is too soon to tell. As of the end of 2001 not only had the Kyoto Protocol not entered into force but it showed no sign of doing so in the foreseeable future. States continue the process of meeting in high-level negotiations to attempt to determine how to implement the controversial aspects of the agreement, while others suggest that the agreement is a flawed effort that either cannot hope to accomplish sufficient reductions to have a measurable effect on human-induced climate change or is even the wrong type of effort more generally.[59] Yet there are signs that individually states and non-state actors are changing their behavior in a way that might ultimately have an impact on the ability of the world to implement Kyoto and the necessary measures beyond it, to address the problem of climate change.

Participation

The participation of not only developed but developing countries was essential if the Montreal Protocol process was to work. Most developed countries joined the Protocol immediately, but the issue of bringing in developing states was more difficult and equally important. Although at the time the Protocol was signed the per capita consumption of ozone-depleting substances by developing countries was miniscule and production in most of these countries negligible, these figures were likely to grow significantly. Chlorofluorocarbons had been essential in the process of industrialization for the countries of the northern hemisphere, and others at early stages of development were likely to use these cheap, safe chemicals in their process of industrialization as well. It was estimated at the time that India and China alone would account for one-third of the world's consumption of CFCs by 2008.[60] Moreover, the problem had clearly been created by northern industries, and the concern about the environmental problem was most prevalent in the industrialized world. In the absence of sufficient incentives to join the agreement, developing countries showed every sign of remaining outside the regulatory system. By the time of the London negotiations in 1989 the only major CFC-using developing countries that had joined the agreement were Mexico, Nigeria, and Venezuela.[61]

The initial efforts to bring developing countries into the agreement revolved around a grace-period (initially ten years, though it has been renegotiated for a variety of different ODSs) during which developing countries would not have to meet the obligations of the Protocol. This measure allowed member developing countries whose annual per capita consumption of ODS was less than 0.3 kg per capita to continue and even increase their use of these substances. The Protocol acknowledged that these countries had special needs for financial and technical assistance to meet their obligations, but without specifying the way in which these needs would be met, the lag-time was insufficient to convince most developing countries to join.

The second measure was a trade incentive: states that are party to the agreement can only trade in controlled substances with those that are in the agreement.[62] For states that did not produce ODSs but hoped to use them, joining the agreement was the obvious way to guarantee their access to these chemicals. The scenario would only work, however, if the developing countries capable of producing ODSs were brought into the agreement as well. Otherwise a separate trading bloc could emerge outside of the agreement that could undermine, rather than encourage, participation. Mexico was the only developing country producer of ODSs that initially signed the Protocol.[63] The reluctance of other producer states such as China and India to join the Montreal Protocol initially indicated that the trade sanctions would be insufficient to bring developing countries into the agreement. These states, potentially unaffected by the sanctions, would have to be convinced to join.

The most innovative and essential element in bringing these states into the agreement was the elaboration of a financial transfer mechanism. The Multilateral Fund, as the mechanism was ultimately named, was the factor that allowed for universal participation in the agreement, and facilitated the process of moving away from ozone-depleting substances in developing countries. It is a generally well-designed instrument for bringing developing states into the Montreal Protocol and helping their implementation of the agreement.

The creation of this fund can be attributed to the power that a commons issue gives to those states whose participation is essential to addressing the environmental problem but for whom it is not a priority. A number of states explicitly tied their participation in the treaty process to the creation of a funding mechanism. India and China, whose participation in the agreement was essential due to their large and growing populations, rapid industrialization, and ability to produce ozone-depleting substances, refused to join the agreement unless an aid package with which they were satisfied was created.[64] The resulting funding mechanism is specified in Article 10 of the Protocol (as amended), and involves funding from developed countries based on the UN scale of assessments, put into a multilateral fund overseen by a committee composed both of donors and recipients.[65]

The creation of the Fund had the intended effect. China joined the Protocol immediately, followed by India and Brazil in 1992 and eventually by almost all developing countries. Importantly, the operation of the Fund has gone a long way toward helping some developing countries avoid ozone-depleting substances or change over their use of ODSs to ozone-safe chemicals or processes. By early 2001 developed countries had contributed more than $1.22 billion to the fund, and the Executive Committee had approved nearly 3500 projects in 124 developing countries, expected to result in the phaseout of the consumption of more than 142,000 ODP tonnes and the production of 39,000 tonnes of ODSs. Approximately 85 percent of that amount has already been phased out.[66]

Developing countries have been dubious of participating in agreements to prevent or mitigate climate change, but so have a number of developed countries. The FCCC is making some progress in addressing developing country concerns; in some aspects it promises more than the ozone regime, but in the absence of specific abatement measures it is difficult to tell how far the agreement will go towards meeting the concerns of developing countries. Following shortly after the specification of a funding mechanism under the London Amendments to the Montreal Protocol, developing country negotiators of the FCCC were insistent that aid be included in the agreement as a quid pro quo for signing.[67]

In a victory for the developing countries, the idea that there would be funding (and that it would be new and additional) was essentially assumed to be a given; it was the format for it that was more contentious. In this case, a mechanism had already been created outside of the FCCC framework. The Global Environment Facility (GEF), run largely by the World Bank (with assistance from UN agencies), had been set up to provide multilateral funding to address four global environmental issues: ozone depletion, climate change, biodiversity, and international waters. Industrialized countries wanted to use the GEF as the funding mechanism for climate change because they had a larger degree of influence over funding through that organization than they thought they would over a new mechanism; developing countries opposed the use of the GEF for precisely the same reason.[68] Developed countries essentially refused to provide serious levels of aid if the GEF was not chosen as the interim funding mechanism for the convention, and they were successful. Developing countries did make a credible threat to reject the FCCC if the GEF were not at least restructured to give them more influence over its activities; the restructuring that resulted made the decision processes in the GEF similar to those in the Multilateral Fund.[69]

The Framework Convention on Climate Change requires that developed country parties provide 'new and additional financial resources to meet the agreed full costs incurred by developing country Parties' in meeting their obligations under the convention.[70] At this point the obligations referred to pertain to gathering and communicating information about the sources and sinks of greenhouse gases, but it is likely that any new obligations will be undertaken only with the financial assistance to meet them. The funding obligation outlined in the FCCC goes further in some ways than that under the Montreal Protocol; the convention specifies that 'the extent to which developing country Parties will effectively implement their commitments ... will depend on the effective implementation by developed country Parties of their commit-ments ... related to financial resources.'[71] The Kyoto Protocol indicates further commitments for transfer of financial resources and technology.[72]

Other questions about the role developing countries will play are as yet unresolved, and relate to the issue of the participation of the USA, the largest greenhouse gas emitter. The US Senate voted 95–0 on a declaration that it would reject any climate agreement that requires abatement measures from industrialized countries without also requiring obligations to be undertaken by developing countries.[73] But as of late 2001 developing countries did not have obligations under the Kyoto Protocol, and there was no serious international discussion of requiring them. Most of the states that had ratified the Kyoto Protocol as of late 2001 were either developing countries or former Soviet-bloc countries that will be able to benefit from emissions trading.

The Kyoto Protocol addressed some of the concerns of developed countries both through the flexibility mechanisms it included, and by taking the relatively unusual step of differentiating levels of developed country abatement obligations under the Protocol. The 'Qualified Emission Limitation or Reduction Commitments' for developed country parties varies from 92 percent of 1990 emissions to 110 percent.[74] Although the Convention indicates the need to take into account 'specific national and regional development priorities, objectives, and circum-stances' there is no specific formula for arriving at the differentiated commitments of the parties. Instead, commitments agreed to were those that were politically feasible: as much as each individual party was willing to commit to. In order to reach an agreement that had a chance of including the major developed country parties, negotiators agreed to targets that states were more or less willing to accept.

Compliance and Effectiveness

It is too early to address the issue of compliance with measures to address climate change, because there are few legal abatement obligations as this book goes to press. Measures to protect the ozone layer, however, require extensive action. While there are instances of non-compliance, they are almost the exception that proves the rule: states have fundamentally changed the way their industries operate in order to live up to a set of ever-tightening international agreements to protect the ozone layer.

There are two types of non-compliance with the Montreal Protocol that have taken place. The first is state-level non-compliance, that happened as former Soviet-bloc states found their economies in disarray at the time when they were supposed to be phasing out their use of many ODSs. Due to an accident of timing, under the agreement they are considered developed countries, but the fall of communism in this region in the late 1980s and early 1990s left them in economic and political situations that were more similar to those of developing countries. In particular, Belarus, Bulgaria, Poland, Russia, and Ukraine were not able to meet the 1996 deadline for complete phaseout of a set of ODSs. The non-compliance was obvious, but no one wanted to accuse the states of actual non-compliance, so they were persuaded by the treaty secretariat to turn themselves in to the non-compliance procedure developed under the Montreal Protocol. This process allowed for increased funding and flexibility in the phaseout dates to be negotiated for the states that went through this process.[75]

The black market that has emerged in ODSs is also important. Chlorofluorocarbons (CFCs) are smuggled into the USA, Europe, and other developed countries where CFC manufacturing for domestic consumption is no longer allowed. High excise taxes (particularly in the USA) made legal purchase of these substances too costly even before the total developed-country phaseout, and some who want cheap access to these chemicals have been willing to skirt the law to obtain them. Chlorofluorocarbons are currently the main component of the black market for ODSs, and although it is feared that other ODSs will also reach the black market, that is unlikely.

The extent of the black market, although unknown, is significant. In some US ports CFC smuggling is second only in value to the smuggling of narcotics.[76] Industry estimates suggest that up to 20 percent of CFCs currently in use may have been purchased on the black market.[77] Predictions of when the ozone layer will recover have been based on consumption numbers that assume complete compliance with Montreal Protocol requirements, and the increase in CFC use that is made possible by the black market is certain to delay the environmental recovery foreseen by the treaty process. Jerry Mahlman, then of the U.S. National Oceanic and Atmospheric Administration, suggested that a 'cheating rate of only 10 percent can keep stratospheric CFC levels from declining.'[78] The lack of progress in fixing the ozone layer can be seen already in the fact that the concentration of one of the two main types of CFC in the atmosphere changed not at all during the 1990s, and the other has increased during that period.[79] In addition, the Montreal Protocol regulatory system as a whole depends on the adoption of substitute chemicals and processes in a way that reinforces the phaseout process and is undermined when CFC smuggling becomes prominent.[80]

The causes of the black market are several. First, the differential phaseout dates between developed and developing countries means that production is allowed in some states even when consumption in the developed world is supposed to cease. Moreover, even after the phaseout date, production of these chemicals is allowed in developed countries, if made for export.[81] Production is also allowed for 'essential' use even after phaseout of particular chemicals. The fact that some production is legal means that the mere presence of these substances cannot be taken as a sign of their illegality, making detection of illegality more difficult.

Second, the Eastern European countries that did not comply with their original phaseout deadlines also have had difficulty controlling their borders. The financial incentives to sell these illicit CFCs on the black market for foreign currency increase with the other forms of economic hardship that often accompany the process of economic transition. It is suggested that much of the black market in CFCs can be traced to Russian production.[82] Third, smuggling CFCs and other ozone-depleting substances is relatively easy. It is difficult to distinguish virgin CFCs from those that are recycled (and therefore legal to use).[83] Some of the same factors that initially made these substances so attractive to use – their stability and lack of toxicity – make them simple to hide, and the fact that they can be produced cheaply in Mexico or (before the phaseout) bought with low excise taxes in Canada has made them easy to purchase and bring across the border with the USA. Similar smuggling takes place between Eastern and Western Europe.[84] Another strategy some countries use is to claim they are exporting recycled CFCs when they do not have the capability to recycle them; in all probability these exports are of virgin CFCs.[85]

The most important cause for the black market in ozone-depleting substances, however, is the demand in developed countries. In the case of ozone-depleting substances, the demand comes from two main factors, neither of which is directly connected to the Montreal Protocol itself. The first is the excise tax that most developed countries have placed on ozone-depleting substances in an effort to increase the attractiveness of the phaseout process, as discussed above. The other demand-side element of the black market involves the high cost of retrofitting some CFC-based equipment to use other non-ozone depleting substances. The primary culprit in this case is automobile air conditioning, which exists in 90 percent of US automobiles[86] and to a lesser degree in Europe and other developed countries. Air-conditioning units that had been made to use CFCs could either be recharged using increasingly expensive and less available CFCs, or could be retrofitted to use substitute chemicals. The retrofitting can cost between $200 and $800,[87] depending on the model year of the car. Garages that buy cheap, black-market CFCs can charge their customers significantly less for recharging their air conditioners, while at the same time making a profit of up to $2000 per canister of CFCs.[88]

Although the black market in CFCs is less than ideal and should be ameliorated to the greatest extent possible, its existence does not pose a long-term threat to the health of the Montreal Protocol system. The demand for black market CFCs is already smaller than it could have been and is likely to have a finite time period. It has, for instance, generally been limited to the mobile air conditioning sector. Large industrial users of CFCs have been reluctant to invest in CFCs of questionable origin. This reluctance stems in part out of concern for the legality of the interaction – legitimate businesses are unlikely to risk difficulties with the tax authorities from using black market products. More importantly, black-market CFCs that have been seized often contain a high degree of impurities; those who are responsible for large-scale refrigeration or cooling units are unlikely to risk refilling them with CFCs whose origin is uncertain.[89]

Even within the mobile air-conditioning sector, the cost of retrofitting automobile air conditioners has been steadily falling.[90] Moreover, the type of equipment most likely to make use of black-market CFCs is small, easily replaceable, and has a finite, and rather short, life cycle. Air conditioners, particularly those found in automobiles (the major recipients of illegal CFCs), tend to have life cycles shorter than large industrial equipment. With all new air conditioners made in ozone-friendly ways, the demand for illegal CFCs will rapidly diminish.

The existence of non-compliance with the Montreal Protocol suggests that the behaviors it requires are not simple and costless. That observation makes the great extent of compliance all the more impressive. This issue then also raises the question of whether the Montreal Protocol and its amendments have been effective at addressing the environmental problem.

Without a doubt, states have changed behavior due to the Montreal Protocol, as suggested above. The environment has not been as quick to follow, largely because of the long atmospheric residence times of many ozone-depleting substances. But it is generally agreed that the process has done as much to combat the environmental problem, in a relatively quick time frame, as any other international environmental agreement.

What is interesting is the extent to which states have changed behavior with respect to emission of greenhouse gases as well. A number of states have undertaken pilot programs to make use of the flexibility mechanisms under Kyoto, even when they may not count towards ultimate emission reductions, and most are attempting to increase energy efficiency. China, one of the largest greenhouse gas emitters, appears to have been able to decouple greenhouse gas emissions from energy efficiency, managing to increase its energy output by 50 percent while decreasing its coal consumption by 30 percent.[91] The UN Environment Programme (UNEP) reports that China, with no abatement obligations under Kyoto, has reduced its greenhouse gas emissions by at least 10 percent since 1996. The UNEP released a study in 2001 suggesting that renewable energy projects and governmental action will save 'the equivalent of 1 billion tons of carbon dioxide' annually by 2005. Even the USA, whose greenhouse gas emissions have grown, has decreased by 11 percent the amount of CO_2 emitted per unit of GDP growth.[92] It is difficult to determine whether these changes are caused by the specific anticipation of Kyoto implementation, by broader concern about climate change, or by other local environmental advantages of the actions taken. However, it is clear that there will be changes by states and non-state actors to reflect a generally accepted understanding that climate change is happening.

WHALING

When the whale gets strike
And the line runs o'er,
And the whale makes a plunder with her tail,
And the boat capsized, and four men were drowned,
And we never caught that whale, brave boys,
We never caught that whale.

'Greenland Whale Fisheries', traditional folk song

Commercial whaling has taken place since at least 1100, and has captured the imaginations of folklorists, the economies of nations, and, eventually, so many of the great whales that they nearly became extinct. Whaling is a complex issue to address in examining environmental protection, involving problems of management of a shared natural resource, the difficulty caused by uncertainty, and ultimately the role of ethics. It has a longer history of international regulation than the other issues examined here and a more controversial one as well.

The effort to regulate whaling raises important issues for the protection of the environment. Like ozone depletion and climate change, conservation of whales is a global issue that involves a global commons – the oceans. Technology plays a role in this case as in others. With the invention of factory whaling ships that could travel long distances, stay out for months, and process and preserve their catches on board, previously abundant whale stocks quickly became depleted.

There are aspects of whaling that should make it easier to regulate than some other international environmental issues. In the first place, the same actors who create the problem (whalers) are the ones who suffer from it; whale depletion is not a standard externality in which an unrelated industry is causing harm to an entirely different set of actors.[1] The universe of actors is not only circumscribed and known but potentially self-interested; as the preamble to the International Convention for the Regulation of Whaling explains 'whale stocks are susceptible to natural increases if whaling is properly regulated and ... increases in the size of whale stocks will permit increases in the number of whales which may be captured without endangering the natural resource.'[2] If whalers can sufficiently self-regulate, they will ultimately help themselves. Nevertheless, conservation of whales presents the potential for exactly the sort of 'tragedy of the commons' that Garrett Hardin identified,[3] and there are several aspects of whaling that make it even more complicated to regulate than herders on Hardin's cow pasture.

Regulation of whaling is difficult in part because of the uncertainty involved in regulating a resource that you cannot directly measure; it has been uncertain at any given time how many whales were in the oceans and how many of them could be taken sustainably. When scientists themselves disagreed about how depleted a particular whale stock was, what incentive did whalers have to undertake sacrifices to protect a stock that might not even be depleted? Early regulatory efforts, intended to protect the whaling stocks from over-harvesting, met with difficulty as whalers were wary of individual sacrifice for collective gain or certain limits in the present for the uncertain prospect of future benefits. More importantly, because of concern that whaling states would pull out of the IWC rather than adhere to a quota they considered to be too restrictive, the quotas were set consistently higher than the organization's own Scientific Committee recommended.[4]

As the international whaling regime matured and began to impose strict limits on whaling, individual whalers, or even entire whaling fleets, found ways – both legal and illegal – around international regulations, and thus contributed further to the depletion of the whales on which their livelihoods depended. Some whaling ships registered in states not belonging to the International Whaling Commission (IWC).[5] Some traditional whaling states chose initially not to join the agreement. Whaling states within the organization took advantage of the ability to opt out of quotas that would have hurt the livelihood of their whalers, or resorted to using 'scientific' whaling to allow whale fleets to persist, and to meet local demand for whale products, when commercial whaling was restricted. Compliance, difficult to monitor for most environmental issues, is even harder when addressing obligations involving ocean resources. The ocean is huge, and few states want to submit either to searches or to an international observer program (although the latter was ultimately implemented in a limited way for whaling in the Antarctic). Such searches or monitoring programs are also likely to be costly. It is up to individual whalers or states to report their catches. Since information is self-reported and the IWC only has the power to ask the individual states to investigate and punish infractions, it is difficult to determine non-compliance, but there has been consistent evidence throughout the history of the IWC that some states or ships were not living up to their obligations. More recent evidence has indicated that there was wide-spread non-compliance by the former Soviet Union, well-hidden from the IWC until later revealed. This non-compliance contributed to scientific uncertainty because misreported catches were used to make stock estimates; in this case the non-compliance was sufficient to undermine scientific models of whale populations. Moreover, the recent evidence of past non-compliance with whaling regulations demonstrates the ever-present possibility of non-compliance with international obligations more broadly, and the need to find ways to detect or prevent it.

Environmental activists have played an important role in this process as well, first in publicizing the depletion of the ocean's great mammals. 'Save the Whales!' became the rallying cry of environmentalists in the 1970s. The actions of non-governmental organizations, both within their countries and across borders, changed the attitudes of some whaling states and ultimately the composition of the international body charged with the regulation of whaling. Eventually some non-governmental organizations attempted to shift the terms of the debate about the regulation of whaling. They argued that whales should not be seen as a resource to be exploited, but should be protected as individuals. These organizations convinced non-whaling states to join the IWC, which is open to membership regardless of whaling activity, with the goal of restricting – or ending – commercial whaling. Occasionally, they even paid the dues of these anti-whaling states they convinced to join.[6] These organizations raised awareness of the issue of whaling, and ultimately an alliance between those opposed to whaling on moral grounds and those who supported a ban on whaling in order to replenish the stocks was sufficient to support a moratorium on commercial whaling. As some whale stocks have replenished, this coalition is breaking down and providing the focal point for the debate over the future of commercial whaling.

Power politics has also played a role in the whaling debate in its recent history. The USA used threats of economic sanctions to persuade states whaling outside of the agreement to join and to submit to the regulations passed by the organization. Pro-whaling states have also tried to influence the members of the IWC through promises of aid or threats of its removal depending on a state's participation in the commission.

The most serious regulatory step taken by the IWC was a moratorium on commercial whaling, which began in 1986. By this point it was clear that all stocks were seriously depleted, and scientists and NGOs lobbied hard for the protection of whales. The moratorium was initially supposed to last 10 years, but it has not yet been removed, despite the fact that some stocks have recovered substantially. Some states have withdrawn from the organization and/or recommenced commercial whaling, which they believe can be done sustainably. The issue for many at this point seems to be a possible conflict between the issue of sustainable harvest and the issue of whether (as some environmentalists believe) there are some species that for moral reasons should not be subject to harvesting at all.

Currently the future of whaling is in doubt. Iceland withdrew from the IWC in order to protect its rights to catch whales commercially. Norway is engaging in commercial whaling while still in the organization, legally accepted because of its objection to the commercial whaling moratorium. Japan is engaging in scientific whaling and trying to expand the definition of aboriginal subsistence whaling to allow whaling to be done by whalers in coastal communities. An additional organization, the North Atlantic Marine Mammal Commission (NAMMCO), is gaining greater claim as a forum for the possible regulation – but acceptance – of commercial whaling. The future of both whaling and the international efforts to regulate it is in doubt.

EARLY WHALING HISTORY

The first large-scale whalers were probably the Basques and the Vikings, although human interaction with whales has been recorded from the time of Alexander the Great.[7] The first important resource whales provided was oil, used for lamps and as a lubricant, and as an ingredient for soap, paint, and medicine. Whalebones and baleen (the flexible strips of bone in the mouths of non-toothed whales) were used in the construction of corset stays, umbrellas, and a wide variety of other products. Whale products also became an important source of protein for much of the world.[8]

Initially whalers hunted those whales close to their shores, faced them from small boats and towed dead whales back to shore for processing. By the mid-fifteenth century, however, Basque whalers were already venturing far from home in search of whales. Doing so necessitated the construction of larger vessels that could travel across the oceans and bring back the barrels of oil gained from whales off the Eastern coast of Canada. Whalers from other regions joined the hunt, and by the beginning of the seventeenth century whale ships from a number of countries were hunting for whales in the Arctic, and coming into conflict with each other as each vied for use of the best whaling grounds.[9] As the intensity of the whale hunt increased, so too did the level of technology to allow the whalers to hunt more efficiently. Whaling companies established permanent whaling stations in the Arctic so they could leave their equipment year round, rather than having to transport it and assemble it for each whaling season. They then began to hunt whales further out to sea, and created processing facilities for boiling the blubber into oil on the ships themselves so whales would not have to be towed to shore for processing. New whales, such as the sperm whale whose head contains a wax-like substance useful for making bright-burning, nearly smokeless, candles (and whose intestines sometimes contained ambergris, which fetched a high price as an ingredient in perfume), could be found further from shore, and provided new targets for the whaling industry. England and the USA became the predominant whaling countries, and their vessels spanned most of the globe. By the mid-nineteenth century the American whaling industry reached its peak with 735 whaling vessels, accounting for approximately 80 percent of the world's whaling fleet.[10]

It was not until the middle of the nineteenth century that the human effect on the world's population of whales became apparent. The response of whalers, however, was to improve technology so as to be able to find and hunt whales more efficiently. Steam was introduced to power whaling vessels, and hand-held harpoons were replaced by lances shot from vessels and designed to explode once in the whale.[11] Improvements in processing techniques ultimately resulted in 'industrial whalers' – ships powered by steam, equipped with harpoon cannons, and capable of processing and storing oil on board, pioneered by the Norwegian whaling fleet. Other innovations, such as the electric lance, invented initially by German whalers, allowed for easier (and, some argued, increasingly humane) killing of whales. The addition, in the twentieth century, of refrigeration increased the parts of the whale that could be taken and the length of time vessels could remain at sea. The whalers had the tools with which to capture whales, but there were fewer and fewer whales to hunt.

INTERNATIONAL REGULATION OF WHALING

Concern by the whalers about possible depletion of the whales on which they depended for their livelihood led to early domestic and international efforts to regulate whaling. Norway passed legislation beginning in 1904 to limit whaling in its coastal waters and in 1929 to limit whaling on the high seas of depleted species such as right whales, as well as all whale calves.[12] The first international agreement, The Geneva Convention for the Regulation of Whaling, was negotiated under the auspices of the League of Nations in 1931. It contained rules similar to the Norwegian restrictions, but several of the important whaling states, most notably Japan, Germany, and the Soviet Union, did not sign it. The two former countries in particular used whale products to support their international political ambitions (Nazi Germany to reduce its dependence on edible oil from abroad and Japan for export of whale oil to fund its activities in China and Manchuria), and maintained whaling vessels for strategic uses.[13] Without several of the most important whaling states (accounting for up to 30 percent of whaling at the time), the agreement was incapable of regulating whaling effectively. In the absence of effective international whaling regulation individual whaling companies attempted cartel-like agreements through an organization called the International Association of Whaling Companies.[14] This was an effort to stabilize world whale oil prices by limiting total production of whale oil and dividing it into individual quotas for each company. This effort went the way of most cartels, however: voluntary agreements were routinely ignored when they hurt competition, were subject to free riding, and could not survive the increased market importance of those – such as Japan – that refused to go along with agreements.[15] An additional effort was made by whaling states to gain cooperation in limiting whale catches in 1937, with the negotiation of the International Agreement for the Regulation of Whaling. This agreement set catch size limits and designated a whaling season, but neither was sufficiently stringent, especially in the absence of actual catch limits, to have an effect at protecting whale stocks.[16]

Further negotiations on protocols followed annually with some progress, but the greatest effect on protecting whale stocks was due to the near-cessation of commercial whaling that came during World War II, suggesting the advantage of warfare for the recovery of at least some species. One agreement was reached in 1944 in anticipation of the need for whale oil that would emerge at the war's conclusion, regulating whaling by categorizing whales by how much oil they contained and then restricting catches based on those units of measure. A blue whale was the standard unit of measure and the other species of whales were expressed in 'blue whale units,' (BWU) or how many whales of different species contained the amount of whale oil in a blue whale. One BWU, for example, was equal to two fin whales, two and a half humpbacks, or six seis.[17] Whale quotas would then be set in terms of how many BWUs could be caught.

The end of the war provided the best opportunity yet to finally gain true international regulation of whaling. Japan's whaling fleet, used as wartime vessels, was in ruins, and Germany's whaling industry was destroyed to the extent that it was never rebuilt. Moreover, the war years gave whaling stocks sufficient time to recover so that, when whaling states began negotiations at the end of the war on how to prevent over-harvesting of whales, they could set realistic catch limits that could (at least potentially) allow both for the protection of whales and the survival of the industry. The agreement that still governs most commercial whaling in the world, the International Convention for the Regulation of Whaling, was signed on 2 December 1946. The objective of the Convention is the 'proper and effective conservation and development of whale stocks' in order to enable 'the orderly development of the whaling industry.'[18]

The states negotiating the agreement attempted to remedy some of the problems of the earlier whaling agreements while unquestioningly adopting some of their structures in ways that caused later difficulties. One important goal was to create an agreement that would not have to be renegotiated and reratified every year, and could nevertheless allow whaling restrictions to be changed from year to year, responding to information on the health of whale stocks. To do so, the Convention created the International Whaling Commission. The IWC is global; it has regulatory control over all whales caught wherever whaling takes place, even within coastal seas claimed by adjacent nations.

The convention established three committees for the IWC: Scientific, Technical, and Finance and Administration. These committees meet and make recommendations to the IWC as a whole. The Scientific Committee (SC) was instructed by the original Rules of Procedure to 'keep under review the statistical, biological, and other technical information ... and to make recommendations thereon.'[19] The Scientific Committee reports on and analyzes research results achieved from scientific studies conducted within individual states, but does not carry out research itself. The Committee was reorganized in 1977, to include advisors from the United Nations Environment Programme, the Food and Agriculture Organization, and the (then) International Union for the Conservation of Nature (IUCN), and its meetings were opened to NGO observers. The Technical Committee (TC), under the Rules of Procedure of the IWC, was constituted to 'review regulations, consider questions involving time, manner, and intensity of whaling operations, [investigate] infractions reports,' among other things; and to make recommendations. It was charged with including non-scientific factors in consideration of proposed regulations.[20] Its role was changed in 1978 to include screening the business for the Plenary sessions, in order to speed up the work of the IWC meetings.[21] Both the Scientific Committee and the Technical Committee can consider and report on proposed changes to whaling regulations. The Finance and Administration Committee advises the IWC on issues of contributions, budgets and other related matters.

Importantly, the IWC creates regulations through a 'schedule,' passed each year, which denotes how many of each types of whale are allowed to be caught in each area. Passage of the schedule requires an affirmative vote of three quarters of the IWC members and then becomes binding on all members. As international law cannot bind those who choose not to participate, however, there is a procedure by which states can opt out of any of the provisions of the schedule with which they do not agree. To do so a state lodges an 'objection' to any amendment to the schedule within 90 days after it has passed, and it is thereby not bound by the regulation.[22] Under the agreement, the IWC is not allowed to limit the number of ships engaged in whaling, nor may it pass national quotas.[23]

IWC REGULATION IN PRACTICE

There have been several different management approaches in the history of the Commission. Initially, quotas were not on individual species; the Commission instead continued the practice of expressing catch limits in terms of numbers of Blue Whale Units (BWU) that could be taken. The organization thus had no ability to regulate stocks separately. In 1972 the IWC divided stocks into individual species which were regulated separately; occasionally sub-species had different quotas. This set of regulations was codified and further developed in a 'new management procedure.'[24] Stocks were divided into 'initial management stocks,' 'sustained management stocks,' and 'protected stocks,' for the basis of regulation.[25] The catching of some species was banned altogether. The current system, a moratorium on commercial whaling, was actually created under the normal regulatory process, by reducing the quotas to zero beginning for the 1986 whaling season. There is current pressure to lift the moratorium for some species, but the IWC has not yet taken that step; in preparation for such a time a 'revised management procedure' has been created.

Quotas during the periods of whaling were global and not allocated among specific states, which would have been prohibited by the convention. However, the race for whales in the region, and the uncertainty for each whaling company of what that year's catch might be, created economic difficulties for the industry and contributed to the depletion of whale stocks. Whalers had to compete with each other in what came to be known as the 'Whaling Olympic,' as each industrial whaling ship worked around the clock to catch as many whales as possible before the season was declared to be over. This scramble led to overcapitalization, as whaling ships had to be better prepared to beat others to the catch. In the five-year period from 1946 to 1951 the number of days in the whaling season fell from 112 to only 64, as ships grew increasingly efficient at catching whales; the cost of building a whale fleet concomitantly doubled by 1960.[26] Britain proposed in 1958 that the states engaged in open ocean whaling in the Antarctic consult outside the auspices of the organization to divide up the allocated catch into national quotas.[27] The states were able to agree initially on a scheme that limited the number of factory whaling ships a state could have in the region and to allocate 20 percent of the total catch in the region to the Soviet Union. Difficulty agreeing on the division of the rest of the catch, however, almost led to the collapse of the organization, as the Netherlands, Norway, and Japan threatened to withdraw from the IWC because of lack of agreement on national quotas in the Antarctic and the suspicion that the USSR was not abiding by the quota it had been given. These states gave official notices of withdrawal but intimated that they would reconsider if quotas were allocated.[28] The withdrawal of the first two states actually took effect, and quotas were not assessed during the time they were not members of the commission. The two rejoined and the issue of national quotas was finally resolved in 1962.[29]

The Role of Science

Decisions of the IWC with respect to restrictions on whaling are to be 'based on scientific findings.'[30] In practice, however, this instruction has been contentious and subject to abuse in a number of different ways. It has been suggested that the IWC history through 1970 'is one of almost constant failure to set the ... quotas at levels commensurate with scientific advice.'[31] The post-moratorium time period has also been filled with allegations that the organization is neglecting its obligation to base decisions about quotas on science, continuing the moratorium when scientific consensus is high that some species of whales have reached population levels that would allow them to be harvested sustainably. On the other hand, continued scientific uncertainty is invoked by those who do not want a return to commercial whaling.[32] Because of the IWC's requirement that decisions be based on science, all sides in the whaling debate have couched their arguments in the guise of science and uncertainty, whether or not it actually provided the reasons for the positions taken.

There has legitimately been a consistently high degree of uncertainty about whale populations. The Scientific Committee of the IWC, charged with resolving the uncertainty and making catch recommendations, faced a number of problems in doing so. Scientists on the committee often held different opinions about the number of whales that could be sustainably caught, with some of the highest estimates from scientists from whaling states. Japan, the Netherlands, and the Soviet Union (three of the major whaling states), for example, often had higher estimates of the stocks than did scientists from other countries.[33] Even the meaning of the different assessments is hard to interpret: did traditional whaling states have better informed whale specialists, or were Scientific Committee members from major whaling states influenced by the short-term desire of the whaling industries in their states for higher catch levels?

The composition of the committee compounds this uncertainty. It is supposed to be composed of 'qualified experts,' though there is no requirement of scientific qualifications and the members are often representatives and sometimes employees of the whaling industries within their countries. In some instances states appoint committee members who are not scientists, and some members of the committee 'are under instructions to argue in support of a position adopted by their government for reasons other than science alone.'[34]

The way in which decisions about quotas are made has always been contentious, and clearly based on more than scientific recommendations. Because of initial concern that whaling states would pull out of the IWC rather than adhere to too small a quota, the quotas were set consistently higher than even the Scientific Committee or other scientists recommended.[35] Any scientific errors or misjudgments by the Scientific Committee were probably compounded when its recommendations were debated in the Technical Committee and then in the IWC as a whole, both of which take economic and social interests of member states into consideration, along with the health of the whale populations.[36]

This self-interested action in the face of genuine uncertainty is exactly what one would predict. When it is unclear what the optimal solution is, individual actors should be expected to 'pick and choose from the existing often diverging scientific reports or opinions' in the calculation of advantage.[37] But this calculation ultimately led to the creation of unrealistic quotas. For most of the 1960s and the early 1970s the quotas set were never reached, a clear indication that quotas were set too high: despite the efforts of the whalers they could not catch as many whales as they were allowed to. Moreover, the concomitant decline in whale stocks (suggested in part by the annual lowering of whaling quotas) supports the assertion that quotas were set far above those that would protect the resource.

The stock evaluations and the understanding of the level of sustainable harvest was clearly flawed, as the population levels of most species plunged. It is necessary to differentiate, however, between the assessments of the members of the Scientific Committee and the quotas set by the IWC. Although quotas suggested by the Scientific Committee were probably too high, the Commission as a whole often did not heed even those suggestions and set the quotas still higher. A notable example came in the late 1970s: for two years in a row the Scientific Committee recommended that the catch limit for sperm whales in the North Pacific be set at 763; the IWC chose instead to set a quota of 6444 in 1977 and 6344 in 1978 for the region, almost ten times higher than the scientific recommendation.[38]

The IWC also failed to heed other advice given to it by its Scientific Committee. One major example is the continued use of the BWU as a tool for regulation longer than any scientific advice supported its use. When whales were regulated only in terms of the proportion of BWUs they represented, individual threatened species could not be specifically protected. When individual species, including the blue whale itself, were threatened with possible extinction, a collective quota could not protect them, nor could it prevent other whale species from facing the same problems in the future. Outside organizations even joined the effort to convince the IWC of the wisdom of changing its regulatory unit. The Food and Agriculture Organization (FAO) was involved with the process because it cooperated with the IWC to do whale-stock assessments. By the mid-1960s, when whale stocks were clearly being depleted and the IWC was unable to pass strict quotas to protect them, the FAO threatened to cease cooperation on research unless the IWC adopted quotas that fit the scientific consensus for the level of management required; specifically the IWC would have to end the use of the BWU and reduce the catches of fin and sei whales below the assessed sustainable yield.[39]

The IWC commissioned additional scientific evaluations during this period of disagreement over management. The first of these was the creation of a Committee of Three in 1961 after the discussion over quotas had repeatedly broken down over disagreement about management practices and sustainable yield. This Committee was composed of experts in whale (or fish) population dynamics, and 'drawn from countries not engaged in pelagic whaling in the Antarctic.'[40] The Committee was later broadened to four. The committee operated from 1961 to 1964. The IWC pledged itself to heed the recommendations of this Committee. The Committee found extreme depletion of some whale stocks, and therefore recommended a complete ban on the catching of humpbacks and blue whales, as well as a low quota on fin whales. It also proposed ending the use of the BWU. The Scientific Committee concurred with most of the Committee of Three/Four's recommendations, though the Scientific Committee representatives from Japan and the Soviet Union could not agree with the recommendation to abandon the BWU, and demanded more scientific information before a change in regulatory procedure be made. Their dissention gave the commissioners from those countries what one analyst referred to as a 'scientific alibi' when voting against the change.[41] The chair of the Scientific Committee threatened to resign if the new quotas were not adopted. The IWC began by protecting specific stocks through disallowing all catches of blue and humpback whales, but retained the BWU quota for fin and sei whales. It was only in 1972 that the BWU measure was finally abandoned.

Scientific discourse played an important role in the creation of the commercial moratorium. After decades of catch limits higher than the IWC's own scientists recommended it was becoming virtually certain that some stocks were so severely depleted that they could not be harvested sustainably in the short run. The initial efforts of the new management procedure, while more scientifically justified than management by BWU, did not succeed in preventing some whale stocks from becoming seriously endangered. At the same time, uncertainty about the actual size of whaling stocks remained strong in this period.[42] When the idea of a moratorium was first proposed in 1972 the Scientific Committee argued that it was not scientifically justified. As the option increasingly debated, the opinions of some in the SC shifted, with some arguing that a moratorium would allow for increased emphasis on science.[43] Some members of the Scientific Committee also came to believe in the precautionary principle: without certainty that whale stocks at the time could withstand continued hunting, doing so should not be allowed so as to prevent the possibility of extinction.[44] The Scientific Committee as a whole did not propose or even support the moratorium, and other organizations such as the FAO opposed it as well. Nevertheless, the clear evidence of severely depleted whale stocks probably influenced some of the support behind the halt to commercial whaling.

The controversy over the use of science in the organization did not end with the creation of the moratorium on commercial whaling; it is argued that the organization is now failing to heed scientific advice that favors allowing whaling, when earlier it failed to heed the advice to restrict it. As part of the decision on the commercial moratorium, the Scientific Committee was directed by the IWC to do a 'comprehensive assessment' of whale stocks by 1990,[45] which would guide the Commission in its decision about whether to continue or lift the moratorium. The committee reported some of its results in 1990, and by 1991 drafted a Revised Management Procedure. On minke whales, the most contested stock, it reached a variety of conclusions. It concluded that the eastern north-Pacific stock of minke whales numbered at least 21,000, had been increasing by 3 percent per year from 1967 to 1988, and might approach the region's carrying capacity. It found that the minkes in the Southern hemisphere numbered 760,000. In the north Atlantic there was a range of estimates due to survey difficulties.[46] Overall, though, its conclusions pointed to the likelihood that such whales could be harvested sustainably. The recommendations of the Scientific Committee have not been adopted because of the politicized nature of whaling brought about in large part by non-governmental organizations (as discussed below), and the requirement of agreement of three-quarters of the IWC's membership to change the schedule.

NON-COMPLIANCE

Compliance is always at least an underlying concern in international agreements; in the case of whaling this concern turns out to have been well-founded. The Convention itself has no procedure for detecting or responding to non-compliance; instead 'each Contracting Government shall take appropriate measures to ensure the application of the provisions ... and the punishment of infractions ... in operations carried out by persons or by vessels under its jurisdiction.'[47] As with most international agreements, data on compliance (in this case, whaling catch-statistics) are self-reported. Under the ICRW, whalers transmit their catch data to the Bureau of International Whaling Statistics in Norway.[48] Although technically not part of the IWC, this bureau functions as part of the commission by deciding when to end the whaling season each year that commercial whaling occurs, based on the information it receives.[49] This system creates several different types of incentives for non-compliance.

The first concerns the role of self-reported information used to determine the closing of the whaling season. Individual whalers who correctly report their catches run the risk of reducing the number of whales they can catch overall, as their reports serve to hasten the closing of the season. This process creates the possibility for systemic non-compliance without being able to ascribe individual responsibility. It is possible that during the final days of the whaling season as determined by the BIWS the collective catch will exceed the quota, but responsibility for this excess could be ascribed to no individual whaling vessel or state. Such a system can make non-compliance harder to detect, prevent, or punish.

From early on IWC members expressed concern over whether the whaling ships of the member states were following the rules on catch limits and sizes. There was some evidence examined by the Technical Committee suggesting that whalers were misreporting catch sizes. For instance, in 1965 when the minimum size limit for baleen whales was 38 feet, 90 percent of female baleen whales caught were reported to be between 38 and 39 feet long – a statistical absurdity.[50] Whalers were almost certainly catching undersize whales and reporting them at or near the minimum size. All information was self-reported and the IWC only had the power to ask the individual states to investigate and punish infractions,[51] so there is not much information on this type of non-compliance beyond suspicions extrapolated in this manner.

Suspected lack of compliance with catch limits in the Antarctic made states overall less willing to accept substantial restrictions on their whaling activities.[52] Commission members suggested that the creation of some kind of inspection process would increase the willingness, particularly of the Antarctic pelagic whaling states, to accept greater cuts in the whaling quotas, because they could be more certain that their competitors were not defying the regulations. The IWC considered creation of an international observer scheme to address this potential problem, but the issue was contentious and the observer scheme was discussed from 1957 until it was finally implemented for the Antarctic whaling states in 1972. The ultimate scheme involved the whaling states nominating commissioners, who were then appointed to go along on Antarctic whaling voyages to monitor compliance. Such a scheme was only created for Antarctic whaling, however, and not seriously considered for whaling vessels overall.

More serious is non-compliance that was not reported or observed and was therefore hard to detect. In the 1990s reports from Russia indicated that whale statistics reported by the former Soviet Union were incorrect. The Russian Commissioner to the IWC in 1994 suggested that Soviet whale catches from the 1960s to the 1980s were nearly twice the number reported to the organization.[53] Moreover, the USSR had a systematic program to misreport the species of whale that were caught, taking prohibited whales such as humpbacks and right and blue whales in large numbers, and reporting their catches as other species. Ernst Cherry, a member of Russia's team investigating illegal Soviet whaling, commented that 'the data on violations of whaling rules contained in official Soviet reports bore no resemblance to the real situation.'[54] It is also likely that the Japanese knew about and even assisted such non-compliance, by buying whale carcasses at sea from Soviet vessels.[55] Before the implementation of an international observer scheme, there was no way to ascertain whether reported catches were in compliance with regulations. It is worth noting, however, that the great bulk of illegal Soviet whaling happened outside the Antarctic, and the international observer scheme could not prevent illegal whaling in areas in which it did not operate. It does suggest, however, both the advantage of such a scheme and the reasons why some of the major whaling states resisted it so strongly.

The effect that Soviet non-compliance had on the use of scientific models for whale conservation is also important. The models examined by the Scientific Committee to set whaling quotas were based on reported catch statistics; projections of stock recovery were likely thrown off by non-compliance.[56]

Finally, the issue of non-compliance with the whaling regime shows the ease of non-compliance with international environmental regulations more broadly. In this instance, there was probably non-compliance (with size limits, for instance) by individual whaling vessels, made possible in an arena as vast and difficult to monitor as the ocean. We also saw non-compliance at the officially sanctioned state level, something that is perhaps somewhat less likely in the post-Soviet era of increased information and political openness, but not necessarily a phenomenon entirely relegated to history. Ironically, however, it also shows the importance that states accord to the perception of compliance: the USSR could easily have objected to specific quotas or withdrawn from the IWC altogether and accomplished its whaling legally. That it chose to hide its excessive whaling behind a cloak of respectability suggests that the norms of the whaling regime, and the norms of compliance more broadly, do have some effect.

Non-participation

An important difficulty faced by those who want to regulate whaling internationally is gaining the participation of all those likely to be catching whales. Several aspects of this have been challenging in the history of whaling regulation. The first was an attempt to secure the involvement of all the whaling states in the Commission, or, failing that, to gather information on their catches that could be used to determine a sustainable harvest. The Commission passed numerous resolutions over the years aimed at encouraging non-member whaling states to sign the agreement. The second was an effort to ensure that all IWC members actually accepted all of the regulations passed by the commission. In both cases unilateral threats of economic sanctions by the USA had the greatest effect in bringing non-members into the IWC, and encouraging members to accept the organization's restrictions on whaling.

The USA used domestic legislation passed initially in 1971 for the purpose of threatening states that did not accept provisions of fisheries treaties. The legislation, the Pelly Amendment to the Fisherman's Protective Act, allows the US President to refuse to accept imports of fish when the Secretary of Commerce 'finds that nationals of a foreign country, directly or indirectly, are conducting fishing operations under circumstances which diminish the effectiveness' of an international fishery conservation program. The legislation was left intentionally broad, and defines 'international fishery conservation program' as 'any ban, restriction, regulation, or other measure in force pursuant to a multilateral agreement to which the United States is a signatory party, the purpose of which is to conserve or protect the living resources of the sea.'[57] In other words, whaling was an acceptable target of the legislation, and the legislation could be – and in fact generally has been – used against states that are themselves not members of the agreement in question. A second piece of US legislation was passed to decrease the amount of discretion the President has when the Secretary of Commerce has 'certified' that a state is diminishing the effectiveness of the International Whaling Commission. The Packwood-Magnuson Amendment to the Magnuson Fishery Conservation and Management Act, passed in 1979, required that states certified as such under the Pelly Amendment automatically have their fishing allocation in US waters cut by at least 50 percent, and cut off entirely the following year if the issues that led to certification have not been remedied.[58]

The main whaling states that had not initially signed the agreement were Chile, South Korea, Peru, and Taiwan. After IWC efforts failed to bring them in, the USA certified each under the Pelly Amendment, thus threatening them with the loss of the US market for their fish and fish products. The USA certified Chile, Peru, and South Korea in 1978; all three took immediate steps to join the organization.[59] The USA certified Taiwan for the same reason in 1980; although it did not sign the ICRW it did agree to stop all foreign whaling and then banned whaling altogether in 1981.[60]

An additional – and in the IWC case, earlier – instance of this type of non-participation was the presence of what came to be known as 'pirate whalers'; whaling ships that flew flags of states that were not members of the IWC so that their activities would remain unregulated. This non-participation differs slightly, however, from state-level non-compliance, because in this instance it is an individual whaling vessel that finds a way to engage in whaling without falling under international regulation.[61] The main whaling organization engaged in this type of whaling was the Olympic Whaling Company, run by Aristotle Onassis. The company's main whaling vessel, the *Olympic Challenger*, was registered in Panama; other whaling vessels run by the company were registered in Honduras. The company itself was incorporated in Uruguay. None of these states were IWC members, so the vessels were not bound by IWC regulations. In the early 1950s the *Olympic Challenger* and its associated whale catchers caught whales by contravening nearly every IWC rule, while trying to negotiate deals with some of the major whaling vessels.[62] The IWC repeatedly discussed how to prevent such pirate whaling, with specific reference to the *Olympic Challenger*. Most efforts were aimed at convincing Panama, the state under which it was flagged, to join the Commission, or to at least enforce IWC provisions. The IWC had little success, however, and it is likely that had Panama joined at the time, Onassis would simply have registered his operations elsewhere. In 1956 the Peruvian Navy seized the vessel for fishing in Peruvian waters and sold it to the Japanese,[63] ending the most serious case of individual non-participation in the convention process.

A second type of non-participation occurs when members of the organization opt out of specific commitments. This practice is legal, but it also undermines the ability of the organization to accomplish effective regulation. The practice has been widespread at points in IWC history. Unfortunately, at times, this procedure has meant that none of the major whaling states have been bound by some of the regulations passed by the organization. In 1964, for example, the IWC passed a complete ban on the catching of blue whales, which were quite endangered in the Antarctic at that point. But all five of the Antarctic whaling states objected to the quota, and thus were not bound by it. States used the objections practice strategically as well. For instance, in 1956 the Soviet Union indicated that, although it approved a lowering of the whaling quota that year, seven states objected to it, and it would not abide by the lower quota if the other major whaling states did not.[64] Such strategic use of the objections procedure makes sense in the ocean commons; if one major whaling state restricts its catches and others do not it loses twice: first by having to forego the whales it could have caught, and second because its conservation behavior will not even serve to protect the stock in the long run if others continue to catch whales.

Efforts to remedy this situation also had mixed effects; in the 1970s and 1980s US threats to deny entry to fish products from states because of their whaling behavior had an important effect on the willingness of member states to accept specific whaling regulations. This influence culminated in threats that convinced the most reluctant whaling states to abide by the moratorium on commercial whaling, but has waned in more recent times. The first use of these threats came in 1974 with US certification of Japan and the Soviet Union for lodging objections to the quota for minke whales in the Southern hemisphere. Both were certified under the Pelly Amendment and both agreed to abide by the quota. In 1980 Spain objected to the quota on fin whales and South Korea to the ban on the use of the cold harpoon; both withdrew their objections when the USA threatened certification under the Pelly Amendment.[65] The adoption by the IWC in 1982 of a moratorium on commercial whaling as of the 1986 whaling season drew official objections from many of the major whaling states, primary among them Japan, the USSR, and Norway. The USA certified the latter two; domestic battles over whether it was required to certify Japan were fought judicially all the way to the US Supreme Court, leaving unclear whether Japan would ultimately be certified.[66] In the interim, Japan withdrew its objection, arguing later that it had done so in an 'involuntary' manner, 'coerced by a certain nation.'[67] Norway and the Soviet Union responded by agreeing to halt whaling, but did not withdraw their objections.

THE ROLE OF NON-GOVERNMENTAL ORGANIZATIONS

Non-governmental organizations have been some of the harshest critics of the operations of the IWC, and their influence has been unquestionable. Unlike much of the debate about whaling, their campaigns have not been conducted so much in terms of science as in terms of ethics and images. Non-governmental organizations such as Greenpeace attempted to shift the terms of the debate about the regulation of whaling. They began by using the same scientific terms more broadly discussed in the organization, suggesting that depletion of whales required a commercial moratorium in order to protect the species. Ultimately, however, the organizations most central to the whaling debate believe that whales should not be seen as a resource to be exploited, and should not be killed at all.

Organizations such as Greenpeace, the Sea Shepherd Conservation Society, the Animal Welfare Institute, and many others have had a considerable effect on whaling policy worldwide through a number of types of strategies, many subverting (or even coming to redefine) the traditional role of activist organizations. They have engaged in direct action campaigns, putting themselves between whale boats and whales with the hope of protecting the whales and, more importantly, dramatizing the whale hunt. Using this approach as well as other publicity- and awareness-raising campaigns they have worked not through their own states to change their views on whaling, but across state lines to influence the views of others in whaling states and through them to change the policies of those states. At the same time activist organizations worked through the international process created by the IWC, working to convince non-whaling states to join the IWC, which is open to membership regardless of whaling activity. Because a three-quarters majority is needed to amend the schedule, convincing a sufficient number of anti-whaling states to join the organization could – and did – have an important influence on the policies adopted.

Beginning in the early 1970s, conservation organizations, primarily in the USA and the UK, took up the plight of the whale as an important symbol of environmentalism. Some of these groups were broader environmental organizations for which the whale could serve as an important symbol; other organizations, such as the American Cetacean Society, were formed solely for the purpose of protecting whales. While a number of organizations worked in standard awareness-raising fashion with a goal of influencing the political stands of their own governments, other organizations took on increasingly radical approaches that brought the issue even more publicity.

Working through national political channels should not be discounted as an effective way to change international environmental policy. Environmental activists within the USA clearly influenced the passage of the 1972 Marine Mammal Protection Act (MMPA), which effectively ended any potential remaining US whaling industry and, more importantly, helped to turn the USA against whaling internationally. It was in the context of the MMPA that the USA was pressured – and able – to use the Pelly and Packwood-Magnuson Amendments to persuade whaling states to join the organization and accept its regulations. Non-governmental organizations also formed branches in other IWC member states to work to convince local populations to turn against whaling. Two such states that eventually changed from pro-whaling to anti-whaling were Argentina and Uruguay.[68] Working within the state was thus an important role for anti-whaling activists.

Working through other channels allowed these organizations to have an even greater impact, however. Some tactics, such as collecting evidence of violations of whaling agreements, helped raise awareness of those within the organization that current whaling regulations were not sufficiently constraining member states. Even simply documenting legal whaling practices, through videotapes of whaling vessels slaughtering the whales they caught, could help dramatize the brutality of the whaling industry to those who simply had not thought much about it previously.[69] Greenpeace activists often put themselves physically in between whaling vessels and whales, both in the hopes of preventing whalers from catching individual whales (because of the risk that an activist would be harmed in the process) and to indicate their level of commitment to the cause. In doing so, they also hoped to change the image of whaling in the minds of average people, who could see large factory whaling vessels taking on committed activists and facing defenseless whales.[70] In the case of whaling it seems likely that these actions outside of the traditional political arena were more effective at changing whaling policy than traditional political action would have been.[71]

In the short run, the greatest success of anti-whaling environmental organizations was through persuading anti-whaling states to join the IWC. In some cases this process happened through the conversion of pro-whaling states, such as Australia, into anti-whaling states, with domestic electoral victories.[72] Some former whaling states ceased participation in the organization once they stopped whaling. The Dutch had not actually left the organization but were not active participants; environmental organizations persuaded the Netherlands to become active in the organization in the campaign to halt commercial whaling. Non-governmental organizations focused additional efforts on bringing in non-whaling states that had never or had not recently been members of the organization, so as to increase the number of votes against whaling. The Seychelles membership in the IWC in 1979 was an important victory for the anti-whaling organizations, because it was the first anti-whaling developing state to join the organization.[73] A number of states in the agreement that have traditionally not cared about whaling joined in the time period when a commercial whaling moratorium was being discussed in the organization. Antigua and Barbuda, Oman, Egypt, and Kenya, for example, are all states that joined in the early 1980s, with no previous history of concern about whaling issues, that voted consistently against commercial whaling.[74]

Non-governmental organizations contributed financially to bringing states into the agreement as well. A former Greenpeace consultant tells of a plan that added at least six new anti-whaling members in the period from 1978 to 1982 through the paying of annual dues, drafting of membership documents, and naming of commissioners to represent these countries, at an annual cost of more than $150,000.[75] Japan's representatives at the 47th IWC annual meeting in 1995 pointed out that 'some individuals are listed as government delegates attending the preliminary meetings of working groups and sub-committees but registered as NGO observers in the plenary week.'[76] While NGOs were not the only ones to play this game,[77] their efforts to recruit non- (and anti-) whaling states to the organization ultimately resulted in raising the membership of non-whaling states in the agreement to just above three-quarters of the membership, the number required to amend the schedule to create a temporary moratorium on commercial whaling.

Through this variety of techniques, these organizations raised awareness of the issue of whaling, and ultimately an alliance between those opposed to whaling on moral grounds and those opposed to whaling in order to replenish the stocks was sufficient to support a moratorium on commercial whaling. Although the goal of these organizations was to change the terms of the debate, they also called attention to the lack of sustainable management by the Commission over time, and thus provided the information used by those who supported the moratorium on conservation rather than preservation grounds. What resulted was an uneasy coalition of those who supported a halt to commercial whaling for a variety of different reasons, and that, through an increased voting bloc and increasing evidence of severe depletion of whale stocks, managed to create a moratorium on commercial whaling.

THE COMMERCIAL WHALING MORATORIUM

By the early 1970s whale stocks were clearly depleted and it seemed likely that only drastic measures could remedy the situation. A number of scientists and other organizations began to recommend a temporary suspension of commercial whaling to allow stocks to recover. The 1972 UN Conference on the Human Environment in Stockholm criticized IWC practices and recommended that the IWC implement a ten-year commercial moratorium.[78] The USA re-proposed the idea at IWC meetings in the following years.

Several elements had to come together before the IWC could adopt such a radical change in whaling policy. The increasing evidence that whaling stocks were depleted, while never quite convincing the diehard whaling states that a moratorium was necessary, did at least serve to persuade those that generally favored whaling but felt that their economies and the cause of whaling could best be served by allowing whale stocks to recover. The conversion of some states within the IWC from whaling states to non-whaling states through the decreasing economic viability of the industry meant that the universe of states whose behavior had to change decreased. The increasing transformation of some of these former whaling states into vehement anti-whaling states, as their domestic populations came to believe that the whales must be saved, was brought about largely by publicity and made possible by the conviction and activities of activist organizations. That one of these was the USA, willing to put economic threats behind its anti-whaling stance, could only help the move in this direction. At the same time, the conviction of other non-whaling states, some of it aided in a number of ways by activist organizations, that commercial whaling must be at least temporarily stopped, eventually resulted in a non-whaling supermajority in the IWC. It was not until 1982, ten years after the original Stockholm Conference Proposal, that agreement was reached within the IWC for a temporary halt to commercial whaling, for the purpose of allowing stocks to recover. Even then, the moratorium was not to take effect until the 1986 whaling season, to allow whaling industries time to adjust. Actual commercial whaling ceased later than that, as it took several years longer to convince all whaling states to participate.

AFTER THE MORATORIUM?

The commercial whaling moratorium was supposed to last, at most, a decade. The status of whale stocks was to be evaluated in 1990, with a view toward considering the resumption of commercial whaling. Instead, while many estimates suggest that some species of whale – particularly Minke – could be harvested sustainably, the moratorium remains. The supermajority of non-whaling states that passed the moratorium would need to agree to remove it, and many of them have refused to change their position. The debate, however, and the activities of whaling states, have changed.

Three of the four primary whaling states that went along with the moratorium only reluctantly have indicated a renewed interest in whaling. (The fourth, the former Soviet Union, ceased an interest in commercial whaling in the wake of the other political and economic changes it faced during the decade of the 1990s, although Russia has suggested the possibility of renewed whaling eventually.) Iceland pulled out of the IWC in 1992 to reserve its right to catch whales (although it rejoined in 2001, hoping to influence the organization from the inside to allow whaling).[79] Norway, which maintained its objection to the moratorium and therefore is not legally bound to uphold it, resumed commercial whaling that same year. It catches only minke whales, for which it sets its own quota annually. Japan continues to hunt whales for 'scientific' purposes, as allowed – and not regulated – by the IWC. While the Secretary of the IWC has suggested that there is a legitimate scientific purpose served by lethal whaling studies,[80] this Japanese scientific whaling kills enough whales to keep the former commercial whaling industry operational and the whale meat from whales caught for these studies is sold in Japanese food markets. Moreover, testing of whale meat labeled as from minke whales determined that one-quarter of it came not from minkes but from other protected whale species, even during the period when Japan claimed to only be killing minke whales for scientific purposes.[81] Japan has also labored within the IWC to redefine its coastal whaling, as allowed under the agreement.

Greenpeace members, however, continue to argue that no killing of whales is acceptable. 'Even if humanity thinks that it has an ironclad 'scientific' banner under which to kill the whales, is that enough? Is the paradigm under ... which it is okay to take the maximum number of a particular species according to a complicated calculation of "sustainability" defensible?'[82] Some of the states in the Commission are persuaded by this logic. The IWC delegate from the UK indicated in an opening statement to the 50th IWC annual meeting in 1998 that 'We do not believe that any whaling is justified' and would like to see 'the introduction of a permanent, comprehensive moratorium on all whaling other than aboriginal subsistence whaling.'[83]

Others fall somewhere in the middle. They acknowledge that whaling has been poorly regulated in the past, and new revelations about Soviet non-compliance only serve to underscore the past inability of the organization to prevent depletion of whales. As witnessed in the case of elephant protection under the Convention on International Trade in Endangered Species of Wild Fauna and Flora (CITES) as well as other environmental regimes, a complete ban on an activity is easier to monitor and enforce than one that allows for, but limits, a potentially harmful environmental activity. Others argue that a whaling regime that does not include the major whaling states in its regulatory process (if they withdraw, as Iceland has done and Japan and Norway have threatened to do, or if they catch whales – for science or for commercial purposes – in ways not regulated by the organization while still members) would be better off relaxing its moratorium to allow its continued oversight of the process. Fewer whales may be caught under a commercial whaling regime overseen by the IWC than under an IWC moratorium with non-participation.[84]

Some promising compromise positions have recently been proposed. An Irish proposal in 1998 would have allowed whaling within exclusive economic zones with the whale meat used only for local consumption, in return for a ban on whaling on the open ocean. The interesting aspect of the potential Irish-brokered compromise is that it exposed the game-playing that states have been doing in representing their negotiating positions. States like the UK and the USA, which have largely opposed whaling for ethical reasons but have couched it in language of science, sustainability, and compliance, found themselves faced with a plan that would actually meet their stated goals if not their underlying concerns. Conversely, states like Japan and Norway that have attempted to couch their desire for commercial whaling in other guises, would be faced with the choice of either exposing their true intentions or giving up some of their goals. Japan would need to admit that whale conservation is possible without the type of 'research whaling' it currently undertakes, a position it has staunchly avoided. This specific proposal is not likely to pass, but it has paved the way for additional creative discussion of the conditions under which commercial whaling might be deemed acceptable, and sufficiently regulated to prevent depletion or extinction. There are new predictions that the moratorium may end in the near future, and the fear that if it does not, the IWC, for all intents and purposes, will.[85]

Yet for those who find the killing of marine mammals to be morally repugnant, would such a compromise be acceptable? As Greenpeace activists continue to put themselves between whalers and whales, would they be willing to accept a politically expedient compromise that might result in the killing of fewer whales but enshrine in international law and practice the principle that killing whales is simply the acceptable harvesting of a sustainable resource? Should they be?

AMAZONIAN BIODIVERSITY

The Amazon is ... a remarkable self-contained system that depends crucially on the integrity of the whole to sustain itself ... the soils are among the poorest on the planet – yet the vegetation and the unparalleled richness of living organisms seem to suggest a luxuriance that derives from the plenty rather than from deprivation. That paradox is the miracle of the rainforest.[1]

Biodiversity is an unusual global environmental issue. For the most part any particular species or part of an ecosystem is located in the territory of a state and thus can be seen as a private good. For a number of reasons, however, the destruction of biodiversity and the efforts to protect it are inherently global issues. First, the concern about them is international: people all over the world care about potential future benefits, existence value, or associated environmental problems that come from biodiversity or the failure to protect it. Second, the idea of biodiversity, as separate from species protection, suggests that what is important is not only individual species or even ecosystems, but the world-wide diversity of these things. Thus no one state alone can guarantee worldwide biodiversity; in order to have a diverse array of species, ecosystems, and genetic material efforts must be made in a variety of places worldwide to protect such diversity. Third, and most controversially, the causes of much biodiversity loss, even when taking place on a primarily local level, are often international. These include pressures to overuse resources to pay back debt, international markets and multinational corporations that value the use rather than the protection of natural resources, and governments that are so impoverished by a number of historical (and often international) causes that they have short time horizons, leading them to undervalue local resources.

This issue is thus inherently global, but because ecosystems (unlike the atmosphere or even ocean species) exist in specific locations, the efforts to protect them take on a different character from other forms of international environmental cooperation. State sovereignty is an important factor, both in constraining and in inspiring solutions to biodiversity problems. Developing states, host to most of the world's biodiversity, have strongly supported wording in international declarations and treaties that supports states' 'sovereign rights over their own biodiversity,'[2] and that acknowledges that 'states have, in accordance with the Charter of the United Nations and the principles of international law, the sovereign right to exploit their own resources pursuant to their own environmental and developmental policies.'[3] The important effect of these principles is that countries have been wary to take on any international obligations to significantly constrain what they can do with their biodiversity resources, and that developed states that place a high value on biodiversity have needed to make deals with biodiverse states in order to gain access to the resources or increase the likelihood that they will be protected. Non-governmental actors have also been particularly involved in these approaches, either out of environmental concern or interest in access to resources, and many of the most notable approaches to biodiversity protection have been private, rather than intergovernmental.

Issues pertaining to biodiversity are examined here in the context of the Amazonian rainforest. Doing so allows a specific focus to be put on a global phenomenon and thus allows for a closer examination of both global and local activities to protect biodiversity in a particular region. The Amazon in particular is relevant both for its importance to global biodiversity and for the creativity – along with occasional failure – of the efforts to protect species and ecosystems. The Amazon rainforest, which is present in eight different South American countries,[4] has been declared by biologist Norman Myers to be one of the world's biodiversity 'hotspots.'[5] Tropical forests generally are considered to contain between 50 and 90 percent of all the world's species.[6] The Amazon constitutes only 7 percent of the earth's land surface, but accounts for 35 percent of its tropical forests. Sixty percent of the rainforest is in Brazil.[7]

Although the Amazon rainforest is spread across eight countries, it functions in many ways as a unitary ecosystem. It plays an important role in the global climate system, acting as a giant 'heat pump' sending energy from the tropics to moderate the climate of the colder, higher, latitudes.[8] The ecosystem functions additionally in the global climate system by acting as a carbon sink, taking up carbon dioxide that would otherwise enter the climate and contribute to global climate change. In fact, with increasing deforestation worldwide, a carbon sink can be transformed into a carbon source, as cut or burned trees release the carbon they had stored. While the amount of carbon emissions from tropical deforestation vary widely, it is suggested that somewhere between 0.4 and 5 billion tons of carbon enter the atmosphere annually from tropical deforestation.[9] Deforestation is the second most important source of human contribution of CO_2 to the atmosphere.[10]

The Amazonian rainforest has an importance far beyond its role in the global climate system. Tropical forests account for a large percentage of the world's species that may become extinct with increased levels of deforestation. These species may be valued for their potential uses (as genetic material or for potential future medicinal products that can be made from them) or simply because of the belief that it is wrong to cause the extinction of species. Moreover, the ecosystem as a whole interacts; when one part of it is removed the rest has difficulty functioning. Deforestation can lead to local problems like soil erosion and decreased land productivity.

It must also be pointed out how little we know, both in the Amazon and elsewhere, about the level of biodiversity generally. It is suggested that the approximately 1.4 million species identified represent as little as 15 percent of the total existing species.[11] For that reason, estimates of biodiversity loss vary greatly. While many estimates suggest that approximately 5 percent of the world's species become extinct each decade, estimates even within the relatively conservative community of specialists range between 1 percent and 11 percent per decade.[12] Even within the region of the Amazonian rainforest, estimates differ widely as to how much land is being converted from rainforest. Two estimates from the late 1980s put the total rainforest area lost up to that point between 7 percent and 12 percent.[13]

THREATS TO AMAZONIAN BIODIVERSITY

Biodiversity loss in the Amazonian region is caused primarily by agricultural and development activities, in addition to direct harvesting of natural resources. There are deeper causes, however, to these activities, including subsidies, social pressures, transnational capital and trade, the debt crisis, and land distribution. Additional related threats to biodiversity are the over-harvesting of wild species, the introduction of non-native species (including agriculture), habitat destruction, pollution by toxins, changing nutrient balances, or physical contaminants and local or global climatic changes.

Agricultural activity of a variety of types is a major source of biodiversity loss in the Amazonian region. Estimates in the early 1990s put the amount of land in the Amazon each year eliminated by cattle ranching at around 15,000 square kilometers.[14] Cattle ranching is responsible for the greatest percentage of forest loss overall, accounting for more than 72 percent of the deforested area of the Brazilian Amazon.[15] Up to 65,000 square kilometers of the forest loss in the region can be attributed to farmers who cut or burn down trees in order to plant crops. Small-scale farming is seen as responsible for up to 11 percent of all deforestation in the region, as farmers from various regions migrate into the rainforest in an effort to support themselves.[16] Similarly, palm, rubber, and oil plantations add to the rainforest destruction.[17] More importantly, the increased wealth of local populations contributes to more, rather than less, pressure on the land, as wealthier rainforest settlers are likely to see cattle ranching, among the most land intensive of rainforest activities, as a route to a better life.[18]

Development, broadly construed, also contributes to the loss of Amazonian rainforest biodiversity. Brazilian government policies to 'open up' the rainforest to settlement and economic activity began as early as 1946.[19] These policies generally involved the construction of major highways. The first major effort of this sort came in 1956 with the construction of a highway through the rainforest between several major cities, that made possible the colonization of rainforest land, increased the flow of foreign capital into Brazil, and increased the dependence of the Brazilian economy on oil.[20] Further road projects made access to the Amazon even easier. The most controversial of these road-building exercises was the Polonoreste project, financed by the World Bank to pave a major highway cutting through the Brazilian state of Rondônia. This project began as military rule in Brazil was ending in the early 1980s and people moved at great speed into areas of the Amazon that the military had previously controlled as national security zones. Military presence had at least kept order in this region, and without it, land conflicts in the region increased. The World Bank included provisions in the project designed to protect the environment and indigenous people, but activists believed that increased ease of transportation would simply increase settlement and deforestation in the area, at the expense of indigenous populations. As a result of multinational protests the World Bank suspended payments to Brazil in 1985.[21] Despite this controversy, efforts to encourage Brazil to make the Amazon more accessible to populations and those wanting to engage in economic activity have had a clear impact on deforestation.

Finally, natural resource extraction is a major threat to biodiversity in the Amazon region. The most obvious activity of this sort is logging. In the Brazilian region of Amazonia, logging and the associated wood products industries have been among the fastest growing contributions to the national economy. Commercial logging intersects with agricultural use because, once an area has been stripped of its trees, settlers and subsistence farmers often move in. The roads created by the logging industry make access by settlers possible into areas of the rainforest that would have been previously impenetrable.[22] Moreover, mining of copper and other minerals can have a huge impact on the biodiversity of the region. The Brazilian Amazon contains what some suggest is the world's largest deposit of iron ore, manganese, and other minerals. While mining can theoretically be done in a way that has minimal impact on the surrounding ecosystem, development of this region includes an open ore mine and a variety of smelters, with serious environmental impacts.[23] Similarly, mining for gold, found in some rivers of the Amazon region, leads to an influx of people and pollution of the rivers by mercury, which is used (often illegally) to amalgamate gold.[24] Oil, present in various places in the Amazon but particularly in Ecuador, is harvested by companies that travel far into the forest by helicopter, clear the forest for oil drilling, and then often leave waste products or spill oil in the process of transporting it out.

Underlying these specific rainforest destruction activities are broader social forces and policies that create the incentives for the patterns of land use and development seen in the Amazon region. Social pressures created by poverty and population growth are important background factors that force settlers into the rainforest in search of subsistence and land. The rainforest has often functioned as a 'safety valve' for social and agrarian crises,[25] allowing people room to expand or escape local difficulties. Population growth and unequal distribution of non-forested land gives incentives to people to claim and deforest land.[26]

These factors combine with governmental policies that give incentives to those who settle in the rainforest. At minimum, the land tenure system in Brazil, in which 5 percent of farmers occupy 70 percent of the land, and 70 percent occupy 5 percent,[27] suggests that there is little non-forested room for expansion. Government policies designed to deal with these problems grant land to people in the rainforest. In the Brazilian region of Amazonia 'the right to possession of land is granted to the party who clears it,'[28] which gives an obvious incentive to those who destroy rainforested area rather than conserve it. Between 1982 and 1986 approximately half a million people moved to Rondônia to farm, lured by grants of between 100 and 250 hectares per family. During this time period, the forests of the region shrank by 3 percent. The World Bank estimates that 24 percent of the Brazilian state of Rondônia was burned, in efforts to make it suitable for agricultural use.[29] Brazil has spent more than $2.5 billion subsidizing cattle ranching in previously forested areas,[30] which allows ranchers to make a profit even if cattle ranching is an otherwise inefficient source of income. And it frequently is; previously rainforested land tends not to be especially productive either agricultu- rally or for grazing of cattle.[31]

Also important is the incentive that the international market gives to cattle ranchers or lumber companies. The spread of cattle ranching to the Amazonian region can be at least partially attributed to the demand in North America for inexpensive beef.[32] Oil exports, primarily from exploitation in the Amazon, account for more than half of Ecuador's export income.[33] In Brazil, it is argued, the 'international market to a large extent determines the course of development,'[34] with increases in the international price of tropical timber increasing the incentive to cut down trees as earlier international demand for rubber increased the use of the rainforest for rubber plantations. The relationship works the other way as well, however; as world prices for commodities fall, countries that depend on their exports for generating income must export more, rather than less.[35]

Debt is a major underlying factor in development strategies to provide income from the Amazon. The pressures work in several ways. First, the need to pay increasingly large debt service gives an incentive to states to increase their exports, to bring in foreign currency with which to pay the debt. Doing so by increasing the export of primary products found in the rainforest (timber, oil, minerals) is a traditional method for debt-strapped states to earn money to help pay off their debt. Beginning in the 1960s in Brazil small coffee farms were replaced with large-scale agriculture, pushing into the Amazon region to produce soybeans for export; in the 1960s alone these new agricultural activities caused the eradication of 400 million trees from coffee plantations in the rainforest.[36] In order to pay their debt service, countries may be forced to cut social programs, which also result, in the case of Amazonian countries, in more people moving into the forest to try to make a living off of the land.[37] In addition, the more a country is indebted, the higher interest rate it must pay. This translates into what is called a higher discount rate, or a shorter a time horizon. In other words, the state values gains in the present much more than gains in the future, as it struggles to pay off its debt. That also leads to an increased desire to use resources to gain economic advantages in the present, rather than taking a longer view of the advantages of biodiversity. In a particularly interesting example of this phenomenon, Nicaragua allowed a Taiwanese timber company to log one-eighth of its remaining forests in return for a $30 million loan to help Nicaragua pay its foreign debt.[38] The debt crisis in Latin America in the 1980s certainly correlates with increased deforestation, with 9.2 million hectares per year of rainforest lost in the 1970s and 16.8 million hectares per year lost in the 1990s.[39]

There are also important security elements to rainforest development. For Brazil, in particular, the undeveloped forest was seen as a source for wealth in a newly emerging industrial power.[40] Additionally, protection of borders is more difficult in a densely forested area, and in countries with potential domestic unrest the difficulties of monitoring activities of the population gives additional incentive to develop previously forested land.

APPROACHES TO PROTECTION

International Agreements

There are few international agreements that provide serious protection for biodiversity as a whole. Treaties to protect specific species were among the first international environmental agreements, beginning at the end of the nineteenth century and focusing first on migratory species or those in danger from overhunting. Among the most important international species protection agreements is the Convention on International Trade in Endangered Species of Wild Fauna and Flora (CITES), signed in 1973, which restricts trade in species listed in several appendices to the treaty. This agreement has probably been responsible for the increased protection of some individual species, but is unlikely to have a large effect on biodiversity as a whole. It also demonstrates the difficulties of creating invasive restrictions to protect natural resources: by regulating only trade in endangered species it protects state sovereignty by allowing states to do whatever they want with species inside their own borders.

Given the important role of forests in biodiversity generally and Amazonian biodiversity in particular, it is also worth mentioning the International Tropical Timber Agreement, signed initially in 1983 and renegotiated in 1994. This commodity agreement attempts indirectly to conserve tropical forest resources by addressing uncertainty and fluctuation in the international market for tropical timber, with the idea that a more stable international market will allow states to choose when to harvest and sell their forest resources, rather than being driven to do so by market pressures or opportunities. The 1994 renegotiation focused more directly on sustainable use of tropical timber, setting an (un-reached) goal for producers of tropical timbers to be able to export only sustainably harvested timber by the year 2000,[41] and by setting up the Bali partnership fund to 'assist producing members to make the investments necessary' to meet the sustainability objective.[42] It is not clear that the treaty has fulfilled its main objective of facilitating (and regularizing) trade in tropical timber, and even less clear that it has contributed significantly to an increase in sustainable management of these forests. The treaty organization itself suggests that at the end of the 1990s less than 1 percent of tropical forests were under sustainable management.[43]

The international agreement most directly concerned with the protection of the world's biodiversity, the Convention on Biological Diversity (CBD), was negotiated in conjunction with the UN Conference on Environment and Development (UNCED) in Rio di Janiero, Brazil, in 1992. This agreement is a framework convention, to which the Cartagena Biosafety Protocol was added in 2000.

In large part due to the level of uncertainty about current levels of biodiversity and the extent of existing threats, the major substantive obligation of the CBD is the identification, monitoring, and assessment of existing biodiversity. Countries are required to determine the extent of their biological diversity and monitor it on ongoing basis, particularly those aspects 'requiring urgent conservation measures.'[44] The agreement requires all parties to develop 'national strategies, plans or programmes for the conservation and sustainable use' of biodiversity.[45] The treaty also puts forth an obligation to protect existing biodiversity resources, though it leaves the form of implementation entirely to the discretion of the states involved. As such it is hardly a substantive obligation to which states could be called to account. An additional important aspect is the funding mechanism, described in Article 20 of the treaty and implemented by the Global Environment Facility. This obligates developed countries to pay the 'full incremental costs' that developing countries incur in meeting the obligations of the treaty.

As suggested above, the CBD continues the move in international law away from the principle of 'free access' by anyone to biodiversity resources. Again 'recognizing the sovereign rights of States over their natural resources,' the treaty agrees to facilitate access to genetic resource, but requires that such access be on the basis of prior informed consent and 'on mutually agreed terms.'[46] It thus increases the ability of states to keep others from their biodiversity resources to a much greater extent than it requires them to protect such resources. The idea in part may be that states, when guaranteed control over their own resources, will be able to profit from them in a way that will increase the likelihood of preserving them. Nevertheless, as many of the factors involved in biodiversity loss suggest, short-term considerations will often trump the long-run advantages to an individual state of protecting a piece of the world's biodiversity heritage. The sovereignty rights affirmed by states in the CBD were made possible primarily because states cannot be forced to join international environmental agreements. Since most biodiversity is located within the territory of states, those states with high biodiversity resources were loathe to accept specific restrictions but eager to increase their control over their resources. These states had the ability to keep substantive conservation obligations from the agreement. What resulted was a treaty that provides a general approach to the protection of biodiversity and an agreement that doing so is important, while requiring little substantive action to accomplish that goal. The funding mechanism and the information generated from national biodiversity inventories are likely to be among the most important features of the agreement, largely because they will reduce some of the uncertainty and scientific disagreement associated with discussions of biodiversity.

The one existing protocol to the CBD is the Cartagena Biosafety Protocol (2000), again showing a concern by developing countries to protect their territorial integrity from outside interference, rather than an obligation to preserve ecosystems in any way. The Protocol concerns trade in what it calls living modified organisms (LMOs); another term for genetically modified organisms (GMOs) or biotechnology. Trade in these organisms is regulated through a prior-informed-consent-like procedure termed advanced informed agreement (AIA). Under this process, countries that wish to export LMOs must inform and receive consent from the importing country before such an activity can take place.[47] Additional obligations require all states to notify each other in the case of unintentional transboundary release of LMOs and take responsibility for the removal of any LMOs illegally transferred. The agreement spells out the ability of states to restrict imports of LMOs based on risk assessment, 'carried out in a scientifically sound manner.'[48] While the Biosafety Protocol may serve to protect ecosystems from being taken over by genetically modified organisms unwittingly imported and thus help conserve biodiversity, the converse argument is made as well: that increased use of biotechnology will allow more people to be fed using less land and with less damage to ecosystems, and thus ultimately benefit biodiversity.[49] More importantly, the fact that the first protocol to the CBD is again about protecting the rights of the countries in which the most biodiversity is found, rather than requiring obligations of them, suggests the importance of the issue structure in determining what types of biodiversity protection may be most useful.

Private Solutions

The nature of the biodiversity conservation problem suggests that states are likely to be most moved by measures to protect biodiversity that enable them to profit from the protection of their resources. While, to some extent, sustainable use of any resource, and in particular the protection of rainforest ecosystems that otherwise are subject to soil degradation and erosion, is in the interests of the countries in which the resource is located, that interest is collective and long term. The forces that lead to rainforest destruction tend to be individual (as farmers or ranchers move into the Amazon in search of profits) and driven by short-term considerations. A number of innovative private solutions have helped to mitigate some of the underlying causes for rainforest destruction. They provide benefits to individuals as well as the state for protecting nature, and increase the likelihood that the long-term benefits of protecting biodiversity resources will be accomplished. These efforts rely predominantly on actions of non-governmental actors, who also play a broader role in general pressure to address issues of biodiversity protection.

Debt-for-Nature Swaps

One of the most inventive strategies for protection of biodiversity is the idea of debt forgiveness in exchange for conservation activities under-taken by the indebted country. As first proposed by Thomas Lovejoy of the World Wildlife Fund in 1984,[50] this process traditionally happens when a seriously indebted country is unlikely to be able to pay back its debt. The bank to which it owes the debt sells the debt at a discounted rate on the secondary market for fear that it will not receive the full payment from the country in question. A non-governmental organiza-tion (NGO), interested in conservation, buys a piece of the country's debt at a discounted rate. The NGO then negotiates with the environment and finance ministries of the indebted country for some amount of money – usually higher than the NGO paid for the debt but lower than the actual value of the debt – to be put in national currency into local conservation. The first debt-for-nature (DFN) swap, in Bolivia in 1987, required the setting aside of specific land areas for conservation. Concerns about sovereignty and disrespect of local priorities led to a general shift of approach allowing DFN funding to be put to any agreed-upon conservation goal, including environmental education, increases in the budgets of the national parks, funding for a local conservation organization, or employment of rangers to patrol protected areas. Swaps still almost always focus on increasing conservation in a specific area of the indebted state.

DFN swaps build on the idea that highly indebted countries are likely to use natural resources unsustainably in order to meet their immediate economic needs. Because of the Latin American debt crisis the mechanism was also able to build on the advantages of a secondary market in debt to increase the value of money that NGOs put towards conservation. Rather than simply donating money to a country to convince it to protect its biodiversity, the NGO invests that money in buying debt and thus multiplies the amount of conservation its donation can buy. For example, Conservation International spent $750,000 on a DFN swap in Brazil. If it had simply donated that amount of money to Brazilian conservation, it would have purchased $750,000 in conservation measures in Brazil. Instead, it purchased $2.2 million in debt and (in a slight departure from the usual process) Brazil agreed to put all of the funding towards conservation locally.[51] The NGO thus spent $750,000 to purchase $2.2 million in conservation measures in Brazil. That is the marvel of the DFN swap mechanism.

Between 1987 and 1994 (the height of the first generation DFN swaps) there were 32 swaps completed in 15 states, which reduced foreign debt by $177 million and generated approximately $130 million in local conservation funding.[52] Most swaps were in Latin America. Early DFN swaps in the Amazon region included two in Bolivia, two in Ecuador, and one in Brazil.[53] More recent DFN swaps have followed a different pattern, with governments forgiving debt in exchange for conservation measures, the first of these involving Germany forgiving $500 million in Kenyan debt in exchange for environmental protection.[54] The US Tropical Forest Conservation Act of 1998 promises to provide $325 million for DFN swaps,[55] and other states plan or have executed these types of swaps.

It is clear that DFN swaps are a mechanism more suited to addressing conservation needs than solving the debt crisis given the relatively small amount of debt that is forgiven overall,[56] although that may change with second generation, bilateral, swaps. But the mechanism has already had a noticeable impact on conservation and that may only increase with larger, government-driven, swaps. For example, the first Ecuadorian DFN swap relieved only $1 million in debt of an overall debt of $8.3 billion, but the amount put to conservation more than doubled the budgets of the national parks.[57]

There are criticisms of this mechanism even within the framework of conservation, however. These focus either on the failure of external

NGOs to effectively influence domestic conservation or on the ethics of doing so. The first concern is that funding does not necessarily accomplish much; Rhona Mahoney complains that DFN swaps produce only 'paper parks' that give the illusion of environmental protection without actual on-the-ground conservation. She points out that 'protected areas are invaded by loggers, miners, or the landless.'[58] While this observation is certainly true in some instances, NGOs have learned from DFN failures and have designated increased funding to help protect park borders and provide alternative economic activities for people affected by the protection of land they might otherwise occupy. A recent study of 93 national parks in tropical areas concluded that 83 percent of the parks were unaffected by agricultural encroachment, and also suffered less than nearby areas from other human-induced change such as hunting, grazing, and logging.[59]

Others point to the inflationary pressure that can be created domestically by the influx of currency used to pay for environmental measures.[60] This happens particularly if the government responds to the need to put local funding into conservation by simply printing additional currency. States do not have to follow that approach, however, and in most cases the amount of internal money generated in debt-for-nature swaps is small enough relative to the overall national budget to have at most a minimal inflationary effect. In addition, it is suggested that the mechanism rests on an incorrect assumption of a relationship between debt and deforestation.[61] It is clear that debt is not the only or even necessarily primary factor leading to Amazonian deforestation, but when you consider that DFN swaps provide increased funding for conservation, while reducing small amounts of debt, this criticism seems irrelevant. Whether deforestation in the Amazon is caused by debt, the fact that it can be ameliorated by a mechanism that involves debt relief seems clear.

A bigger concern may be ethical. The mechanism has been called 'eco-imperialistic.'[62] Developing countries often see such agreements as threats to sovereignty, which may have prevented some from participating. Some are concerned that the mechanism takes place without developed countries acknowledging their role in environmental degradation, and operates by affecting the lives of local subsistence farmers in the Amazon rather than changing the lifestyles of people in the wealthy industrialized countries.[63] It is also suggested that no real transfer of funding takes place, since the funding from NGOs goes to the banks, and the country protects biodiversity with its own money. While all of these criticism are to some extent fair, if conservation of biodiversity is a relevant goal, the actions of debt-for-nature swaps are one way to accomplish it. The fact that states do not have to choose to participate removes at least some of the sovereignty concerns. To the extent that biodiversity conservation is advantageous in the long run for the country it takes place in, DFN swaps may be one way to help states to realize their own long-term self-interest.

It is also interesting to note that initial DFN swap successes helped sow the seeds of their own decline. During the height of the Latin American debt crisis debt could be bought for a highly discounted rate on the secondary market, because banks believed the chances of being paid back were slim; few others wanted to buy debt that was so unlikely to be paid back and so the price was low. During the 1990s the price of Latin American debt on the secondary market increased, largely because banks became more cautious about loaning money to those who had previously failed to pay it back and there was thus less debt to be sold. Even in cases where the price of debt decreased, governments have responded to increased NGO demands for swaps by agreeing to put a lower percentage of the swapped debt value into conservation. So while the price of Costa Rica's debt on the secondary market fell from 30 cents per dollar of debt to only 10 cents in the first few years of the mechanism's operation, the country responded by moving from paying 75 percent of the debt's face value for conservation goals to paying only 30 percent.[64] While bilateral governmental debt forgiveness in exchange for conservation measures may be of increasing importance in the future, first-generation debt-for-nature swaps appear to have been a somewhat time-limited mechanism.

Bioprospecting

Since one of the arguments for protecting the rainforest is the potential future use of its products for medical advances, ensuring that states in which it exists benefit from those medical advances could help increase the odds that those states will undertake measures to protect their biodiversity. It was estimated that, as of 1990, the global sale of products derived from traditional medical practices in tropical countries earned $32 billion annually,[65] and 25 percent of drugs sold in the USA (to say nothing of the emerging market in dietary supplements) have active ingredients derived from plants.[66] Bioprospecting involves the extraction and examination of biological samples from an area to determine whether they are useful for pharmacological purposes. While this activity is not new – Eli Lilly and Co. developed cancer treatments from the rosy periwinkle native to Madagascar in the 1950s,[67] and specific removal and use of local plants likely dates back to colonial times – its specific contribution to conservation is. The countries in which bioprospecting takes place, buoyed by increasing international safeguards on their rights to their own resources, demand compensation for allowing pharmaceutical companies to examine their resources. This compensation comes in several forms: companies may pay states to protect an area in which they want to bioprospect and simply to allow them access, local people are often paid to collect and evaluate samples and are provided with technology and training to do so, and if a product is developed from this process the state that has a bioprospecting deal with the company has probably negotiated for some share of the royalties. More generally, the idea is that a state will itself gain the incentive to protect an area that might be the source of economic benefits in the near future, particularly if threats to the area originally came for economic reasons.[68]

The first large bioprospecting deal took place not in the Amazon but in Costa Rica in 1991, when the pharmaceutical company Merck paid that country approximate $1.1 million plus access to royalties (half of which are to be put into conservation) in return for samples and protection of a specific region. Merck and Costa Rica renewed the contract in 1994 for an additional $1 million.[69]

There have been at least a few bioprospecting agreements specifically in the Amazon region. A firm called Shaman Pharmaceuticals, Inc., draws on the knowledge of practicers of traditional medicine in the Amazon to identify the plants that might have medicinal potential. Working in the Amazon, among other locations, this firm includes biodiversity conservation as part of its mission and shares the benefits of its developments with the communities in which it works, through a non-profit organization it created called 'Healing Forest Conservancy.' It employs local people. In its operations in Peru, the company made an agreement with a federation representing 30,000 indigenous people to harvest plant samples for its operations.[70] While Shaman has had remarkable success at finding products to bring to drug trials, the company recently filed for Chapter 11 bankruptcy protection[71] and it is unclear what its future will be. At minimum it appears to have left the pharmaceutical development process and has focused its efforts on dietary supplements, which require less government oversight.

The Massachusetts Institute of Technology (MIT) began a $5 million bioprospecting project in the Amazon region of Brazil. Under this arrangement, MIT agreed to establish a biotechnology center in the Amazon region, and make use of faculty resources to help develop a variety of appropriate economic activities for the region. In addition, the plan called for screening natural resources in the area for suitability for pharmaceutical use. Brazil had previously been wary of entering into bioprospecting agreements, but this one differed from the standard model in that development of any products with commercial potential was to take place inside Brazil, rather than in pharmaceutical industries outside the country.[72] Unfortunately, this agreement was never fully implemented, and MIT pulled the plug with the project in arrears when Brazil did not contribute the funding it agreed to provide.[73]

Bioprospecting agreements appear to be a way for states to earn funding from their biodiversity resources and thus increase the reasons to protect it. Certainly some of these agreements fulfill that function, although the two examples given here suggest that initial optimism was likely overstated. There are also dangers in the widespread use of this approach. One is that the mechanism may be likely to be less profitable as it becomes more popular, in ways similar to debt-for-nature swaps. The more states there are with high levels of biodiversity that are willing to agree to enter into bioprospecting agreements, the less each state's negotiating advantage becomes. This is observed particularly with respect to the negotiation for royalties from the rainforest products that lead to successful drug development. Where once the expected range for royalties was between 1 percent and 15 percent,[74] royalties in some cases now range as low as 0.2 percent.[75] Another criticism of the mechanism is that even when royalties are substantial, little may go to the actual communities in which the bioprospecting takes place.[76] Eli Lilly receives profits of up to $100 million annually from the drugs developed from the rosy periwinkle and Madagascar receives none of these profits.[77] Even when local communities are expected to receive the profits, the time-frame is longer than may be ideal to help prevent more immediately profitable and less sustainable uses of forest resources. The first marketed product from Shaman's Amazon bioprospecting, a dietary supplement to treat AIDS diarrhea derived from the Amazonian *Croton lechleri* (or Dragon's Blood) tree, reached the market in 2000, nearly 15 years after the company first began bioprospecting in the Amazon. This product appeared sooner than it would otherwise have done because the company, dismayed by delays by the US Food and Drug Administration, decided to offer it for sale as a dietary supplement,[78] a category with less strict regulation (but also probably lower profits). Even so, this timeline is common; it is estimated that the average time for a pharmaceutical company to develop and bring a new drug to market is between twelve and fifteen years.[79] Some pharmaceutical companies, initially interested in bioprospecting deals, have recently been unable to accomplish their goals and have given up. Pharmaceutical giant Pfizer apparently tried to buy access to a 3 hectare plot of land in Ecuador for $1 million, working on the details of the deal for nearly four years before Ecuador cancelled the deal without explaining why.[80]

A similar but more fundamental criticism of the idea of bioprospecting is that it can become – either potentially or inherently – what people refer to as 'biopiracy.' Some object to the mere idea of patenting a life form or something derived from it, and thus suggest that any pharmaceutical companies that do so (such as Merck) are fundamentally engaged in illegitimate activity. Ironically, the criticism is more often applied to smaller firms like Shaman that rely specifically on indigenous knowledge to help identify local uses of natural products and thus increase the likelihood of finding effective medical treatments. These firms are seen as taking and patenting local knowledge, with the (generally unsubstantiated) critique that local people will no longer be able to use traditional remedies. It is true that these groups do not then profit from the sale of resulting products to the same extent that the companies that develop them do. Local people may earn income from gathering plant samples for bioprospecting agreements, but the agreements themselves are ultimately between the government of the country and the pharmaceutical company, and thus indigenous people may not see the prospective future income from royalties.[81] The jury is out about whether the advantages of environmental protection outweigh the seeming unfairness of such a situation. More serious yet are the true biopirates – those who come to take samples without permission and then use them to develop and profit from drugs. The rights of ownership to genetic material agreed to in the CBD, which is one of the reasons for the reluctance of the USA to fully participate in the agreement, is an effort to prevent or mitigate such outcomes.

Ecotourism

Opening the Amazon, or other areas of high biodiversity, to environmentally-friendly tourism offers another option for earning income from the resource and thus increasing the advantages to making sure it is protected. Cited as the fasted growing form of tourism but without a generally accepted definition, ecotourism generally involves enticing people to visit (presumably in an ecologically responsible manner) the very places one hopes to protect from destruction. Some argue that 'of all the economic alternatives contemplated for threatened habitats in the developing world, none appears to hold as much commercial promise as the business of accommodating people who wish to experience those habitats firsthand.'[82]

Some of the most widely practiced ecotourism takes place in Kenya, Costa Rica, and the Galapagos islands of Ecuador,[83] but ecotourism in the Amazon region is increasing. Brazil in 1997 launched a $200 million program to help an ecotourism industry develop in the Amazon region. At that point, Latin American states had invested approximately $21 billion to develop ecotourism.[84] There are numerous examples of specific ecotourism programs in the Amazon region, many of which appear to genuinely return money to the local community in which they take place, and may have the effect of increasing concern for biodiversity protection among those who take part in them. One Brazilian example is the Silves Association for Environmental and Cultural Preservation, which began an ecotourism program when the area's fishing industry had over-harvested the fish stocks. The funding from ecotourism goes to fund ranger patrols, habitat restoration, and education for the local fishers.[85] In the Ecuadorian Amazon, the Kapawi lodge aims to help an indigenous tribe protect its lands and earn an income, while protecting its local culture. This venture is jointly run by a for-profit tourism agency, and the local tribe's federation. The lodge was built by the local people using materials from the forest, and people who visit learn about both the local ecosystem and culture.[86] For every ecotourism project that carefully protects the area in which it operates and returns funding to the local community, however, there are plenty that prey on the desire of tourists to visit nature, without actually protecting it along the way.[87]

Ecotourism is another mechanism that can sow the seeds of its own demise. In essence it succeeds when it is profitable, but profit as a driving motive can overtake environmental protection. Any visitors to endangered habitats can have an impact on the ecosystems, and large numbers of visitors create problems of erosion and solid waste. At its extreme, tourism in fragile ecosystems may sufficiently impact the environment, or even simply the ability to enjoy being 'alone' with nature, that it can lead to either a total destruction of the area or a decline in true opportunities for ecotourism.[88] Moreover, the infrastructure needed to make ecotourism desirable and thus profitable, such as roads into remote areas, can then create opportunities for depletion of the resources of the area by commercial actors, such as loggers who are more able to reach virgin forest.[89]

Other concerns expressed are for the wellbeing of local people in remote areas. They may gain income from ecotourism, and thus be able to avoid engaging in (or being subject to) activities that destroy the ecosystems on which they have traditionally depended, but their own cultural diversity may suffer. Particularly in previously unvisited areas of the Amazon, local peoples become part of a cash economy that they may not have previously participated in, and are exposed to Western lifestyles they may not have previously encountered.[90] While it is as paternalistic to deny indigenous people the opportunity to change their lifestyles if they want to as it is to impose a new way of life upon them, this potential impact of ecotourism poses ethical concerns about its benefits for the very people it may be intended to help.

Alternative Rainforest Products

From Ben and Jerry's 'Rainforest Crunch' ice-cream to Body Shop toiletries made from 'sustainably' harvested rainforest products, the world has been made aware that products from the Amazon can be harvested in a way that can provide local economic benefits without destroying the ecosystem. The most influential academic argument in this effort came in a 1989 article in *Nature* in which the authors argued that rainforest land in the Amazon could be more economically valuable when sustainably harvested than when logged and converted to agricultural uses, even in the short run. They came to this conclusion after studying an area of Amazon rainforest in Peru, and concluded that production rates and world prices of rainforest products in the area would yield two to three times the value of the harvested timber of the region, and would be available over the long run if harvested sustainably.[91]

One of the best known efforts to put this observation into practice comes from the non-governmental organization Conservation International (CI). Conservation International's 'Sound Environmental Enterprise Development' program began in 1990 with the Tagua Initiative. This project focuses on encouraging sustainable harvesting of the tagua nut, which has properties much like ivory, and linking local suppliers with manufacturers nationally and internationally who can make use of products derived from this nut. In particular, CI worked on this project with the Fundacion de Capacitacion e Investigation para el Desarollo Socioambiental (CIDESA), an Ecuadorian community development organization, and with residents of a buffer zone of an Amazonian ecological reserve, from which the nuts could be harvested.[92] By 1995 the initiative had sold 1600 tons of tagua nuts within Ecuador, and the price had increased 200 percent. It had also involved more than 1500 people and resulted in the sales, at that point, of more than 35 million buttons.[93] The government of the region in which the initiative operates agreed to create a reserve to protect forests and also refused to allow the clearing of forested land in the area for a banana plantation.[94]

There are dangers from the successes in creation of a demand for sustainably harvested forest products. Less scrupulous organizations might use the marketing advantage of selling to environmentally concerned customers without taking the care that NGOs like Conservation International do to ensure the protection of the ecosystem from which such products are harvested. R. David Simpson suggests that 'virtually anything that can be harvested from a diverse natural forest can be even more profitably cultivated in that same area by eradicating competing species.'[95] While there is little evidence so far of widespread occurrence of this phenomenon with the Tagua Initiative, his example of such a danger, some have noted that a typical forest where tagua products are being harvested 'bears little resemblance to an undisturbed primary forest.'[96] Later studies have suggested that the economic advantage in using alternative rainforest products is less than half what the *Nature* article suggested.[97]

INTERNATIONAL AID

Aid from external governments, non-governmental organizations, or international organizations can provide funding for study or conservation of biodiversity, as seen in a number of such efforts underway in the Amazon region. Often this aid is in conjunction with some of the abovementioned private initiatives or international agreements, but it is worth mentioning separately nonetheless.

The Global Environment Facility (GEF), established in 1990 with provision of funding for biodiversity conservation as one of its four original focus areas, was later also designated the funding mechanism for the Convention on Biological Diversity. The GEF, which receives its funding from developed states, had by early 2000 allocated more than one billion dollars worldwide to nearly 350 biodiversity programs, which had been matched by nearly $1.7 billion in co-financing.[98] This funding included not only projects and 'enabling activities' for states (including those in the Amazon region) to do national biodiversity surveys and create national biodiversity plans under the CBD, but also four large programs focused specifically on protecting Amazonian biodiversity funded at $49 million total. The programs are the Amazon Region Protected Areas Program in Brazil, the Indigenous Management of Protected Areas project in Peru, and two Amazon-wide projects to provide 'Regional Support for the Conservation and Sustainable Use of Natural Resources in the Amazon' and 'Action for a Sustainable Amazonia.'[99]

Other governmental funding for Amazonian biodiversity comes from governments outside the GEF framework. In 1991 the G-7, European

Union, and the Netherlands pledged $250 million for a 'Pilot Program for the Protection of the Tropical Forests' to be managed by the World Bank. This project was intended to increase education about the contribution of the Amazon to global emissions of greenhouse gases, to demonstrate the potential compatibility between economic and environmental objectives in tropical forests, and protect genetic resources.[100]

Given that uncertainty both about the number and types of species and about the role of biodiversity in other environmental issues has been a stumbling block in efforts to protect ecosystems, many international programs attempt to provide financial or technical aid to help answer these questions. One important such initiative in the Amazon is the Large Scale Biosphere-Atmosphere Experiment in Amazonia (LBA). This project is an international effort to understand the 'climatological, ecological, biogeochemical and hydrological systems' of the Amazon region. The project is intended to operate between 1996 and 2003, and uses satellite data to measure environmental changes and impacts from various activities. This project is headed by Brazil's Ministry of Science and Technology, but has received assistance from a wide variety of states and relied on satellite images provided by many sources.[101]

Similar monitoring of biodiversity more broadly, and in the Amazon in particular, has been done by non-governmental organizations. The World Conservation Monitoring Center (now a part of the UN Environment Programme, but originally an independent organization) created the Biodiversity Management Program, designed to help states produce sufficient information to create national strategies to assess and protect biodiversity. On other biodiversity-related issues, NGOs such as the organization TRAFFIC have been invaluable players in the effort to monitor trade in endangered species. Concern about biodiversity, in the Amazon and beyond, reaches across borders and past governments, as a wide variety of actors contribute to efforts to better understand and protect it.

CONCLUSION

The differences between biodiversity conservation, which may conceptually be part of the common heritage of humankind, and climate change, ozone depletion, and whaling, which are truly global commons issues, is that biodiversity protection can simultaneously be accomplished and avoided by various states. No one state can undermine biodiversity protection worldwide, nor can any one state accomplish it fully.

Biodiversity protection has implications for a wide range of both local and global environmental issues. Locally, protecting ecosystems helps prevent soil degradation, erosion, and desertification. Globally, forests (as well as other plants) are carbon sinks that may mitigate human impact on the climate. In fact, a US 'Greening of the Globe' initiative proposed in 2000 by then President Clinton specifically to reduce greenhouse gas emissions included a proposed $37 million in debt-for-nature swaps, suggesting that biodiversity protection can help address other global environmental problems. Likewise, increases in such transboundary pollution problems as acid rain in Latin America can harm biodiversity in the Amazon. Biodiversity loss is more broadly associated with the very underpinnings of modern environmental problems: increased industrialization, population pressure, and international economic incentives. It thus serves as a virtual canary in the coal mine, indicating the health of the global environment.

Also important in the biodiversity protection efforts examined here is the role of non-governmental actors who, as Cord Jacobeit put it in his discussion of debt-for-nature swaps, are 'leading the way'[102] in addressing biodiversity. While states hold the trump card – their sovereignty – in allowing or denying access to their biodiversity, it is often both environmental organizations and various industries that are more able to offer states incentives to protect their biodiversity than other states. This experience suggests the importance of non-state actors, not only in influencing the behavior of the states in which they operate, but in making reasonably direct changes in the environmental policies of other states.

ACID RAIN IN EUROPE AND NORTH AMERICA

'If acid rain controls were cheap, there wouldn't be any disagreement on the science.'

William Ruckleshaus, EPA Administrator[1]

Acid rain is the same phenomenon, with minor variations, in most places where it occurs. Industrial activity, such as transportation or power generation, emits air pollutants like sulphur dioxide (SO_2) nitrogen oxides (NO_x), ammonia (NH_3) and volatile organic compounds (VOCs). These and related substances are changed chemically to sulfuric and nitric acids and carried by air currents until they are deposited in areas away from where the pollutants were initially generated.[2] Wind patterns may affect the way pollution is distributed, characteristics of the natural environment may vary in their ability to absorb acidification without suffering serious damage, and the types of industrial activities practiced in a given region may influence the components of the air pollutant precursors to acidification. In general, however, the problem is a common and commonly experienced effect of industrial activity.

It is a fundamentally different type of atmospheric pollution problem, for several reasons, than ocean fisheries or global climate change. These differences have important implications for the ways it has been addressed internationally. In terms of the nature of the problem, the primary difference is that acid rain has a directional character. How affected a country is by acid rain has everything to do with prevailing wind patterns and its own geographical characteristics and, most importantly, where the emissions come from. Unlike ozone depletion where a ton of ozone-depleting substances emitted anywhere in the world has the same impact on the ozone layer as the same amount emitted anywhere else, location matters for acid rain. States can be net importers or net exporters of acidifying substances, depending on whether they receive more acid rain than they send out on wind currents, or vice versa. This directionality has huge impacts for political efforts to address the problem.

Another important difference is the role of science and uncertainty. While the causes and effects of the environmental problem are now well understood and there is little uncertainty, understanding the phenomenon that has come to be called acid raid took a different and in many ways more traditional path than that of more global atmospheric pollutants. While the effect of coal burning on acid levels in the air was known as early as the 1850s and the term 'acid rain' was coined as early as 1872,[3] the modern discussion of transboundary acid rain began in Sweden in the 1950s and 1960s. Swedish scientists monitoring lakes over decades began to notice an increase in lake acidity. In 1968 a scientist argued the probable cause was air pollutants travelling long distances from other areas of Europe,[4] but this assertion was widely disputed and the true cause of acidification of Scandinavian ecosystems was not fully understood for more than a decade. As Marc Levy suggests, the initial scientific discussion broke down into at least two separate questions that had to be addressed separately: whether sulphur dioxide could travel long distances, and whether its deposition from the air could harm local ecosystems.[5] This environmental issue was thus addressed beginning with the observation of an environmental problem leading to the search for its cause, followed by a regulatory process, a model quite different from some other current international environmental issues.

Despite the similarity of the acid rain problems experienced in different geographic areas and shared scientific understanding, the regulatory process to address acid rain has followed a somewhat different timetable and pattern in North America and Europe. The process in North America has taken a longer period of time and resulted in generally weaker obligations. The specifics of the obligations differ as well. In the European experience a wider range of pollutants, including those that are not directly related to acid rain, has been regulated. The European experience has also, although imperfectly and tentatively, addressed the issue of targeting emission reductions to the sources that cause the most environmental damage, based on a consideration of a combination of emissions, wind patterns and natural vulnerability of areas to acidification. Both processes allow a lot of latitude in how specific reduction obligations will be implemented domestically; perhaps not surprisingly, the ways that Canada and the USA have chosen to reduce their transboundary air pollution allow for a greater use of market mechanisms than do those undertaken in Europe. These differences exist despite the fact that the USA and Canada participated in the European regulatory process and are signatories both to the European framework convention to protect against acid rain and to some of its protocols, and despite the fact that they were taking place at roughly the same time and with access to the same scientific information.

In addition, this case shows the role of security factors in influencing environmental cooperation in ways that challenge the standard environment and security model. In this case, cooperation in Europe to address acid rain came not so much because there was an environmental problem with security implications but because environmental cooperation could help address an entirely unrelated security issue: how to obtain cooperation between Western and Eastern Europe during the Cold War. International organizations cast about for a low-politics issue on which to create East-West cooperation, and built upon Scandinavian concerns about transboundary acid rain to put forward an international negotiation, not so much due to great international concern about acid rain, but largely because such concern did not exist and acid rain thus seemed a safe issue on which to negotiate.

The European cooperation that has resulted from this first step has been impressive; states have changed their positions on emissions cuts and abatement policies more generally, in part due to public pressure and in part due to a scientific process that made the effects of the problem more clearly visible to those who did not realize they were suffering from it. The directional nature of the problem, however, makes the political dynamics of cooperation more difficult, as those who cause but do not suffer as much from the problem are less willing to change their behavior than those who experience the greatest effects. The power of those who want to resist regulation based on self-interest is thus clear in this instance, and an important lesson to remember in global environmental politics.

THE ENVIRONMENTAL PROBLEM

The precursor pollutants to acid rain can stay in the atmosphere for up to twenty days and can travel several hundred kilometers or more. The acidity, or pH, of rainfall varies naturally to some extent, but industrial activities have greatly changed the composition of precipitation in many areas.[6] Acidification can also be deposited in dry form. Moreover, there is something like a tipping point for acidification in many contexts; until a threshold point additional acid deposition may cause little damage, but afterwards small additional deposition can be responsible for extensive environmental damage.

There are a number of environmental problems that result from acid deposition. The pH of lakes and other bodies of water can be lowered to the point where they cannot sustain aquatic life. Forests can suffer damage from acid deposition. Soils can be made more acidic, which, if they do not have substances with which to buffer the acid, can influence plant growth. Acid rain is also corrosive and has caused damage to buildings, statues, and cultural artifacts.

ACID RAIN POLITICS IN EUROPE AND NORTH AMERICA

Regulatory History

International discussion of European acid rain began at the UN Conference on the Human Environment in Stockholm in 1972 at the behest of Scandinavian states, although no actual negotiations about the problem took place at the conference. Following Stockholm, the Organization for Economic Cooperation and Development (OECD) decided to study the issue, in part through monitoring. A report from this process published in 1977 suggested that long-range transport of air pollutants took place and had significant effects on many of the European countries involved in the study.[7] Meanwhile, diplomatic efforts following the 1975 Helsinki Conference on Security and Cooperation in Europe were searching for a low-politics issue on which East and West Europe could negotiate a cooperative agreement. The UN Economic Commission for Europe (ECE) suggested that an environmental issue would provide a suitable avenue for negotiation, and ultimately selected acid rain.[8] These negotiations were thus pushed by Eastern bloc countries for political reasons and Scandinavian countries for environmental reasons, with mild resistance from much of the rest of Western Europe. Negotiations toward a convention took place in 1978 and 1979, with the Convention on Long-Range Transboundary Air Pollution (LRTAP) signed in 1979. Canada and the USA participated in the LRTAP process, as signatories to the framework convention and participants in negotiations, probably in part because of the security goals of negotiating East-West cooperation.

Due in large part to the lack of environmental concern about the problem in most Western European countries, LRTAP was negotiated as a framework convention with little in the way of substantive abatement requirements. Signatory states agree in principle to limit and reduce their production of air pollutants. Parties commit to the idea that transboundary flows of air pollutants should be reduced as much as possible, as long as doing so is economically feasible.[9] The treaty also includes a process for collaboration in research and exchange of information on emissions and transboundary flows of air pollutants, abatement technology, and the effects of the major air pollutants.[10] Efforts were then made to negotiate protocols to create specific obligations. The first effort was for regulations to control SO_2. The Scandinavian countries had been pushing for a commitment to a 30 percent reduction of SO_2 emissions since before LRTAP negotiations were even completed, but this proposal met with resistance particularly from the rest of Western Europe. Some in the East were willing to agree, although Russia was concerned that it should only be required to reduce its transboundary flows of pollutants rather than emissions more generally. Research presented during the period of negotiations indicated that forests could be harmed by acid rain and that Germany's famous Black Forest was experiencing problems. Germany then joined the call for large cuts in SO_2 emissions. In 1983 a number of states committed to 30 percent reductions despite the lack of formally agreed obligations to do so. By the end of 1984 twenty states had joined the '30 percent club' and an agreement became possible.[11] By the time negotiations over a second sulphur protocol took place, in the 1990s, the approach had changed from one that focused on flat-rate reductions undertaken by all signatories to scientifically based differentiated reduction commitments taking account of the differing effects of emissions by and on states in different geographic and ecological situations.[12] Although accepted as scientific principle, the process of determining politically acceptable implementation of this concept in its purest form proved difficult.

The second protocol to be discussed, on control of nitrogen oxides, was proposed by the Scandinavian countries in 1985, immediately after the completion of the sulphur protocol. There was an important disagreement over how to regulate emissions from mobile sources, as automobile emissions are one of the major sources of NO_x. The extent of the emissions controls was also controversial, with several states pushing for 30 percent reductions, and others calling only for a freeze in emissions or even allowing for an increase. When in 1988 the middle option prevailed, a new 30 percent club formed, with half of the signatory states also signing (non-binding) pledges to decrease their emissions by 30 percent of 1987 levels by 1995. The Protocol also suggests that states work to decrease emissions further, and begin to apply the idea of critical loads.[13] A critical load is the amount of pollutant a particular area can receive before suffering negative environmental consequences; the idea is that emissions should ultimately be regulated to below that point, which requires different states to have different abatement obligations.

A third protocol, on the control of volatile organic compounds, was negotiated beginning in 1989. Controversy here was more pronounced, with no agreement on the type of emissions controls. Many states were willing to reduce their emissions by 30 percent, but some that did not suffer domestic damage from their own VOC emissions wanted only to reduce the transboundary flow of their pollutants. Eastern European states, newly moving towards democracy and capitalism, were unsure of their ability to comply with rigorous cuts and therefore suggested only a freeze on emissions. The protocol, agreed to in 1991, lists three types of regulatory options from which states must choose (along with the base year from which reductions will be calculated) upon signing the agreement. A state can choose to reduce VOC emissions by 30 percent, it can specify certain management areas that are the sources of transboundary flows of VOC pollutants and reduce emissions from those areas by 30 percent (along with a national freeze by 1999 at 1988 levels) or it can implement a freeze by 1999 at 1988 levels alone if 1988 VOC emissions were sufficiently low.[14]

The second sulphur protocol calls for states to ensure 'as far as possible, without entailing excessive costs,' that their deposition of acid rain from sulphur compounds does not exceed critical loads. The specific obligations are set out in an annex and involve a complex array of different emissions reductions required for each state over a set of years, determined in part by environmental circumstances and in part by what states were willing to accept.[15] It entered into force in August 1998. Two other protocols, negotiated in 1998, addressing the control of heavy metals and persistent organic pollutants,[16] are of minimal importance to the issue of acid rain particularly, although they do indicate the spillover effect of the agreement into cooperation on related issues. An additional protocol deals with the financing of the Cooperative Programme for the Monitoring and Evaluation of the Long-Range Transmission of Air Pollutants in Europe, and a 1999 Protocol 'to Abate Acidification, Eutrophication, and Ground-Level Ozone' attempts to take most cuts even further based on critical loads and the cost effectiveness of reductions.

Discussion of regulation of transboundary acid rain in North America began in the late 1970s. Both the USA and Canada had domestic air pollution laws regulating the substances that are involved in acid rain production already. Some even mentioned the need to prevent transboundary damage, but did not have any specific regulatory mechanism to do so. In 1977, the Canadian Minister of the Environment called for negotiations towards an agreement, which led to the formation of the Bilateral Research Consultation Group on the Long-Range Transport of Air Pollutants but no actual negotiations. The US Senate passed a 'sense of the Senate' resolution in 1978 that asked the President to negotiate an agreement with Canada, driven in part by US concerns about new construction of Canadian coal-burning power plants near the border.[17] When Canadian officials responded by pointing out the effects of US emissions on Canada, discussions went nowhere fast. After continued Canadian pressure the US agreed in 1980 to a Memorandum of Intent (MOI). It committed the two states to upholding existing domestic air pollution legislation, and created five working groups to study the issues. Negotiations began as intended by the Memorandum, but were suspended shortly thereafter.

Canada attempted at several points to persuade the USA to undertake domestic regulations. In 1982 it proposed that the USA adopt a 50 percent reduction in SO_2 emissions, but then President Reagan refused to consider such an option. Meanwhile, the various scientific processes set up by the MOI and other independent groups made available more information about the transport of and damages from acid rain. Canada also signed the sulphur protocol to LRTAP, committing it to reductions in SO_2 emissions of 30 percent. By 1985 the two heads of state appointed special envoys to study the issue. Their report eventually called for increased funding on research for new ways to produce less SO_2 in the process of coal-burning.[18] A report by the US National Research Council involving both Canadian and American scientists, released in 1986, indicated that acid deposition was occurring as a result of emissions of SO_2, but the USA would agree only to further research, arguing that the problem was not serious enough to justify expensive abatement measures.[19] The National Acid Rain Precipitation Assessment Program (NAPAP), a USA-based evaluation of acid rain initiated in 1980, released its interim report in 1987 with its summary report concluding that the effects of acid rain were not serious or widespread. It was inconsistent with most other assessments of the problem and was accused of being highly politicized.[20] Its release only made negotiations on the issue between the USA and Canada more difficult. In the interim, Canada took steps to reform its own domestic regulations, taking leadership in controlling the emission of pollutants that contribute to acid rain.

Canada continued to push the USA rhetorically on acid rain. In 1989, after George Bush became US President, discussions began again in earnest. The US was at the same time revising its national Clean Air Act to include provisions to respond to acid rain. The US executive branch proposed regulations in which SO_2 reductions would take place through creating a tradable permits system, which would make US reductions less costly and more efficient. With these measures passed as the Clean Air Act Amendments of 1990, the USA was once again willing to negotiate with Canada.[21] Negotiations began in 1990 and were concluded in the space of less than a year. The final result, eleven years after the MOI, and twelve years after both countries had already committed themselves to mitigating acid rain under LRTAP, was the United States-Canada Air Quality Agreement.

This agreement creates bilateral obligations to mitigate the acid rain problem. Its provisions are fairly general. It commits both states to set specific reductions to 'reduce transboundary flows of ... acidic deposition precursors.'[22] It also commits the parties more generally to environmental impact assessment, prior notification, and mitigation measures, and to conduct coordinated or cooperative scientific, technical, and economic research.[23]

An annex to the agreement sets specific reduction targets for SO_2 and NO_x for each state. Canada committed to reducing SO_2 emissions in its seven eastern provinces to 2.3 million tonnes per year by 1994, not to exceed that level annually through 1999, and to set a permanent annual cap of 3.2 million tonnes by 2000. The USA committed to SO_2 reductions of 10 million tons below 1980 levels by 2000 (with several exceptions relating to existing domestic legislation), a permanent cap on national emissions at 8.95 million tons for electric utilities by 2010, and the creation of new limits on SO_2 from industrial sources if they are expected to exceed 5.6 million tons annually.[24]

For NO_x, Canada agreed to reduce emissions from stationary sources by 2000 to '100,000 tonnes below the year 2000 forecast level of 970,000 tonnes,' and develop further reduction requirements by 2005 at the latest. For mobile sources the agreement sets out a minimum control program for motor vehicles that depends on the size and age of the vehicles. The USA agreed to a goal of reducing overall annual emissions of NO_x by 2 million tons from 1980 levels by 2000. For stationary sources it would do so by an agreed emission rate for boilers and the requirement that the Environmental Protection Agency set emission standards for other types of boilers and some other stationary sources of NO_x by 1997. For mobile sources the US agreed to a minimum control program that is more elaborate than, but comparable to, the standards accepted by Canada.[25] How these reductions are made is left up to the states.

Through participation in the LRTAP process, the USA and Canada have undertaken some obligations in that forum as well, despite the fact that their emissions do not contribute to European acid rain. Canada signed the first sulphur protocol although the USA has not. Both states signed the NO_x protocol (without the additional pledge of 30 percent reductions) and the VOC protocol, with the USA choosing an overall 30 percent reduction and Canada choosing a 30 percent reduction in specified areas.[26] Canada has signed, and was one of the of the early states to ratify, the second sulphur protocol under LRTAP; the US has neither signed nor ratified.[27] Canada is also one of the few states to have ratified the 1998 LRTAP protocols on heavy metals and persistent organic pollutants.[28]

SCIENTIFIC UNCERTAINTY

The resolution of unknown factors about acid rain in the European process contributed to the increasing willingness of states in the region to undertake environmental controls. Uncertainty – or its resolution – can legitimately be seen to have played a role in European acid rain negotiations. When discussions began in the early 1970s there was little available evidence indicating that pollutants could travel such long distances or cause serious acidification of ecosystems. The research begun by the negotiating process and institutionalized within LRTAP contributed new understanding of the existence and extent of long-range transboundary air pollution. Although not traceable solely to the resolution of uncertainty, the increased willingness to negotiate further cuts in emissions and include new substances is certainly related to new scientific evidence about the extent of acidification. Moreover, the willingness to base cuts in emissions, at least in theory, on the idea of critical loads, reflects an acceptance of the scientific understanding of transport of air pollutants and ecological vulnerability that would not have been seen a decade earlier.

Scientific uncertainty does not explain the differences in timing or content between European and North American regulations, however. Uncertainty about the acid rain problem was given as the main reason for delay in the North American regulatory process. For example, during the negotiations following the MOI, the US took the position that more research was required to confirm that there even was a cause-and-effect relationship between pollution and transboundary acid rain.[29] It is true that there are region-specific differences in weather patterns and ecosystems that need to be understood, but the overall scientific understanding available because of the European regulatory process gives convincing evidence of the existence and mechanisms of acid rain. If uncertainty were the cause of inaction, the regulations in North America, beginning slightly later than those in Europe, should in fact have proceeded more quickly and with greater depth, because they could build on the scientific understanding gleaned in the European case. As signatories to LRTAP the USA and Canada participated in and had access to the scientific research. The fact that most US claims of uncertainty were not about geographically specific elements of acid rain but were calling into question the scientific understanding of the process more generally indicates that uncertainty functioned at least partly as a smokescreen to hide other reasons for lack of cooperation.

Politics of Science

The politics of science has been found to differ in the two regions generally. Sheila Jasanoff and others have examined the way that European and North American decision-making relating to harmful pollutants operates, arguing that similar concerns lead to varied outcomes in part because of the way science is used in the process. In the case of chemical regulation, for instance, the US was found to insist on common regulations and to address the broadest range of substances, taking risk assessment strongly into consideration, whereas Britain regulated in an entirely opposite way, and German regulations fell between the two.[30] Jasanoff points to features of political culture that influence the way science is interpreted and acted upon, not necessarily in consciously self-interested ways.

In the case of acid rain it is argued that the way in which research was conducted influenced its acceptability to the process. Roderick Shaw suggests that the scientific evidence in the European context was widely accepted because it was conducted as part of the overall regulatory process, by the regulatory organization (the UN Economic Commission for Europe).[31] It was also important that it was conducted internationally. The lack of acceptance by US actors of the scientific evidence for harm from acid rain could possibly be attributed to the fact that much of the basic research was done in a European context, although given that it was a context in which the USA participated, that explanation seems weak. Interestingly, studies on US regulatory styles suggest generally that it is more willing to respond to situations of risk than other states and that it is less cost-conscious in the process of doing so.[32] The case of North American acid rain regulation would suggest the opposite.

More important than the issue of scientific uncertainty per se or even institutional constraints on the interpretation of science may be the way that science is used within the decision-making process by those with pre-determined interests. The USA's distrust of the mounting scientific evidence of damage from acid rain was certainly self-serving, and helped to delay agreement in North America. Some have argued that in the North American context more generally the institutions that sponsor reports 'seem to shade the assessment results more than might be expected just from national differences.'[33] Scientists may be unwitting but important players in this process. Oran Young explains that the scientific community addressing the question of acid rain presented 'the relevant scientific evidence in ways that both sides in the debate have been able to exploit for partisan purposes.'[34] It is clear that the USA used the spectre of scientific uncertainty as a way to avoid taking international regulatory action that it would prefer not to take. In Europe too, states that would prefer not to bear the costs of international regulation, such as Britain, pointed to scientific uncertainty to justify their reluctance. It is important to acknowledge the political uses to which uncertainty can be put, but it is not clear that self-interested uses of uncertainty alone provide a sufficient explanation for the differences between the North American and European processes.

INTERESTS

The interests of the individual states involved with an international problem are likely to have an effect on the extent and type of regulation, nowhere more than in a directional pollution problem in which interests are likely to differ. These interests collectively can shape both the extent to which a cooperative outcome is likely and the particular form of an agreement that does emerge. Realist international relations theory at its most basic, seeing any international cooperation that does emerge as epiphenominal, would suggest that the interests of the individual states are paramount. This phenomenon is, if anything, more likely in issues relating to the environment. Detlef Sprinz and Tapani Vaahtoranta are among those who see states as rational self-interested actors. Specifically, they expect states that are the victims of pollution to seek international environmental protection, and those that are net contributors to the problem to resist.[35]

Their hypothesis can be used easily to explain responses to acid rain in both regions, as well as the differences between the two regions. The directional character of acid rain, combined with differences in the natural ability of various ecosystems to resist harm from acidifying substances, means that the extent to which states are harmed by acid rain varies, often through no action of their own. Some states are net exporters and some are net importers of acid rain. Examining the interests of a state as a single entity, of course, oversimplifies the situation, because within any of the states examined there are actors who are harmed by acid rain or who would be harmed by the regulation of emissions to prevent acid rain. Nevertheless, there are certain wider generalizations that can help explain the negotiating positions taken by various states. In both the European and North American cases, the net exporters are less willing to undertake cooperative action than the net importers. In the case of North America, more than 50 percent of the acid rain Canada receives is thought to come from the USA, whereas only 15 percent of US acid rain is thought to originate in Canada. In addition, Canada is more vulnerable to acidification, not necessarily for ecological reasons, but because it relies more heavily for income on the natural resources (such as forestry products and fisheries) that are harmed by acid rain than does the USA.[36] Given those overall statistics, it is not surprising that the USA was a reluctant participant in negotiations. With US reluctance, agreement was likely to be problematic.

Sprinz and Vaahtoranta examine their interest-based approach in the context of acid rain in Europe, specifically looking at the first sulphur protocol. They suggest that a variable approach combining the ecological vulnerability of a state and the cost to that state of reducing the pollutants that cause acid rain can explain the willingness of a state to adopt the first sulphur protocol. Although their theory cannot account for the case of the UK, judged to have high ecological vulnerability and low abatement costs (and which did not sign the protocol),[37] it otherwise explains the actions of states that chose to push for, go along with, or refuse to participate in European acid rain controls.

ADDITIONAL FACTORS

Other factors that contribute to explaining the outcomes in both regions include factors that many who examine international negotiations more broadly consider important: the role of power and the number of actors involved in a negotiation. Power is difficult to define and even more difficult to conceptualize in an environmental context, but the fact that acid rain cuts to the heart of industrial activity and was initially negotiated in a security context suggests that the power of the actors is likely to be important. Powerful actors certainly played influential roles in acid rain negotiations both in Europe and North America. Germany's transformation into a supporter of emission controls was an important factor in allowing regulation to move forward in Europe. The disparity in power in the North American case was certainly influential in slowing down the agreement and in keeping its provisions somewhat weaker than those that have been undertaken in Europe. In both economic and security terms Canada is far more dependent on the USA than the reverse, although the USA did rely heavily on Canada as a source for energy.[38] It is important to note, though, that the power of the UK did not prevent agreement in Europe the way that the power of the USA slowed it down in North America. Power alone is, moreover, not a full explanation for the actions of states in international cooperation in the two regions, although the ability of important actors to throw their weight around in international environmental negotiations should not be overlooked more generally.

Also worth discussing in conjunction with power is the number of actors involved. Most international relations theory models international cooperation as a two-player game, and most international agreements are indeed bilateral. In the realm of global environmental politics, however, much is now done through multilateral agreement, and the number of actors involved may make a difference. In the case of acid rain, negotiations in Europe involved a large number of participants compared to the bilateral US–Canada negotiations, and may therefore be a possible source of the different outcomes. Nevertheless, hypotheses about the difficulty of negotiations with greater numbers of actors do not explain the increased difficulty of negotiating the North American Air Quality Agreement, and the decreased stringency of its provisions. They would suggest exactly the opposite.

An important related element that has not been independently examined is the actions undertaken by states prior to international negotiations on an issue, or the actions they would take without international agreement. There is evidence that industrial actors already subject to domestic environmental regulations will work to push for international regulations so that their competitors will have to bear similar costs.[39] States that have regulated unilaterally, or are willing to address a collective issue will benefit greatly if they can persuade others to do so as well. International cooperation can therefore be a reasonable activity by those who have regulated domestically; the question is whether it causes them to undertake action they would not have otherwise taken.

Much of the action undertaken by states in both regions to mitigate acid rain damage reflects what they had already done domestically or would have done in the absence of international cooperation. In Europe, Levy points out, Norway, Sweden, and Germany would have undertaken their LRTAP-related obligations without any international agreement; these states reduced their emissions before they had international obligations to do so.[40] Similarly, France dropped its initial objection to the first sulphur protocol when it realized that its aggressive nuclear energy program would allow it to meet the proposed obligations without changing existing activity.[41] By the time of the second sulphur protocol,

Barbara Connolly points out, most states had exceeded the 30 percent reductions required in the first protocol, many because of domestic reasons, unrelated changes in energy policy, or European Union regulation.[42] In North America, the Air Quality Agreement finally emerged once the US had already taken domestic action, under the 1990 Clean Air Act Amendments, to mitigate the creation of acid rain. Perhaps states are only willing to accept internationally what they have already adopted domestically, or what they are likely to adopt anyway. That pessimism overlooks the role of the international scientific process, particularly under LRTAP, in persuading states that their interests are at stake, but it does suggest that domestic regulation can be an important precursor to international environmental action.

CONCLUSION

In both regions, states have undertaken increasingly strict actions to limit their production, from industrial and transportation sectors, of substances that contribute to acid rain. What began as a concern by Swedish scientists about lake acidification has ultimately led to an understanding that a wide variety of air pollutants can travel long distances across national borders to impact other states, and a willingness to take action based on this knowledge. The directional element of this pollution provides an example of a situation where neither contribution to, nor suffering from, environmental damage is universally distributed across states.

The collective scientific undertaking generated by the LRTAP process convinced states that they had interests in controlling acid rain they might otherwise not have discovered independently until much later.[43] Germany became an advocate of strong mitigation measures when it discovered damage to its own forests from acid rain. That looks to be an example of self-interest, but it was self-interest made possible by the resolution of scientific uncertainty. A counterpoint to the political ways states choose to use science for self-interested reasons is the fact that scientific information may inform and thereby change self-interest in a way that can make cooperation or regulation more likely.

Consideration of the number of actors in a negotiation becomes more useful when taken in conjunction with other explanations. In particular, the smaller numbers in the North American context meant that if one of the actors wanted to undermine the process it could do so in a way that was less likely in Europe with far more actors. Moreover, when that actor is the more powerful of the two, it has an easier time undermining cooperation. When you combine the issues of interests and numbers in this case you see that the directionality of the environmental problem actually made it more likely that a larger group of (smaller) states would be able to agree to collective mitigation measures than a smaller group of states with less mutual geographic dependence. If the European case had involved negotiations only between Germany and the UK the scenario might have looked similar to that in North America.

It is unlikely that domestic preferences account for all the activity we see in the case of acid rain. Levy points to the 'tote-board diplomacy' effect of essentially shaming states into agreeing to emissions cuts because other states have publicly accepted them. So states may take action they wanted to take domestically, but take it publicly in a way that may help induce others to do so as well. Similarly, some of the domestic action may be undertaken in the service of trying to persuade others to regulate. In the North American context, Canada increased the stringency of its acid rain protection probably in part to shame the USA into taking similar action (or at least because its willingness to regulate was called into question early in the process). Simply looking at what action states have already taken domestically may not take into account the strategic nature of their domestic actions.

It is also worth noting, in the acid rain case, that, to an extent greater than in many other international environmental agreements, states have accepted different levels and types of obligations under the various different acid rain agreements. The obligations for the USA and for Canada differ under the North American agreement. Under LRTAP there are *de facto* differences to the extent that different states may agree to different LRTAP protocols or that some states agree only to reduce their transboundary fluxes rather than overall emissions; by the VOC protocol and particularly the second sulphur protocol the obligations undertaken by the different European states vary widely, and this trend continues with more recent protocols. This level of differentiation is unusual. Those who examine global environmental agreements are unused to seeing different levels of obligations within treaties, although it is more common in bilateral treaties where the norm of equity may be less pronounced for precisely the reasons discussed in examining the effects of numbers. It is also interesting to observe that this trend is appearing even in multilateral agreements. In agreements where states take on different levels of commitments, particular when not tied directly to environmental conditions, the effects of numbers, uncertainty, interests, and domestic politics may be even greater than they would otherwise be.

CONCLUSION

The experience of responding to global environmental issues suggests a number of conclusions. Addressing environmental issues is not easy, but it is possible. The right combination of information and interests, politics and persuasion, can bring states to commit to changing behavior, and people to actually do so, in ways that influence the environment beneficially. People's ability to degrade the environment is increasing, but so is our understanding of how natural systems work and intersect, and the same technological and economic innovation that can be seen as creating environmental destruction can also be harnessed to mitigate it.

The cases examined here suggest that it is not only difficult to gain international cooperation to protect the environment, as in the case of global climate change, but also that it is difficult to ensure compliance with international agreements, as demonstrated by illegal Soviet whaling and the black market in ozone-depleting substances. Even when there is large-scale behavior change, as with developed countries' near complete phaseout of ODSs, the environment does not necessarily respond quickly. Under such circumstances, it can be difficult to determine whether lack of environmental improvement is due to an inaccurate or incomplete understanding of the environmental problem, undetected cheating, or natural environmental fluctuations. More importantly, it can be politically difficult to take potentially costly action when the outcome is uncertain or when it will be beneficial only in the distant future.

These cases nevertheless also demonstrate the willingness of states to work together, and non-state actors to undertake cooperative action with states, in order to address problems that affect the global environment. There are strong (and in Europe, innovative) controls on emissions of acid rain, despite the varying effects on states of acidifying substances. There are innovative policies that bring together industry or environmental organizations with governments in efforts to protect biodiversity in the Amazonian rainforest. A commercial whaling moratorium was declared when it became clear that human activity had depleted whaling stocks to the extent that they would not be able to recover without drastic action. And, although efforts to mitigate climate change are only in their early stages, protection of the global atmosphere through strict regulation of ODSs has been among the most successful international efforts to protect the environment.

Certainly self-interest has played an important role in making these policies possible. But it is interesting to note a subtle redefinition of what constitutes self-interest, from one based on strict power resources of states. When Germany dropped its opposition to acid rain controls after scientific processes initiated by the Convention on Long-Range Transboundary Air Pollution indicated that it, too, was harmed by acid rain, did it change its interests, or simply learn new information that allowed it to realize its broader interest in protecting its environment? When the USA passed restrictions on the use of ODSs in non-essential aerosols after citizens demanded alternatives and scientists expressed precautionary concern about a potential environmental problem, the state was reflecting the concerns of some of its component parts to protect the environment over the long term, at the expense of other, traditionally more politically powerful, elements. This then gave regulated industry an incentive to internationalize that regulation. Environmental politics also makes strange bedfellows out of political actors, when domestic industries may work together with environmentalists on international environmental policy; the latter concerned about the wellbeing of the earth and the former concerned about their international competitiveness.

Studying the politics of the manner in which global environmental problems are addressed also suggests broader lessons for those who examine international relations. The nature of international relations has probably changed across a number of issues areas in the last century. The extent of international cooperation, the transformation of what constitutes 'security', the role of uncertainty, and the importance of non-governmental actors are all factors examined in international relations more broadly but that stand out particularly in efforts to manage the global environment.

While few who study international relations truly believe the characterization of the world as composed of unitary self-interested state actors, there are few areas of international relations in which non-state actors matter more, and in more varied ways, than in the realm of environmental politics. Scientists, not only as generators of knowledge, but as political actors, bring issues to the attention of environmental activists. These activists do not always follow the simple political model of lobbying the policy-makers of their own states (although they also do that) to change international negotiating positions. The standard model of the role of activists is linear: people's concerns filter up to policy-makers, who work them out internationally, agree to policies that states will follow, and then states implement those policies domestically, restricting activities by their citizens. And that is, indeed, sometimes the way global environmental politics works. Initial efforts to regulate whaling followed this model to some extent: whalers wanted to be able to continue their livelihood and to ensure that only as many whales be caught as could be sustained, expressed these concerns to their governments, which negotiated an international agreement that thus regulated the activities of the whalers.[1] But we also see citizens' groups working across borders to influence the actions of other states, disseminating information to other activists. We see environmental organizations buying tracts of land to preserve them, or buying and then forgiving commercial debt of foreign countries that do so. We see international organizations of scientists willing to contradict the political wishes of their states in announcing their findings on climate change. We see people changing their behavior not because they are required to by international or domestic regulations, but because they have been made aware of an environmental problem and want to help fix it. It is the actions of those who are not states that will have to change in order to protect the environment, so it is notable that non-state actors have been so influential in efforts to create a situation in which others will do so.

Nevertheless, states do still matter as actors in international environmental politics. They are the ones that sign international agreements, and that – in some cases, anyway – have the ability to make rules that change the behavior of environmentally destructive actors within their boundaries. Some of the traditional elements of international relations are thus present in global environmental politics. The dissociation between political and ecosystemic boundaries may make cooperation to protect the global environment more difficult at the same time that it makes it more necessary. States cannot address environmental problems by themselves but must cooperate to manage any problems of the global commons. Even issues like deforestation that would seem to be purely local have both international causes and international consequences. Environmental politics, although sometimes stymied by the concerns of states for their own wellbeing, can also be helped by that same concern, as states recognize that they cannot address global environmental problems on their own.

The nature of environmental politics gives influence to some states, as well, that would not traditionally be seen as powerful. States that have biodiversity resources the rest of the world cares about located within their borders have the ability to dictate the terms on which the rest of the world can gain access to them, or the conditions under which these resources will be protected. Developing countries whose future (or, in the case of climate change, current) behavior may influence the ability of states to manage a global environmental problem can gain great influence by refusing to undertake action to protect the resource unless it is on their terms. Their threat to refuse to participate is generally credible. Even if they may be harmed by the environmental problem, their time horizons are generally shortened by the need to meet the basic needs of their current populations. And they have an ethical card to play as well: is it fair to ask developing countries to foreswear development in the ways that have benefitted currently industrialized states? Developing countries have thereby seized great negotiating power in efforts to protect the global environment.

This observation suggests that a Cold War view of security is inappropriate for current environmental issues, both because foreign threats come less from the military might of another state than from its industrialization or resource use, and because a traditional focus on security misrepresents the nature of power and influence in the world. Economic might is still important and can be used in the service of environmental goals, but the ability to destroy a resource can be used to leverage additional economic resources. Environmental interconnectedness is an important aspect of interdependence.

Global environmental issues not addressed in depth in this volume follow and may expand many of the patterns explored here. The Basel Convention on the Control of Transboundary Movement of Hazardous Wastes and their Disposal (1989) reflected the recognition by developing countries that they could not always control their borders and required that exporters get prior informed consent before any shipments of hazardous wastes are sent for disposal. The International Convention for the Prevention of Pollution from Ships (1973/1978) attempted to restrict intentional oil pollution in the oceans in several different ways, gaining the most success when it focused regulations on smaller numbers of easily monitored larger actors (shipbuilders) than large numbers of small actors (ship operators) with incentives to cheat. The UN Convention to Combat Desertification in Those Countries Experiencing Serious Drought and/or Desertification (1994), in which developing states failed to leverage significant new sources of funding for their environmental goals, suggests that the influence of developing countries in international environmental agreements may be relevant but is limited to those issues where their participation is necessary for developed countries to accomplish their goals. The problems are becoming more complicated as well; the presence of organochlorides in the food chain far from where they are produced or consumed suggests an interconnectedness of natural systems even greater than we previously believed. What these and still other environmental issues all have in common are the international implications of domestic activities and the uncertainty about the severity of the environmental problems and the costs and benefits of fixing or preventing them.

There are many additional factors that one should take into consideration when examining global environmental politics, which have arisen implicitly in the cases examined in this volume. Population pressures are at the root of almost all environmental problems; at minimum, more people put more stress on environmental resources. Issues of development are important as well, since many environmental problems can be traced to industrialization. The issue of whether the less developed global South will follow the same industrialization path as its predecessors in Europe and North America is essential in determining what will happen to the global environment. To the extent that it would be better for the environment if development happened differently, how to accomplish that goal, in a manner that is both fair and politically feasible, will be one of the most important questions to address.

The globalizing influence of trade and culture are mirrored in environmental issues: to a large extent, all environmental politics are global. People are more capable of environmental destruction as the industrial revolution reaches further around the globe and people find more efficient ways of harvesting resources at the same time as their activities result in greater levels of pollution. The more we understand about the science of ecosystems, the more we realize that very local activities ultimately have global effects, and that the effects of environmental problems that appear to be only global (such as climate change or ozone depletion) are felt in specifically local ways. If ever there were an issue to remove the distinction between domestic politics and international relations, the study of the politics of the global environment is the one. But in removing this distinction, efforts to protect the global environment can often succeed.

NOTES

CHAPTER 2

1 Harold K. Jacobson and Edith Brown Weiss, 'A Framework for Analysis,' in Edith Brown Weiss and Harold K. Jacobson, eds, *Engaging Countries: Strengthening Compliance with International Environmental Accords* (Cambridge, MA: MIT Press, 1998), p. 1.

2 Lynton Keith Caldwell, *International Environmental Policy*, 3rd edn (Durham and London: Duke University Press, 1996), pp. 63–78.

3 Michael Grubb, Matthias Koch, Abby Munson, Francis Sullivan, and Koy Thomson, *The Earth Summit Agreements: A Guide and Assessment* (London: Earthscan Publications, Ltd, 1993).

4 Stephen D. Krasner, 'Structural Causes and Regime Consequences: Regimes as Intervening Variables,' in Stephen D. Krasner, ed., *International Regimes* (Ithaca and London: Cornell University Press, 1982), p. 1.

5 The content of this section is drawn partly from Elizabeth R. DeSombre, 'International Environmental Policy,' in B. Nath, L. Hens, P. Compton, and D. Devust, eds, *Environmental Management in Practice – Analysis, Implementation, and Policy*, Routledge, 1998, pp. 361–77.

6 Patricia Birnie, *International Regulation of Whaling*, vol. 1 (New York, London, and Rome: Oceana Publications 1985), p. 326.

7 Philippe Sands, *Principles of International Environmental Law* (Manchester and New York: Manchester University Press, 1995), p. 244.

8 Patricia W. Birnie, and Alan E. Boyle, *International Law and the Environment* (Oxford: Clarendon Press, 1992), p. 26.

9 Rio Declaration on Environment and Development, 1992, Principle 7.

10 Grubb *et al.*

11 Detlef Sprinz and Tapani Vaahtoranta, 'The Interest-based Explanation of International Environmental Policy,' *International Organization* 41(1) (Winter 1994), pp. 77–105.

12 Discussion of a definition of power can become unwieldy and is not worth addressing at length in this context.

13 Robert O. Keohane, *After Hegemony: Cooperation and Discord in the World Political Economy* (Princeton: Princeton University Press, 1984); Duncan

Snidal, 'The Limits of Hegemonic Stability Theory,' *International Organization* 30(4) (1985), pp. 579–615.

14 Elizabeth R. DeSombre, 'Developing Country Influence in Global Environmental Negotiations,' *Environmental Politics* 9(3) (Autumn 2000), pp. 23–42.

15 Duncan Snidal, 'The Politics of Scope: Endogenous Actors, Heterogeneity, and Institutions,' in Robert O. Keohane and Elinor Ostrom, eds, *Local Commons and Global Interdependence* (London: Sage Publications, 1995), pp. 47–70.

16 While the issue of compliance with an agreement may seen to be one that emerges after an agreement has been reached, the potential for noncompliance can preclude the ability to reach agreement in the first place.

17 Kenneth A. Oye, 'Explaining Cooperation Under Anarchy: Hypotheses and Strategies,' in Kenneth A. Oye, ed., *Cooperation Under Anarchy* (Princeton: Princeton University Press, 1986), pp. 18–20.

18 Snidal, pp. 47, 57–62.

19 Robert O. Keohane and Elinor Ostrom, 'Introduction,' in Keohane and Ostrom, eds, p. 6.

20 See Snidal, p. 48.

21 Arthur A. Stein, 'Coordination and Collaboration: Regimes in an Anarchic World,' in Krasner, ed., pp. 115–40

22 Oran R. Young, *Governance in World Affairs* (Ithaca, NY: Cornell University Press, 1999), p. 69.

23 See, for instance, Volker Rittberger and Michael Zürn, 'Regime Theory: Findings from the Study of 'East-West' Regimes,' *Cooperation and Conflict* 26 (1991), pp. 171–2.

24 Arild Underdal, 'Patterns of Effectiveness: Examining Evidence from Thirteen International Regimes,' paper presented at the International Studies Association Annual Convention, Toronto, March 1997.

25 See, for example, Robert O. Keohane and Joseph S. Nye, *Power and Interdependence: World Politics in Transition* (Boston and Toronto: Little, Brown & Company, 1977).

26 See, generally, Elizabeth R. DeSombre, *Domestic Sources of International Environmental Policy: Industry, Environmentalists, and US Power* (Cambridge, MA: MIT Press, 2000).

27 Garrett Hardin, 'The Tragedy of the Commons,' *Science* 162 (1968), pp. 1243–8.

28 Susan Jane Buck Cox, 'No Tragedy on the Commons,' *Environment Ethics* 7 (Spring 1985), pp. 49–61.

29 See, for example, Robert Axelrod, *The Evolution of Cooperation* (New York: Basic Books, 1984), and Keohane, *After Hegemony*, among others.

30 Oye, pp. 1–24.

31 J. Samuel Barkin and George E. Shambaugh, 'Hypotheses on the International Politics of Common Pool Resources,' in *Anarchy and the Environment: The International Relations of Common-Pool Resources* (Albany, NY: SUNY Press, 1999), pp. 1–25.

32 Marc A. Levy, 'European Acid Rain: The Power of Tote-Board Diplomacy,' in Peter M. Haas, Robert O. Keohane, and Marc A. Levy, eds., *Institutions for the Earth: Sources of Effective International Environment Protection* (Cambridge, MA: MIT Press, 1993, pp. 75–132.

33 Louis Henkin, *How Nations Behave: Law and Foreign Policy*, 2nd ed. (New York: Columbia University Press for the Council on Foreign Relations, 1979), p. 47.

34 See, generally, Brown Weiss and Jacobson, eds.

35 William Zimmerman, Elena Nikitina, and James Clem, 'The Soviet Union and the Russian Federation: A Natural Experiment in Environmental Compliance,' in Brown Weiss and Jacobson, eds, p. 313–14.

36 See, generally, David Victor, Kal Raustiala, and Eugene B. Skolnikoff, eds, *The Implementation and Effectiveness of International Environmental Commitments* (Cambridge, MA: MIT Press, 1998).

37 Abram and Antonia Chayes, *The New Sovereignty: Compliance with International Regulatory Agreements* (Cambridge, MA: Harvard University Press, 1995).

38 David G. Victor, 'The Operation and Effectiveness of the Montreal Protocol's Non-Compliance Procedure,' in Victor, Raustiala, and Skolnikoff, eds, pp. 137–76.

39 See, for example, Brown Weiss and Jacobson, eds, and Victor, Raustiala, and Skolnikoff, eds.

40 Murillo de Aragão and Stephen Bunker, 'Brazil: Regional Inequalities and Ecological Diversity in a Federal System,' in Brown Weiss and Jacobson, pp. 475–509.

41 Zimmerman, Nikitina, and Clem, pp. 291–325.

42 Ronald Mitchell, *International Oil Pollution at Sea: Environment Policy and Treaty Compliance* (Cambridge, MA: MIT Press, 1994).

43 David G. Victor ' "Learning by Doing" in the Nonbinding International Regime to Manage Trade in Hazardous Chemicals and Pesticides,' in Victor, Raustiala, and Skolnikoff, eds, pp. 221–81.

44 K. Sherman, 'Large Marine Ecosystems,' in *Encyclopedia of Earth System Science*, vol. 2 (New York: Academic Press, 1992), pp. 653–73.

45 'Ozone Depletion at Record Level, UN Agency Says,' *Reuters News Service* (9 October 2000).

46 Ozone Secretariat, 'Press Backgrounder,' http://www.unep.org.ozone/Press-Back (date visited: 19 June 2001).

47 William C.G. Burns, 'From the Harpoon to the Heat: Climate Change and the International Whaling Commission in the 21st Century,' An occasional paper of the Pacific Institute for Studies in Development, Environment, and Security, 2000.

48 Peter M. Haas, Robert O. Keohane, and Marc A. Levy, 'The Effectiveness of International Environment Institutions,' in Haas, Keohane, and Levy, eds, pp. 3–24.

49 Oran R. Young and Marc A. Levy (with the assistance of Gail Osherenko),

'The Effectiveness of International Environmental Regimes,' in Young, ed., *The Effectiveness of International Environmental Regimes* (Cambridge, MA: MIT Press, 1999), pp. 1–32.

50 Edward L Miles, Arild Underdal, Steinar Andresen, Jørgen Wettestad, Jon Birger Skjaerseth, and Elaine M. Carlin, *Explaining Regime Effectiveness: Confronting Theory with Evidence* (Cambridge, MA: MIT Press, 2001).

CHAPTER 3

1 Sam Nunn, 'Strategic Environmental Research and Development Program,' Senate Floor Speech, 28 June 1990, quoted in Kent Hughes Butts, 'Why the Military Is Good for the Environment,' in *Green Security or Militarized Environment*, ed. Jyrki Käkönen (Aldershot, England: Dartmouth Publishing Company, 1994), p. 87.

2 Lester R. Brown, 'Redefining National Security,' *Worldwatch Paper 14* (Worldwatch Institute, 1977).

3 Richard H. Ullman, 'Redefining Security,' *International Security* 8(1) (Summer 1983), pp. 129–53.

4 Jessica Tuchman Matthews, 'Redefining Security,' *Foreign Affairs* 68(2) (Spring 1989), pp. 162–77; Norman Myers, 'Linking Environment and Security,' *Bulletin of the Atomic Scientist* 43 (June 1987), pp. 46–7.

5 Matthew Paterson, *Understanding Global Environmental Politics: Domination, Accumulation, Resistance* (London: Macmillan, 2000), p. 19.

6 Butts, pp. 83–109.

7 John Vidal, 'As the World Runs Dry ... Next, Wars over Water?' *World Press Review*, (November 1995), pp. 8ff.

8 Mostafa Kamal Tolba, 'Middle East Water Issues: Action and Political Will,' in Asit K. Biswas, ed., *International Waters of the Middle East* (Oxford: Oxford University Press, 1994) p. 3. There are obviously more now.

9 Neth. v. Belg. 1937 P.C.I.J. (ser A/B) No. 70, p. 4.

10 Paterson, p. 20; see also J. Bulloch and A. Darwish, *Water Wars: Coming Conflicts in the Middle East* (London: Victor Gollancz, 1993); Nurit Kliot, *Water Resources and Conflict in the Middle East* (London: Routledge, 1994); Danel Hillel, *Rivers of Eden: The Struggle for Water and the Quest for Peace in the Middle East* (Oxford: Oxford University Press, 1995); Caroline Thomas and Darryl Howlett, eds, *Resource Politics: Freshwater and Regional Relations* (Buckingham: Open University Press, 1993).

11 Kliot, p. 173.

12 Hillel, p. 163.

13 George Joffé, 'The Issue of Water in the Middle East and North Africa,' in Thomas and Howlett, eds, p. 73.

14 Joffé, pp. 73–80.

15 CBS News, 'Water Fight in the Mideast,' broadcast 2 July 2000; also available at http://cbsnews.cbs.com/now/story/0,1597,211735-412,00.shtml;

(date visited: 3 July 2000).

16 Lauren Fagan, 'Water a Vexed issue for Israel, Palestinians,' *Reuters* (6 July 2000).

17 The fact that the Colorado river is no longer a water source by the time it reaches Mexico is certainly not to Mexico's liking, for instance.

18 Ronnie D. Lipschutz and John P. Holdren discuss climate change, ozone depletion, acid rain, and tropical deforestation as the major potential national security risks: 'Crossing Borders: Resource Flows, the Global Environment, and International Security,' *Bulletin of Peace Proposals*, 21(2) (1990), pp. 121–33. Peter Stoett includes a discussion on the politics of whaling in his overall discussion of environmental security: Peter Stoett, *Atoms, Whales, and Rivers: Global Environmental Security and International Organization* (New York: Nova Science Publishers, Inc., 1995).

19 Kliot, p. 1.

20 Caroline Thomas and Darryl Howlett, 'The Freshwater Issue in International Relations,' in Thomas and Howlett, eds, pp. 9–11.

21 J. Carroll, 'The Acid Challenge to Security,' *Bulletin of Atomic Scientists* 45(8) (1989), pp. 32–5.

22 Trail Smelter Arbitration (US v. Can) (1941), 3 UNRIAA 1938 (1949).

23 Norman Myers, *Ultimate Security: The Environmental Basis of Political Stability* (New York and London: WW Norton & Co., 1993).

24 See, for example, Nico Schrijver, *Sovereignty over Natural Resources: Balancing Rights and Duties* (Cambridge: Cambridge University Press, 1997).

25 J. Samuel Barkin and George E. Shambaugh, 'Hypotheses on the International Politics of Common Pool Resources,' in J. Samuel Barkin and George E. Shambaugh, eds, *Anarchy and the Environment: The International Relations of Common Pool Resources* (Albany, NY: SUNY Press, 1999), pp. 1– 25.

26 Elizabeth R. DeSombre, *Domestic Sources of International Environmental Policy: Industry, Environmentalists, and US Power* (Cambridge, MA: MIT Press, 2000), p. 94.

27 Peter H. Gleick, 'The Implication of Global Climatic Changes for International Security,' *Climatic Change* 15 (1989), pp. 309–25.

28 Marvin Soroos, 'Global Change, Environment Security, and the Prisoner's Dilemma,' *Journal of Peace Research* 31(3) (1994), pp. 317–32.

29 Jeffrey A. Hart, 'The Anglo-Icelandic Cod War of 1972–1973: A Case Study of A Fishery Dispute,' Research Series No. 20, Institute of International Studies, University of California, Berkeley, 1976.

30 J. Samuel Barkin and Elizabeth R. DeSombre, 'Unilateralism and Multilateralism in International Fisheries Management,' *Global Governance* 6(3) (July–September 2000), pp. 339–60.

31 Intergovernmental Panel on Climate Change (1990), quoted in Myers, *Ultimate Security*, p. 189.

32 Myers, *Ultimate Security*, p. 190.

33 Grover Foley, 'The Looming Environmental Refugee Crisis,' *The Ecologist*

29(2) (March–April 1999), pp. 96–7.

34 Michael Renner, 'Transforming Security,' in Lester Brown *et al.*, eds, *State of the World 1997* (New York: WW Norton & Company, 1997), p. 118.

35 David Douglas, 'Environmental Eviction,' *The Christian Century* 113(26) (22 September 1996), pp. 839–41.

36 Curtis J. Paskett, 'Refugees and Land Use: The Need for Change in a Growing Problem,' *Journal of Soil and Water Conservation* 53(1)(Spring 1998), pp. 57–8.

37 See, for example, Myers, *Ultimately Security*, pp. 189–203; Douglas, pp. 839–41; and Foley, pp. 96–7.

38 Catherine Locke, W. Neil Adger, and P. Mick Kelley, 'Changing Places: Migration's Social and Environmental Consequences,' *Environment* 42(7) (September 2000), pp. 24–35. They argue that sometimes 'enhanced human capital' can result from immigration, and that ultimately under the best circumstances migration can lead to fertility change and demographic transition. Much of the beneficial migration they suggest, however, is more voluntary than the situations that produce environmental refugees.

39 Thomas Homer-Dixon, 'Environmental Scarcity and Mass Violence,' in Gearóid O'Tauthail, Simon Dalby, and Paul Routledge, eds, *The Geopolitics Reader* (London: Routledge, 1998), p. 207.

40 Daniel Deudney, 'Environment and Security: Muddled Thinking,' *Bulletin of the Atomic Scientist* (April 1991), pp. 23–8.

41 Daniel H. Deudney, 'Bringing Nature Back In: Geopolitical Theory from the Greeks to the Global Era,' in Daniel H. Deudney and Richard A. Matthew, eds, *Contested Grounds: Security and Conflict in the New Environmental Politics* (Albany: SUNY Press, 1999), pp. 25–57.

42 Matthias Finger, 'The Military, the Nation-State and the Environment,' *The Ecologist* 21(5) (September–October 1991), p. 223.

43 Finger, p. 223.

44 Matthew, 'Scarcity and Security,' p. 164.

45 *Ibid.*

46 Michael Renner, 'National Security: The Economic and Environmental Dimensions,' *Worldwatch Paper 89* (Worldwatch Institute, May 1989), p. 62.

47 Shin-wha Lee, 'Not a One-Time Event: Environmental Change, Ethnic Rivalry, and Violent Conflict in the Third World,' *Journal of Environment and Development* 6(4) (December 1997), pp. 365–96.

48 Marc Levy makes a similar observation. Marc A. Levy, 'Time for a Third Wave of Environment and Security Scholarship?' *Environment Change and Security Project Report*, Woodrow Wilson Center, Issue 1 (Spring 1995), pp. 44–6.

49 Thomas Homer-Dixon, 'On the Threshold: Environmental Changes as Causes of Acute Conflict,' *International Security* 16(2) (Fall 1991), pp. 76–116; Thomas Homer-Dixon, 'Environmental Security and Mass Violence,' in Geróid O'Tuathail, Simon Dalby, and Paul Routledge, eds, *The Geopolitics Reader* (London: Routledge, 1998), pp. 204–11.

50 Thomas F. Homer-Dixon and Valerie Percival, 'Environmental Scarcity and Violent Conflict: The Case of South Africa,' *Journal of Peace Research* 35(3) (1998), pp. 279–98.

51 Homer-Dixon, 'Environmental Scarcity and Mass Violence,' pp. 204–11.

52 Thomas F. Homer-Dixon, 'Project on Environment, Population, and Security: Key Findings of Research,' *Environmental Change and Security Project Report, Woodrow Wilson Center,* volume 2 (Spring 1996), pp. 45–57.

53 Homer-Dixon, 'Environmental Scarcity and Mass Violence,' p. 205.

54 Thomas F. Homer-Dixon, 'Environmental Scarcities and Violent Conflict: Evidence from Cases,' *International Security* 19(1) (Summer 1994), pp. 5–40.

55 Homer-Dixon, 'Project on Environment, Population, and Security,' pp. 45–57.

56 Homer-Dixon, 'Project on Environment, Population, and Security,' pp. 45–57.

57 Homer-Dixon, 'On the Threshold,' p. 78.

58 Homer-Dixon, 'Environmental Scarcities and Violent Conflict.'

59 Quoted in Robert D. Kaplan, 'The Coming Anarchy,' *Atlantic Monthly* 273(2) (February 1994), pp. 44–76.

60 Homer-Dixon, 'On the Threshold', pp. 76–116

61 Alexander Carius and Kerstin Imbusch, 'Environment and Security in International Politics – An Introduction,' in Alexander Carius and Kurt M. Lietzmann, eds, *Environmental Change and Security: A European Perspective* (Berlin and New York: Springer, 1999), p. 18.

62 Kaplan, pp. 44–76.

63 Michael N. Dobkowski and Isidor Wallimann, eds, *The Coming Age of Scarcity: Preventing Mass Death and Genocide in the Twenty-first Century* (Syracuse, NY: Syracuse University Press, 1998).

64 Marc A. Levy, 'Is the Environment a National Security Issue?' *International Security* 20(2) (Fall 1995), pp. 35–62.

65 Homer-Dixon, 'Environmental Change and Acute Conflict,' p. 81.

66 Geoffrey D. Dabelko and David D. Dabelko, 'Environmental Security: Issues of Conflict and Redefinition,' *Environmental Change and Security Project Report* 1 (Spring 1995), p. 6.

67 Rio Declaration on Environment and Development, 1992, Principle 24.

68 Arthur Westing, 'Environmental Warfare: An Overview,' in Arthur Westing, ed., *Environmental Warfare: A Technical, Legal, and Policy Appraisal* (London: Taylor & Francis, 1948), p. 3.

69 Finger, pp. 220–5.

70 Westing.

71 'International – Primates: Congo Civil War Endangering Great Apes,' *Greenwire,* 5 June 2000.

72 'Focus – Interview: Wildlife Protection in West and Central Africa,' *Greenwire,* 11 June 1991.

73 Joan McQueeny Mitrić, 'Who's Going to Clean up Serbia?' *Washington Post,* 9 July 2000, p. Bl.

74 Finger, p. 221.

75 Michael Renner, 'Assessing the Military's War on the Environment,' in Lester

Brown *et al.*, *The State of the World 1991* (New York: Norton, 1991), pp. 137–8.

76 Wendy Williams, 'Toxins on the Firing Range,' *Scientific American* June 2000, pp. 18, 20.

77 United States General Accounting Office, 'Water Pollution: Stronger Enforcement Needed to Improve Compliance at Federal Facilities,' (Washington, DC: GAO, 1988) GAO/RCED-89-144.

78 William Zimmerman, Elena Nikitina, and James Clem, 'The Soviet Union and the Russian Federation: A Natural Experiment in Environmental Compliance,' in Edith Brown Weiss and Harold K. Jacobson, eds, *Engaging Countries: Strengthening Compliance with International Environmental Accords* (Cambridge, MA: MIT Press, 1988), pp. 313–14.

79 Yereth Rosen, 'USSR Leaves Radioactive Legacy,' *Christian Science Monitor* 26 August 1992, p. 8.

80 International Convention for the Prevention of Pollution from Ships (1973), Article 3(3).

81 Convention on the Protection of the Marine Environment of the Baltic Sea Area (1992), Article 4(3).

82 'Methodological Issues Related to a Protocol or Another Legal Instrument: Draft Decision Submitted by the Committee of the Whole,' FCCC/CP/1997/ L.5, 8 December 1997; Joby Warrick, 'Kyoto Pact Includes a Pentagon Exemption; Armed Forces Permitted to Pollute During Some Overseas Missions,' *Washington Post*, 1 January 1998, p. A10.

83 Convention on the Law of the Non-Navigational Uses of International Watercourses (1997), Article 31. This treaty has not yet entered into force.

84 Finger, p. 222.

85 Finger, p. 224.

86 Ronald J. Diebert, 'From Deep Black to Green? Demystifying the Military Monitoring of the Environment,' *Environmental Change and Security Project Report*, Woodrow Wilson Center, Issue 2 (Spring 1996), pp. 28–9.

87 Diebert, p. 30.

88 Nunn, quoted in Butts.

89 Butts, p. 91.

90 Diebert, p. 29.

91 Michael D. King and David D. Herring, 'Monitoring Earth's Vital Signs,' *Scientific American* (April 2000), pp. 92–7.

92 Butts, p. 83.

93 Butts, p. 89.

94 Simon Dalby, 'The Politics of Environmental Security,' in Käkönen, ed., pp. 29–30.

95 Daniel Deudney, 'Environment and Security: Muddled Thinking,' *Bulletin of the Atomic Scientist* (April 1991), pp. 22–8.

96 *Ibid.*

97 Paterson, *Understanding Global Environmental Politics*.

98 See, for example, Jeremy Rifkin, *Biosphere Politics* (New York: Crown Publishers, Inc., 1991).

99 See, implicity, Matthews.

100 Deudney, 'Environment and Security: Muddled Thinking,' pp. 22–8.

101 Daniel Deudney, 'The Case Against Linking Environmental Degradation and National Security,' *Millennium* 19(3) (1990), pp. 461–76.

102 Hugh Dyer, 'Environmental Security as a Universal Value: Implications for International Theory,' in John Vogler and Mark Imber, eds, *The Environment and International Relations* (New York: The Global Environmental Change Program, 1996), pp. 22–40.

103 See, for example, Alexander Wendt, *Social Theory of International Politics* (Cambridge: Cambridge University Press, 1999).

104 Barry Buzan, *People, States, and Fear*, 2nd ed. (Hemel Hempstead: Harvester Wheatsheaf, 1991), p. 103.

105 Paterson, p. 20.

CHAPTER 4

1   R. W. White, 'Introduction,' in M. F. Ulman, ed., *Keeping Pace with Science and Engineering: Case Studies in Environmental Regulation* (Washington, DC: National Academy Press, 1993), p. 4.

2   Oran Young, 'Science and Social Institutions: Lessons for International Resource Regimes,' in Steinar Andresen and Willy Ostreng, eds, *International Resource Management: The Role of Science and Politics* (London and New York: Bellhaven Press, 1989), p. 12.

3   Jan-Stefan Fritz, 'Earthwatch Twenty-five Years On: Between Science and International Environmental Governance,' *International Environmental Affairs* 10(3) (Summer 1993), pp. 185–6.

4   Lawrence E. Susskind, *Environmental Diplomacy: Negotiating More Effective Environmental Agreements* (New York and Oxford: Oxford University Press, 1994), pp. 66–7.

5   Seong-lin Na and Hyun Song Shin, 'International Environmental Agreements Under Uncertainty,' *Oxford Economic Papers* 50(2) (April 1998), pp. 173–85.

6   See John Rawls, *A Theory of Justice* (Cambridge, MA: Bellknap Press of Harvard University Press, 1971).

7   Vienna Convention for the Protection of the Ozone Layer (1985), Articles 2 through 4 and Annexes I and II.

8   LRTAP 1979, Articles 4 and 9.

9   Framework Convention on Climate Change (1992), Article 4(1)(a).

10 Kenneth R. Foster, Paolo Veccia and Michael H. Repacholi, 'Science and the Precautionary Principle,' *Science* 288 (12 May 2000), p. 979.

11 Foster, Veccia, and Repacholi, p. 979.

12 Michele Territo, 'The Precautionary Principle in Marine Fisheries Conservation and the US Sustainable Fisheries act of 1996,' *Vermont Law Review* 24 (Summer 2000), p. 1356.

13 Vienna Convention (1985) Preamble; cited as the first treaty usage in Philippe Sands, *Principles of International Environmental Law*, vol. 1 (Manchester and New York: Manchester University Press, 1995), p. 209.

14 Daniel Bodansky, 'Scientific Uncertainty and the Precautionary Principle,' *Environment* 33(7) (September 1991), pp. 4–5, 43.

15 David VanderZwaag, 'The Precautionary Principle in Environmental Law and Policy: Elusive Rhetoric and First Embrace,' *Journal of Environmental Law and Practice*, 8(3) (October 1999), pp. 355–75.

16 Bodansky, pp. 4–5, 43.

17 Patrick Michaels, 'Environmental Rules Should Be Based on Science,' *Insight* (12 April 1993), p. 21.

18 S. Lichtenstein, P. Slovic, B. Fischhoff, M. Layman and B. Combs, 'Judged Frequency of Lethal Events,' *Journal of Experimental Psychology: Human Learning and Memory* 4 (1978), pp. 551–78.

19 Lichtenstein *et al.*, cited in Lola L. Lopes, 'Risk Perception and the Perceived Public,' in Daniel W. Bromley and Kathleen Segerson, eds, *The Social Response to Environmental Risk* (Boston, Dordrecht, and London: Kluwer Academic Publishers 1992), p. 60.

20 Sylvia Noble Tesch, *Uncertain Hazards* (Ithaca and London: Cornell University Press, 2000), p. 82.

21 Rose McDermott, *Risk-Taking in International Politics: Prospect Theory in American Foreign Policy* (Ann Arbor: University of Michigan Press, 1998), pp. 6–7.

22 Amos Tversky and Daniel Kahneman, 'Judgments of and by Representativeness,' in Daniel Kahneman, Paul Slovic, and Amos Tversky, eds, *Judgment Under Uncertainty: Heuristics and Biases* (Cambridge: Cambridge University Press, 1982), p. 84.

23 Robert Jervis, *Perception and Misperception in International Politics* (Princeton: Princeton University Press, 1976).

24 McDermott, p. 7.

25 McDermott, p. 8.

26 Dale Griffin and Amos Tversky, 'The Weighing of Evidence and the Determinants of Confidence,' *Cognitive Psychology* 24 (1992), p. 411.

27 Griffin and Tversky, pp. 411–35.

28 Robert W. Kates, 'Hazard and Choice Perception in Flood Plain Management,' *Research Paper 78*, Department of Geography, University of Chicago, 1962.

29 Paul Slovic, Baruch Fischhoff, and Sarah Lichtenstein, 'Rating the Risks,' *Environment* 21(3) (April 1979), pp. 14–20, 36–9.

30 Daniel Goleman, 'Hidden Rules Often Distort Ideas of Risk,' *New York Times*, 1 February 1994, p. C1.

31 McDermott, p. 6.

32 McDermott, p. 15.

33 McDermott, p. 16.

34 John von Neumann and Oskar Morgenstern, *Theory of Games and Economic*

Behavior, 2nd ed. (Princeton: Princeton University Press, 1947); McDermott, p. 17.

35 Daniel Kahneman and Amos Tversky, 'Prospect Theory: An Analysis of Decision Under Risk,' *Econometrica* 47(2) (March 1979), pp. 263–92.

36 McDermott, p. 30.

37 Jeffrey Berejekian, 'The Gains Debate: Framing State Choice,' *American Political Science Review* 91(4) (December 1997), pp. 789–805.

38 Robert Jervis, 'Political Implications of Loss Aversion,' *Political Psychology* 13 (1992), pp. 187–204.

39 Amos Tversky and Daniel Kahneman, 'Loss Aversion in Riskless Choice,' *Quarterly Journal of Economics* 41 (1991), pp. 1039–61.

40 Jack S. Levy, 'Loss Aversion, Framing, and Bargaining: The Implications of Prospect Theory for International Conflict,' *International Political Science Review* 17(2) (1996), pp. 179–95.

41 Chip Heath, and Richard P. Larrick and George Wu, 'Goals as Reference Points,' *Cognitive Psychology* 38 (1999), pp. 79–109.

42 Paul A. Kowert and Margaret G. Hermann, 'Who Takes Risks? Daring and Caution in Foreign Policy Making,' *Journal of Conflict Resolution* 41(5) (October 1996), pp. 611–37.

43 McDermott, pp. 45–75.

44 William A. Boettcher III, 'Context, Methods, Numbers, and Words: Prospect Theory in International Relations,' *Journal of Conflict Resolution* 39(3) (September 1995), pp. 561–83.

45 Kowert and Hermann, pp. 611–13.

46 Stephen J. Breyer, *Breaking the Vicious Circle: Toward Effective Risk Regulation* (Cambridge, MA: Harvard University Press, 1993), pp. 18–19.

47 Breyer, pp. 59–63.

48 Breyer, p. 73.

49 Sylvia Noble Tesh, *Environmental Activists and Scientific Proof* (Ithaca, NY, and London: Cornell University Press, 2000), pp. 86–99.

50 Tesh, pp. 95–7.

51 Michael K. Heiman, 'Science by the People: Grassroots Environmental Monitoring and the Debate over Scientific Expertise,' *Journal of Planning Education and Research* 6 (1997), pp. 291–303.

52 Paul Slovic, Baruch Fischhoff, and Sarah Lichtenstein, 'Rating the Risks,' *Environment* 21(3) (April 1979), pp. 14–20, 36–9.

53 Breyer, p. 14.

54 Lisa Heinzerling, 'Political Science,' *University of Chicago Law Review* 62 (Winter 1995), pp. 463–4.

55 Victor B. Flatt, 'Breaking the Vicious Circle: A Review,' *Environmental Law* 24(4) (October 1994), pp. 1707–28.

56 Flatt, p. 1715.

57 Heinzerling, p. 461–3.

58 Mary Douglas and Aaron Wildavsky, *Risk and Culture: An Essay on the Selection of Technical and Environmental Dangers* (Berkeley, Los Angeles, and

London: University of California Press, 1982).

59 Paul Slovic, 'Beyond Numbers: A Broader Perspective on Risk Perception and Risk Communication,' in Deborah G. Mayo and Rachelle D. Hollander, eds, *Acceptable Evidence: Science and Values in Risk Management* (New York and Oxford: Oxford University Press, 1991), pp. 62–3.

60 Peter M. Haas, 'Banning Chlorofluorocarbons: Epistemic Community Efforts to Protect Stratospheric Ozone,' *International Organization* 46(1) (Winter 1992), p. 187.

61 Emanuel Adler and Peter M. Haas, 'Conclusion: Epistemic Communities, World Order, and the Creation of a Reflective Research Paradigm,' *International Organization* 46(1) (Winter 1992), p. 389.

62 Peter M. Haas, 'Introduction: Epistemic Communities and International Policy Coordination,' *International Organization* 46(1) (Winter 1992), p. 1–35.

63 Martin List and Volker Rittberger, 'Regime Theory and International Environmental Management,' in Andrew Hurrell and Benedict Kingsbury, eds, *The International Politics of the Environment* (Oxford: Clarendon Press, 1992), pp. 85–107.

64 Jutta Brunee and Stephen J. Toope, 'Environmental Security and Freshwater Resources: Ecosystem Regime Building,' *American Journal of International Law* 91(1) (January 1997), pp. 26–59.

65 Jonathan Baert Wiener, 'On the Political Economy of Global Regulation,' *Georgetown Law Journal* 87 (February 1999), pp. 749–94.

66 Karen Liftin, *Ozone Discourses: Science and Politics in Global Environmental Cooperation* (New York: Columbia University Press, 1994).

67 Wiener, p. 772

68 See, for example, Jurgen Schmandt, Hilliard Roderick, and Andrew Morriss, 'Acid Rain Is Different,' in Jurgen Schmandt, Judith Clarkson, and Hilliard Roderick, eds, *Acid Rain and Friendly Neighbors: The Policy Dispute Between Canada and the United States*, revised edition (Duke University Press, 1988), p. 12.

69 Sheila Jasanoff, 'American Exceptionalism and the Political Acknowledgement of Risk,' *Daedalus* 119(4) (Fall 1990) pp. 395–406.

70 Ronald Brickman, Sheila Jasanoff, and Thomas Ilgen, *Controlling Chemicals: The Politics of Regulation in Europe and the United States* (Ithaca, NY, and London: Cornell University Press, 1985), p. 187.

71 Young, p. 20.

72 Liftin, p. 13.

73 Susskind, p. 65.

74 Sheila Jasanoff, 'Pluralism and Convergence in International Science Policy,' in *Science and Sustainability: Selected Papers on IIASA's 20th Anniversary* (Laxenburg: IIASA, 1992), p. 161.

75 Dale Jamieson, 'Scientific Uncertainty and the Political Process,' *Annals of the American Academy of Political and Social Sciences* 545 (May 1996), p. 38.

76 Jamieson, p. 39.

CHAPTER 5

1 Thomas Princen and Matthias Finger, 'Introduction,' in Thomas Princen and Matthias Finger, *Environmental NGOs in World Politics: Linking the Local and the Global* (New York: Routledge, 1994), p. 11.

2 Quoted in Kenny Bruno, 'The Corporate Capture of the Earth Summit,' *Multinational Monitor* 13 (July/August 1992), p. 18.

3 Kenneth N. Waltz, *Man, the State, and War* (New York: Columbia University Press, 1959); Hans J. Morgenthau, *Politics Among Nations: The Struggle for Power and Peace* (Boston: McGraw Hill, 1978).

4 Peter J. Spiro, 'New Global Communities: Nongovernmental Organizations in International Decision-Making Institutions,' *Washington Quarterly* 18(1) (1994), pp. 45–56.

5 Peter Willetts, ed., 'Introduction,' *The Conscience of the World: The Influence of Non-Governmental Organisations in the UN System* (Washington, DC: The Brookings Institution, 1996), p. 9.

6 'Citizens' Groups: The Non-Governmental Order – Will NGOs Democratise, or Merely Disrupt, Global Governance?' *The Economist*, 11 December 1999, p. 20.

7 The Yearbook of International Organizations, published by the Union of International Associations, lists more than 20,000 (1993–4, vol, 1, Munich: K. S. Saur, June 1993, cited in Willetts, p. 9). Others, such as the World Watch Institute, count the number of local NGOs in the millions. See 'Citizens' Groups,' *Economist*, p. 20.

8 Willetts, p. 10.

9 John McCormick, 'The Role of Environmental NGOs in International Regimes,' in Norman J. Vig and Regina S. Axelrod, *The Global Environment: Institutions, Law, and Policy* (Washington, DC: CQ Press, 1999), p. 57.

10 Elizabeth R. DeSombre, 'United Nations Conference on the Human Environment,' and 'United Nations Conference on Environment and Development,' in Andrew Goudie, ed., *Oxford Encyclopedia of Global Change* (New York and Oxford: Oxford University Press, 2000).

11 See, for examples, Alan Touraine, *Return of the Actor: Social Theory in Postindustrial Society* (Minneapolis: University of Minnesota Press, 1988).

12 Matthias Finger, 'NGOs and Transformation: Beyond Social Movement Theory,' in Princen and Finger, *Environmental NGOs in World Politics*, pp. 48–65.

13 Miguel Darcy de Oliveira and Rajesh Tandon, 'An Emerging Global Civil Society,' in Miguel Darcy de Oliveira and Rajesh Tandon, eds, *Citizens: Strengthening Global Civil Society* (Washington, DC: Civitas: World Alliance for Citizen Participation, 1994).

14 Claus Offe, *Contradictions of the Welfare State* (edited by John Keane) (Cambridge, MA: MIT Press, 1984); Princen and Finger, *Environmental NGOs in World Politics*.

15 Spiro, p. 47.

16 Ruben Cesar Fernandes, 'Threads of Planetary Citizenship,' in Darcy de Oliveria and Tandon, eds, pp. 319–46.

17 Paul Wapner, *Environmental Activism and World Civic Politics* (Albany, NY: SUNY Press, 1996), pp. 1–6.

18 Spiro, p. 48.

19 Steve Charnovitz, 'Two Centuries of Participation: NGOs and International Governance,' *Michigan Journal of International Law* 18 (Winter 1997), p. 270.

20 Shirin Sinnar 'Mixed Blessing: The Growing Influence of NGOs,' *Harvard International Review* (Winter 1995–6), pp. 54–7, 79.

21 Sinnar, p. 55.

22 See, for example, Tanja Bruhh, 'NGOs and Formation of International Environmental Regimes: Explaining Their Inclusion,' Paper presented at the Third Pan-European International Relations Conference, September 1998, Vienna, Austria; Sheila Jasanoff, 'NGOs and the Environment: From Knowledge to Action,' *Third World Quarterly* 18(3) (1997), pp. 579–94.

23 Margaret E. Keck and Kathryn Sikkink, *Activists Beyond Borders: Advocacy Networks in International Politics* (Ithaca, NY: Cornell University Press, 1998), p. 2.

24 Barbara J. Bramble and Gareth Porter, 'Non-Governmental Organizations and the Making of U.S. International Policy,' in Andrew Hurrell and Benedict Kingsbury, *The International Politics of the Environment* (Oxford: Clarendon Press, 1992), pp. 313–53.

25 John McCormick, 'The Role of Environmental NGOs in International Regimes,' in Regina S. Axelrod and Norman J. Vig, eds., *The Global Environment: Institutions, Law, and Policy* (Washington, DC: Congressional Quarterly, Inc., 1999), pp. 52–71.

26 Paul Wapner, 'Reorienting State Sovereignty: Rights and Responsibilities in the Environmental Age,' in Karen T. Liftin, ed., *The Greening of Sovereignty in World Politics* (Cambridge, MA: MIT Press, 1998), p. 284.

27 Karen Liftin, 'Ecoregimes: Playing Tug of War with the Nation-State,' in Ronnie Lipschutz and Ken Conca, eds, *The State and Social Power in Global Environmental Politics* (New York: Columbia University Press, 1993), p. 100.

28 Wapner, 'Reorienting State Sovereignty,' p. 285.

29 Interview with Ray Gambell, IWC Secretary, 3 June 1997, Histon, UK.

30 Leslie Spencer with Jan Bollwerk and Richard C. Morais, 'The Not So Peaceful World of Greenpeace,' *Forbes*, 11 November 1991, p. 174ff.

31 International Whaling Commission, 'Chairman's Report of the 47th Annual Meeting,' 1996, p. 41

32 International Convention for the Regulation of Whaling (1946), Article VII.

33 Wapner, 'Reorienting State Sovereignty,' p. 286.

34 P. J. Sands, 'The Role of Non-Governmental Organizations in Enforcing International Environmental Law,' in W. E. Butler, ed., *Control over Compliance with International Law* (Dordrecht: Martinus Nijhoff Publishers, 1991), pp. 61–8.

35 Paul Wapner, 'Politics Beyond the State: Environmental Activism and World

Civic Politics,' *World Politics* 47(3) (April 1995), p. 311.

36 Wapner, *Environmental Activism and World Civic Politics*, p. 53.

37 See, for example, Alex Chadwick, 'The Treasured Islands of Palmyra,' *National Geographic* (March 2001), pp. 46–56.

38 Wapner, *Environmental Activism and World Civic Politics*, p. 15.

39 Collette Ridgeway, 'Privately Protected Places,' *Cato Policy Report* (March/ April 1996). http://www.cato.org/pubs/policy_report/pr-xviii2-ridge-way.html. (date visited: 24 August 2000).

40 See David Potter, ed., *NGOs and Environmental Policies: Asia and Africa* (Portland, OR: Frank Cass, 1996).

41 Alan Thomas, 'NGO Advocacy, Democracy, and Policy Development,' in David Potter, ed., *NGOs and Environmental Policies: Asia and Africa* (Portland: Frank Cass, 1996), pp. 38–65.

42 Bernard Eccleston, 'Does North-South Collaboration Enhance NGO Influence on Deforestation Policies in Malaysia and Indonesia?' in Potter, ed., pp. 66–89; see also Charnovitz, p. 275–6.

43 Ricardo Arnt, 'The Inside out, The Outside In: Pros and Cons of Foreign Influence on Brazilian Environmentalism,' in Helga Ole Bergesen, Magnar Nordergaug, and Georg Parmann, eds, *Green Globe Yearbook 1992* (Oxford: Oxford University Press, 1993), p. 22.

44 Eccleston, p. 67.

45 Thomas, p. 61.

46 David Potter, 'Democratisation and the Environment: NGOs and Deforestation Policies in India (Karnataka) and Indonesia (North Sumatra),' in Potter, ed., pp. 9–38.

47 Thomas, p. 62.

48 Thomas Risse-Kappan, 'Ideas Do Not Float Freely: Transnational Coalitions, Domestic Structures, and the End of the Cold War,' *International Organization* 48(2) (Spring 1994), pp. 185–214.

49 Roger A. Payne, 'Nonprofit Environmental Organizations in World Politics: Domestic Structure and Transnational Relations,' *Policy Studies Review* 4(1) (Spring/Summer 1995), pp. 171–82.

50 Sinnar, p. 55.

51 Livio D. DeSimone and Frank Popoff with the World Business Council for Sustainable Development, *Eco-Efficiency: The Business Link to Sustainable Development* (Cambridge, MA: MIT Press, 1997).

52 T. E. Graedel and B. R. Allenby, *Industrial Ecology* (Upper Saddle River, NJ: Prentice-Hall, 1995), as quoted in Braden R. Allenby, *Industrial Ecology: Policy Framework and Implementation* (Upper Saddle River, NJ: Prentice-Hall, 1999), p. 40.

53 DeSimone and Popoff, pp. 31, 39–40.

54 Stuart L. Hart and Guatam Ahuja, 'Does It Pay to be Green? An Empirical Examination of the Relationship Between Emission Reduction and Firm Performance,' *Business Strategy and Environment* 5 (1996), pp. 30–7.

55 Cairncross, 'Cleaning Up.'

56 Charles S. Pearson, *Down to Business: Multinational Corporations, the Environment, and Development* (Washington, DC: World Resources Institute, 1985).

57 Bruce Smart, *Beyond Compliance* (Washington, DC: World Resources Institute, 1992), p. 250.

58 Michael S. Baram, 'Multinational Corporations, Private Codes, and Technology Transfer for Sustainable Development,' *Environmental Law* 24 (1) (1994), pp. 33–66.

59 Anthony J. Barbera and Virginia D. McConnell, 'The Impact of Environmental Regulations on Industry Productivity: Direct and Indirect Effects,' *Journal of Environmental Economics and Management* 18 (1990), pp. 56–65; Gary W. Yohe, 'The Backward Incidence of Pollution Control – Some Comparative Statics in General Equilibrium,' *Journal of Environmental Economics and Management* 6 (1979), pp. 187–98.

60 Michael E. Porter, 'America's Green Strategy,' *Scientific American* (April 1991), p. 168; Michael E. Porter, *The Competitive Advantage of Nations* (London: Macmillan Press, 1990), pp. 647–9.

61 OECD, *Environmental Policy and Technical Change* (Paris: Organization for Economic Cooperation and Development, 1985).

62 Pearson, p. 70.

63 Mancur Olson, Jr., *The Logic of Collective Action: Public Goods and the Theory of Groups* (Cambridge, MA: Harvard University Press, 1977).

64 David Vogel, 'Representing Diffuse Interests in Environmental Policy-making,' in David Vogel, *Do Institutions Matter? Government Capabilities in the United States and Abroad* (Washington, DC: The Brookings Institution, 1993). Vogel examines what types of institutional structures best represent these diffuse interests.

65 H. Jeffrey Leonard, *Pollution and the Struggle for World Product: Multinational Corporations, Environment, and International Comparative Advantage* (Cambridge: Cambridge University Press, 1988), p. 6.

66 Leonard, p. 7.

67 Arik Levinson, 'Environmental Regulations and Industry Location: International and Domestic Evidence,' in Jagdish Bhagwati and Robert E. Hudec, *Fair Trade and Harmonization: Prerequisites for Free Trade? Vol. I: Economic Analysis* (Cambridge, MA, and London: MIT Press, 1996), p. 450.

68 Cees van Beers and J. C. J. M. van der Bergh, 'An Empirical Multi-Country Analysis of the Impact of Environmental Regulations on Foreign Trade Flows,' *Kyklos* 50(1) (1999), pp. 29–46.

69 Both these states are seen as flags of convenience. 'Panama Increases Lead as Merchant Fleet Reaches Record Tonnage,' *Lloyds Register News Release* http://www.lr/org/new/pr/41wfs.html n.d. (date visited: 21 July 1998); Jim Morris, 'Lost at Sea: Accident Underscores Potential Hazards of Foreign Vessels,' *Houston Chronicle*, 16 December 1996, p. 162.

70 Elizabeth R. DeSombre, 'Flags of Convenience and the Implementation of International Environmental, Safety, and Labor Standards at Sea,'

International Politics 37(2), June 2000, pp. 213–32.

71 In the phrase of Ronie Garcia-Johnson, *Exporting Environmentalism: US Multinational Chemical Corporations in Brazil and Mexico* (Cambridge, MA: MIT Press, 2000).

72 *Ibid.*

73 *Ibid.*

74 Kenny Bruno and Jed Greer, *Greenwash: The Reality Behind Corporate Environmentalism* (Penang: Third World Nework/Apex Press, 1997).

75 See, for example, Charles S. Pearson, *Down to Business: Multinational Corporations, the Environment, and Development* (Washington, DC: World Resources Institute, 1985).

76 Charnovitz, p. 277.

77 Wapner, *Environmental Activism and World Civic Politics*.

78 Steve Charnovitz, p. 269.

79 Helmut Breitmeier and Volker Rittberger, 'Environmental NGOs in an Emerging Global Civil Society,' Centre for International Relations/Peace and Conflict Studies, Institute for Political Science, University of Tübingen, No. 32.

80 Eccleston, pp. 71–4.

81 Kal Raustiala, 'States, NGOs, and International Environmental Institutions,' *International Studies Quarterly* 41 (1997), pp. 719–40.

82 M. Shaw, 'Global Civil Society and Global Responsibility,' *Millennium* 21(3) (1992), p. 434.

83 Steven J. Kobrin, 'Testing the Bargaining Hypothesis in the Manufacturing Sector in Developing Countries,' *International Organization* 41(4) (Autumn 1987), pp. 609–38.

84 Matthias Finger and James Kilcoyne, 'Why Transnational Corporations Are Organizing to "Save the Environment," ' *The Ecologist* 27(4) (August 1997), p. 142.

85 Jennifer Clapp, 'Multinational Corporations and Environmental Hazards in the Asia-Pacific Region,' paper prepared for the International Studies Association Annual Meeting, San Diego, April 1996.

86 Frances Cairncross, 'Cleaning Up,' *The Economist*, 8 September 1990, pp. Slff.; Frances Cairncross, *Costing the Earth* (Boston: Harvard Business School Press, 1991).

87 Nick Butler, 'Companies in International Relations,' *Survival* 21(1) (Spring 2000), pp. 149–64.

88 Nazli Choucri, 'The Global Environment and Multinational Corporations,' *Technology Review* 94(3) (April 1991), pp. 52–60.

89 Interestingly, both the WBCSD and its critics agree with this assessment. Jed Greer and Kenny Bruno, *Greenwash: The Reality Behind Corporate Environmentalism* (Panag, Malaysia: Third World Network, 1996), p. 14; Stephan Schmidheiny and Federico Zorroquín Livio with the World Business Council for Sustainable Development, *Financing Change: The Financial Community, Eco-Efficiency, and Sustainable Development* (Cambridge, MA: MIT Press, 1996).

90 Ross Gelbspan, *The Heat Is On* (Reading, MA: Addison-Wesley, 1997), p. 34.

91 Gelbspan, p. 85. See Chapter 6 for more details.

92 Marie Price, 'Ecopolitics and Environmental Nongovernmental Organizations in Latin America,' *Geographical Review* 84(1) (January 1994), p. 55.

93 Keck and Sikkink, pp. 2–3.

94 Keck and Sikkink, pp. 121, 133–5, 155–6. They argue that the idea of tropical deforestation as an issue area did not even exist in the early 1970s, but was framed as an issue by environmental organizations in response to specific problems.

95 Bramble and Porter, pp. 321–2.

96 Cairncross, 'Cleaning Up,' p. S1.

97 Finger and Kilcoyne.

98 Kenneth A. Oye and James H. Maxwell, 'Self-Interest and Environmental Management,' in Robert O. Keohane and Elinor Ostrom, eds, *Local Commons and Global Interdependence: Heterogeneity and Cooperation in Two Domains,* (Newbury Park, CA: Sage, 1995), pp. 191–221.

99 Randall B. Ripley and Grace A. Franklin, *Congress, the Bureaucracy, and Public Policy,* revised edition (Homewood, IL: The Dorsey Press, 1980), p. 123.

100 Elizabeth R. DeSombre, *Domestic Sources of International Environmental Policy: Industry, Environmentalists, and US Power* (Cambridge, MA: MIT Press, 2000).

101 Wapner, *Environmental Activism and World Civic Politics,* p. 120; see also Charnovitz, p. 274.

102 Per Lindstrom, 'The Role of NGOs as Seen by the United Nations and Its Member States,' in Jurgen Schramm, ed., *The Role of Non-Governmental Organizations in the New European Order* (Germany: Nomos Verlagsgesellschaft, 1995), p. 46.

103 Erik Hundewadt, 'The Role of Voluntary Associations (NGOs) in a Democratic Society,' in Schramm, ed., pp. 7–12.

104 Tim Richardson, Jiri Dusik, and Pavla Jidrova, 'Parallel Public Participation: An Answer to Inertia in Decision-making,' *Environmental Impact Assessment Review* 18 (1998), pp. 201–16.

105 Price, p. 57.

106 John Clark, *Democratizing Development: The Role of Voluntary Organizations* (West Hartford, CT: Kumarian Press, 1990).

107 Darcy de Olivera and Tandon, pp. 1–17.

108 Rusli bin Mohd and Jan G. Laarman, 'The Struggle for Influence: US Nongovernmental Organizations and Tropical Forests,' *Journal of Forestry* 92(6) (June 1994), p. 35.

109 Jonathan A. Fox and L. David Brown, 'Introduction,' in Jonathan Fox and L. David Brown, eds, *The Struggle for Accountability: The World Bank, NGOs, and Grassroots Movements* (Cambridge, MA: MIT Press 1998), p. 3.

110 McCormick, p. 60.

111 George Aditjondro, 'A Reflection About a Decade of International Advocacy Efforts on Indonesian Environmental Issues,' paper presented at the International NGO Group on Indonesia Conference, Bonn, Germany, April

1990, p. 16; quoted in L. David Brown and Jonathan A. Fox, 'Accountability Within Transnational Coalitions,' in Fox and Brown, eds, p. 441.
112 Sinnar.
113 Hundewalt, p. 11.

CHAPTER 6

1 Arun Makhijani and Kevin R. Gurney, *Mending the Ozone Hole: Science, Technology, and Policy* (Cambridge, MA, and London: The MIT Press, 1995), pp. 93–114.
2 Makhijani and Gurney, pp. 51–90.
3 Irving M. Mintzer and J. Amber Leonard, eds, *Negotiating Climate Change* (Cambridge: Cambridge University Press, 1994).
4 M. J. Molina and F. S. Rowland, 'Stratospheric Sink for Chlorofluoro-methanes: Chlorine Atom-catalyzed Destruction of Ozone,' *Nature* 249 (1974), pp. 810–12.
5 Vienna Convention for the Protection of the Ozone Layer (1985), Article 2.
6 Vienna Convention, Article 9(4).
7 London Amendments to the Montreal Protocol (1990).
8 Copenhagen Amendments to the Montreal Protocol (1992).
9 Montreal Amendments to the Montreal Protocol (1997).
10 Geoffrey Palmer, 'New Ways to Make International Environmental Law,' *American Journal of International Law* 86 (April 1992), pp. 274–6.
11 Montreal Protocol (as amended), Article 2(9).
12 For a comparison, see Edith Brown Weiss, 'The Five International Treaties: A Living History,' in Edith Brown Weiss and Harold K. Jacobson, *Engaging Countries: Strengthening Compliance with International Environmental Accords* (Cambridge, MA: MIT Press, 1998), pp. 140–4.
13 Discussed in Matthew Paterson, *Global Warming and Global Politics* (London and New York: Routledge, 1996), pp. 17–21.
14 Paterson, pp. 22–3.
15 Marvin S. Soroos, 'The Atmosphere as an International Common Property Resource,' in S. S. Nagel, ed., *Global Policy Studies* (London: Macmillan, 1991), p. 201.
16 See Ian H. Rowlands, *The Politics of Global Atmospheric Change* (Manchester and London: Manchester University Press, 1995), pp. 68–72.
17 Intergovernmental Panel on Climate Change, 'About IPCC,' n.d. http://www.ipcc.ch/about/about.htm (date visited: 24 June 2001).
18 Framework Convention on Climate Change 1992, Articles 2 and 4.
19 Kyoto Protocol to the Framework Convention on Climate Change, 1997.
20 Framework Convention on Climate Change, Conference of the Parties, 'Actions Taken by the Conference of the Parties,' 4th Session, Annex 60, FCCC/CP/1997/7/Add.1, 1997 (1999).
21 Rowlands, p. 55.

22 Richard A. Kerr, 'Antarctic Ozone Hole Is Still Deepening,' *Science* 232 (27 June 1986), p. 1602.

23 Robert T. Watson, F. Sherwood Rowland, and John Gille, *Ozone Trends Panel: Executive Summary* (Washington, DC: NASA, 1988).

24 Karen T. Liftin, *Ozone Discourses: Science and Politics in Global Environmental Cooperation* (New York: Columbia University Press, 1994; see especially Chapter 4.

25 Liftin, p. 82.

26 Edward A. Parson, 'Protecting the Ozone Layer,' in Peter M. Haas, Robert O. Keohane, and Marc A. Levy, eds, *Institutions for the Earth* (Cambridge, MA: MIT Press, 1993), p. 47.

27 Intergovernmental Panel on Climate Change 'Summary for Policymakers: A Report of Working Group I of the Intergovernmental Panel on Climate Change,' 20 January 2001, available at http://www.ipcc.ch (date visited: 24 June 2001), p. 10.

28 IPCC, p. 9.

29 Quoted in Rowlands, p. 78.

30 Richard A. Kerr, 'Rising Global Temperature, Rising Uncertainty,' *Science* 292 (13 April 2001), pp. 192–4.

31 Quoted in Kerr, 'Rising Global Temperature,' p. 194.

32 Jason Webb, 'Scientists Clearing up Clouds' Effects on Climate,' *Reuters News Service*, 10 November 1998.

33 Patricia Reaney, 'Deep Ocean Current Linked to Global Climate Change,' *Reuters News Service*, 3 August 2000; Global Commons Institute, 'Draft Proposals for a Climate Change Protocol Based on Contraction and Convergence,' Section 2.14, September 1996, http://www.gci.org.uk/contconv/protweb.html (date visited: 26 June 2001).

34 Fred Pearce, 'A Cool Trick,' *New Scientist*, 8 April 2000, p. 18; 'Sinking CO_2' *Environment* 43(2) (March 2001), p. 6.

35 Dale Jamieson, 'Scientific Uncertainty and the Political Process,' *Annals of the American Academy of Political and Social Sciences* 545 (May 1996), pp. 35–43.

36 Quoted in Kerr, 'Rising Global Temperature,' p. 194.

37 Alan S. Miller, 'Incentives for CFC Substitutes: Lessons for Other Greenhouse Gases,' in John C. Topping, ed., *Coping with Climate Change: Proceedings of the Second North American Conference on Preparing for Climate Change* (Washington DC: Climate Institute, 1989), p. 547. Miller does not himself make this argument, but mentions others who do. For others who follow this logic implicitly, see Detlef Sprinz and Tapani Vaahtoranta, 'The Interest-based Explanation of International Environmental Policy,' *International Organization* 48(1), pp. 93–4; James K. Sebenius, 'Challenging Conventional Explanations of International Cooperation: Negotiation Analysis and the Case of Epistemic Communities,' *International Organization* 46(1), p. 358.

38 Richard Elliot Benedick, *Ozone Diplomacy: New Directions in Safeguarding the Planet*, enlarged edition (Cambridge, MA: Harvard University Press, 1998),

pp. 31, 33.

39   Alliance for Responsible CFC Policy, *A Search for Alternatives to the Current Commercial Fluorocarbons*, 24 February 1986, as quoted in Miller, p. 549.

40   Miller, p. 547.

41   David Victor, 'The Montreal Protocol's Non-Compliance Procedure,' in David G. Victor, Kal Raustiala, and Eugene B. Skolnikoff, *The Implementation and Effectiveness of International Environmental Commitments* (Cambridge, MA: The MIT Press, 1998), p. 147.

42   This explanation is considered and discarded by Edward A. Parson, 'Protecting the Ozone Layer,' in Peter M. Haas, Robert O. Keohane, and Marc A. Levy, *Institutions for the Earth: Sources of Effective International Environmental Protection* (Cambridge, MA: The MIT Press, 1993), p. 66.

43   Miller, p. 550.

44   Elizabeth DeSombre, and Joanne Kauffman, 'The Montreal Protocol Multi-lateral Fund: Partial Success Story,' in Robert O. Keohane and Marc A. Levy, *Institutions for Environmental Aid* (Cambridge, MA: The MIT Press, 1996), p. 95.

45   Kenneth Oye and James H. Maxwell, 'Self-Interest and Environmental Management,' in Robert O. Keohane and Elinor Ostrom, eds, *Local Commons and Global Interdependence: Heterogeneity and Cooperation in Two Domains* (Newbury Park, CA: Sage, 1995), p. 198.

46   John C. Dernbach, 'Sustainable Development as a Framework for National Governance,' *Case Western Reserve Law Review* 49(1) (Fall 1998), p. 93.

47   Owen Greene, 'The System for Implementation Review in the Ozone Regime,' Victor, Raustiala, Skolnikoff, pp. 97–8.

48   Rowlands, pp. 126–50.

49   Ross Gelbspan, *The Heat Is On: The High Stakes Battle over Earth's Threatened Climate* (Reading, MA: Addison-Wesley, 1997), p. 34.

50   Timothy Gardner, 'Global Warming Business Group Cools Its Message,' *Reuters News Service*, 9 November 2000; Patrick Connole, 'Ford Exits Anti-Kyoto Climate Change Group,' *Reuters News Service* 7 December 1999; 'Texaco Quits Anti-Kyoto Climate Change Group,' *Reuters News Service*, 2 March 2001.

51   Lee Daniels, 'Texaco Buys 20 Percent Stake in Energy Conversion Company,' *Reuters News Service* 7 June 2000.

52   Gelbspan, pp. 88–9.

53   Greg Schneider, 'Taking No Chances: Disaster-conscious Firms Treat Global Warming as a Reality,' *Washington Post*, 26 June 2001, p. E01.

54   'Shell to Provide Solar Power for Chinese Homes,' *Reuters News Service*, 3 July 2001.

55   Abigail Levene, 'Greenpeace Boards "Wrong" Oil Rig in Bush Protest,' *Reuters News Service*, 18 June 2001.

56   Paul Wapner, *Environmental Activism and World Civic Politics* (Albany, NY: SUNY Press, 1996), p. 127.

57   Michele M. Betsill, 'Linking the Local and Global in Climate Change

Policies,' Paper prepared for delivery at the Annual Meeting of the American Political Science Association, September 2000.

58 Tufts Climate Initiative, 'Who We Are,' http://www.tufts.edu/tie/tci/Who-WeAre.html (date visited: 4 July 2001).

59 David G. Victor, *The Collapse of the Kyoto Protocol and the Struggle to Slow Global Warming* (Princeton: Princeton University Press, 2001).

60 Friends of the Earth, *Funding Change: Developing Countries and the Montreal Protocol*, 1990.

61 Richard Benedick, *Ozone Diplomacy: New Directions in Safeguarding the Planet* (Cambridge, MA: Harvard University Press, 1991), p. 151.

62 Montreal Protocol, Article 4.

63 DeSombre and Kauffman, p. 96.

64 Benedick, Chapter 13.

65 Montreal Protocol Article 10; see also Elizabeth R. DeSombre and Joanne Kauffman, 'The Montreal Protocol Multilateral Fund: Partial Success Story,' in Robert O. Keohane and Marc A. Levy, *Institutions for Environmental Aid* (Cambridge, MA: The MIT Press, 1996), pp. 89–126.

66 The Secretariat of the Multilateral Fund, 'General Information,' http://www.unmfs.org/general.htm; date visited: 5 June 2001.

67 Chandrashekhar Dasgupta, 'The Climate Change Negotiations,' in Irving Mintzer and J. A. Leonard, eds, *Negotiating Climate Change* (Cambridge: Cambridge University Press, 1994), pp. 138–9; see also Michael Grubb *et al.*, *The Earth Summit Agreements: A Guide and Assessment* (London: Earthscan Publications Ltd., 1993).

68 Paterson, p. 66.

69 David Fairman, 'The Global Environmental Facility: Haunted by the Shadow of the Future,' in Robert O. Keohane and Marc A. Levy, eds, *Institutions for Environmental Aid: Pitfalls and Promise*, Cambridge, MA, and London: The MIT Press, 1996, pp. 55–87.

70 FCCC, Article 4(3).

71 FCCC, Article 4(7).

72 Kyoto Protocol, Article 11.

73 Helen Dewar, 'Senate Advises Against Emissions Treaty That Lets Developing Nations Pollute,' *Washington Post*, 26 July 1997, p. A11.

74 Kyoto Protocol, Annex B.

75 Brown Weiss, pp. 154–5.

76 Saleem S. Saab, 'Move over Drugs, There's Something Cooler on the Black Market – Freon,' *Dickenson Journal of International Law* 16 (Spring 1998), p. 634.

77 'Chemical Production: Holed Up,' *The Economist*, 9 December 1995, p. 63.

78 Better Hileman, 'Ozone Treaty: Successful But Pitfalls Remain,' *Chemical and Engineering News*, 15 September 1997, p. 24.

79 S. A. Montzka, J. H. Butler, J. W. Elkins, T. M. Thompson, A. D. Clarke, and L. T. Locke, 'Present and Future Trends in the Atmospheric Burden on Ozone-Depleting Halogens,' *Nature* 398 (22 April 1999), pp. 690–3.

80 Frederick Pool Landers Jr., 'The Black Market Trade in Chlorofluorocarbons: The Montreal Protocol Makes Banned Refrigerants a Hot Commodity,' *Georgia Journal of International and Comparative Law* 26 (Spring 1997), pp. 478–9.

81 The amount exported is limited to 15 percent of a country's 1986 consumption level. Jennifer Clapp, 'The Illegal CFC Trade: An Unexpected Wrinkle in the Ozone Protection Regime,' *International Environmental Affairs* 9(4) (1997), p. 261.

82 Duncan Brack, *International Trade and the Montreal Protocol* (London: Earthscan Publications, Ltd, 1996), p. 105.

83 Decision IV/24 of the Parties to the Montreal Protocol Ozone Secretariat, *Handbook for the Montreal Protocol on Substances That Deplete the Ozone Layer*, 3rd edition (August 1993), p. 32; Landers, p. 473.

84 Clapp, p. 265.

85 Clapp, p. 266.

86 Brack, p. 105.

87 Ronald Begley, Allison Lucas, and Michael Roberts, 'Producers Set for CFC Phaseout,' *Chemical Week* 157(23), 13 December 1996, p. 40.

88 David Sheff, 'The Chilling Effect,' *Outdoor Magazine* (August 1997), p. 91.

89 W. Wayt Gibbs, 'The Treaty That Worked – Almost,' *Scientific American* 273 (September 1995), p. 18.

90 Paul Brand, 'Hot Question for Air Conditioner: Recharge or Convert?' *Minneapolis Star Tribune*, 31 July 1999, p. 1M.

91 Paul Eckert, 'Update – EU Says China to Back Climate Pact Without US,' *Reuters News Service*, 10 April 2001.

92 Tim Breen, 'Climate Change II: Voluntary Greenhouse Gas Reductions "Significant" – UNEP,' *Greenwire*, 2 July 2001.

CHAPTER 7

1 The extent to which this statement is true depends on the extent to which whales are simply regarded as a natural resource to be managed; that definition has been called into question politically by non-governmental actors in important ways in the last 30 years.

2 International Convention for the Regulation of Whaling (1946), Preamble.

3 Garrett Hardin, 'The Tragedy of the Commons,' *Science* 162 (1968), pp. 1243–8.

4 Patricia Birnie, *International Regulation of Whaling: From Conservation of Whaling to Conservation of Whales and Regulation of Whale Watching. Vol. I and II* (New York: Oceana Publications, 1985); Steinar Andresen, 'Science and Politics in the International Management of Whales,' *Marine Policy* 13 (April 1989), p. 99–117.

5 This is the decision-making body constituted by the International Convention for the Regulation of Whaling.

6   Interview with Ray Gambell, IWC Secretary, August 1993; Ronald Mitchell, 'Membership Compliance, and Non-compliance in the International Convention for the Regulation of Whaling 1946–Present.' Paper presented at Harvard University, International Environmental Institutions Research Seminar, October 1992 p. 7. Cited with permission.

7   Richard Ellis, *Men and Whales* (New York: Lyons Press, 1999), p. 33.

8   Daniel Francis, *A History of World Whaling* (Ontario: Viking, 1990), pp. 21–2.

9   Francis, pp. 31–5.

10 Francis, p. 79.

11 Francis, p. 143.

12 Daniel Francis, 1990, p. 208.

13 Francis, pp. 209–10.

14 Karl Brandt, *Whale Oil: An Economic Analysis*. Fats and Oil Studies No. 7 (Stanford: Stanford University, 1940), pp. 92–4, quoted in Marc A. Levy, 'Leviathan's Leviathan: Power, Interests, and Institutional Change in the International Whaling Commission,' unpublished paper, Harvard University, June 1986.

15 Levy, p. 6.

16 Francis, p. 210.

17 Andresen, p. 101; Birnie, *International Regulation of Whaling*, pp. 191–2.

18 ICRW Preamble.

19 Birnie, *International Regulation of Whaling*, p. 178.

20 J. N. Tønnessen and A. O. Johnsen, *The History of Modern Whaling* (Berkeley: University of California Press, 1982), p. 511.

21 Birnie, *International Regulation of Whaling*, pp. 180.

22 If an objection is registered there is an additional 90-day period during which other states may decide to object to the same measure. *International Convention for the Regulation of Whaling*, Article 5(3).

23 *International Convention for the Regulation of Whaling*, Article 5(2)(c).

24 The change to quotas on individual stocks was completed by this time; it had, however, begun gradually earlier with some stock quotas in the North Pacific.

25 Birnie, *International Regulation of Whaling*, pp. 453, 461; Andresen, p. 106. This determination involved comparing the current population size to the maximum sustainable yield (MSY).

26 Colin W. Clark and R. Lamberson, 'An Economic History and Analysis of Pelagic Whaling,' *Marine Policy* 6(2) (April 1992), pp. 107–9.

27 Birnie, *International Regulation of Whaling*, p. 243.

28 Birnie, *International Regulation of Whaling*, p. 247.

29 Birnie, *International Regulation of Whaling*, p. 314.

30 International Convention for the Regulation of Whaling, Article 5(2)(b).

31 Birnie, *International Regulation of Whaling*, p. 191.

32 D. S. Butterworth, 'Science and Sentimentality,' *Nature* 357 (18 June 1992), pp. 532–4.

33 See, generally, Birnie, *International Regulation of Whaling*, for reports from the SC.

34 Butterworth, p. 533.
35 G. Elliot, 'Failure of the International Whaling Commission 1946–1966,' 3 *Marine Policy* (1979), pp. 149–55; Birnie, p. 198.
36 Birnie, *International Regulation of Whaling*, p. 364.
37 Steinar Andresen, 'Science and Politics in the International Management of Whales,' *Marine Policy* (April 1989), p. 100.
38 Ellis, p. 421.
39 Birnie, *International Regulation of Whaling*, p. 335; M. J. Peterson, 'Whalers, Cetologists, Environmentalists, and the International Management of Whaling,' *International Organization* 46(1) (Winter 1992), p. 163.
40 Andresen, p. 104.
41 Andresen, p. 105.
42 Andresen, p. 107.
43 Andresen, p. 110.
44 Andresen, p. 107.
45 International Whaling Commission schedule, 1992, ¶ 10e.
46 G. P. Donovan, 'Forty-second Annual Meeting of the International Whaling Commission, June 1989 [sic],' *Polar Record* 24, pp. 631–63.
47 *International Convention for the Regulation of Whaling*, Article IX(1).
48 Andresen claims that the true name of this organization is the 'Committee of International Whaling Statistics,' but it is known by its other name within the IWC. Andresen, p. 103.
49 It does so by informing whalers a week before it predicts the catch limits will be reached of what the closing date of the season will thus be.
50 Birnie, *International Regulation of Whaling*, p. 338.
51 The main form of punishment was to deny a whaler the fee from an illegally caught whale.
52 G. Elliot, 'The Failure of the International Whaling Commission 1946–1966,' 3 *Marine Policy* (1979), pp. 149–55; Birnie, *International Regulation of Whaling*, p. 198.
53 Greenwire, 'Worldview – Whaling: Soviet Kills Could Affect Sanctuary Decision,' 22 February 1994.
54 Paul Brown, 'Soviet Union Illegally Killed Great Whales,' *Guardian*, 12 February 1994, p. 14; interview with Ray Gambell, IWC Secretary, August 1993. The whole Soviet whaling industry was run as a covert operation.
55 Brown, p. 12.
56 'Call Me Smiley,' *New York Times Magazine*, 13 March 1994, p. 14.
57 United States Public Law 92–219, sec. 8.
58 16 *United States Code* 182.
59 Elizabeth R. DeSombre, *Domestic Sources of International Environmental Policy: Industry, Environmentalists, and US Power* (Cambridge, MA: MIT Press, 2000), pp. 210–11.
60 DeSombre, p. 212.
61 This phenomenon is seen more broadly than in just whaling; ships of all sorts register in 'flag of convenience' countries to get around international

regulations. In the case of the Olympic Whaling Company, it chose specifically to register vessels in locations where it would not be bound by international rules.

62 Tønnessen and Johnsen, pp. 534–8.

63 Mitchell, p. 19.

64 Birnie, *International Regulation of Whaling*, p. 235.

65 Gene S. Martin, Jr., and James W. Brennan, 'Enforcing the International Convention for the Regulation of Whaling: The Pelly and Packwood-Magnuson Amendments,' *Denver Journal of International Law and Policy* 17(2) (1989), pp. 293–315.

66 The Supreme Court ultimately ruled that certification was at the discretion of the Secretary of Commerce and could not be required, but lower courts had ruled otherwise, and the possibility seemed real that Japan would be certified. *Japan Whaling Association v. American Cetacean Society* 478 US 221, 105 S Ct, 2860 (1986); DeSombre, p. 209.

67 International Whaling Commission, 1993, *Verbatim Record*, p. 198.

68 Patricia Birnie, 'The Role of Developing Countries in Nudging the International Whaling Commission from Regulating Whaling to Encouraging Nonconsumptive Uses of Whales,' *Ecology Law Quarterly* 12(1985), p. 955.

69 Wapner, pp. 52, 54.

70 Robert Hunter, *Warriors of the Rainbow: A Chronicle of the Greenpeace Movement* (New York: Holt, Reinhart, & Winston, 1979), p. 229.

71 Robert Mandel, 'Transnational Resource Conflict: The Politics of Whaling,' in *International Studies Quarterly* (March 1984), pp. 99–127.

72 Peterson, p. 175.

73 Birnie, 'The Role of Developing Countries,' p. 953.

74 Alan Macnow, a consultant to the Japan Whaling Association, argues that these states in particular, along with ten others, were recruited to the organization by anti-whaling groups. 'A Whaling Moratorium Opposed by IWC's Own Scientists,' Letter to the Editor, *New York Times*, 29 September 1984, p. 22.

75 Leslie Spencer, with Jan Bollwerk and Richard C. Morais, 'The Not So Peaceful World of Greenpeace,' *Forbes*, 11 November 1991, p. 174ff (Lexis/Nexis).

76 International Whaling Commission, 'Chairman's Report of the 47th Annual Meeting' (1996), p. 41.

77 Pro-whaling states did what they could as well to provide support to countries that would vote in favor of continued commercial whaling. See Day, pp. 103–5, 107; Paul Brown, 'Playing Football with the Whales,' *Guardian*, 1 May 1993, p. 26.

78 Mitchell, pp. 6–7.

79 'Iceland Rejoins IWC, But Exempt from Whaling Ban,' *Reuters News Service*, 4 July 2001.

80 Interview with Ray Gambell, June 1997.

81 Douglas H. Chadwick, 'Pursuing the Minke,' *National Geographic* 199(4)

(April 2000), pp. 58–71.

82 'A New Era for the IWC,' *Greenpeace Magazine* (October–November–December, 1991), p. 5.

83 'International Whaling Commission: 50th Annual Meeting: Opening Statement by the United Kingdom Delegation,' IWC/50/OS/UK, 1998.

84 Mitchell.

85 Alex Kirby, 'Whaling Ban Set to End,' *BBC News*, 11 June 2000. http://news.bbc.co.uk/hi/english/sci/tech/newsid 782999/782697.stm (date visited: 12 June 2000); Daniel Mclaughlin, 'Whaling Watchdog Aims to Regain Control over Seas,' *Reuters, Planet Ark*, 13 June 2000.

CHAPTER 8

1 Peter Bunyard, 'Eradicating the Amazon Rainforests Will Wreak Havoc on Climate,' *The Ecologist* 29(2) (March–April 1999), pp. 81–4.

2 Convention on Biological Diversity (1992), preamble.

3 Rio Declaration (1992), Principle 2. Similar wording is found in the Stockholm Declaration from 1972 and elsewhere in customary international law.

4 Bolivia, Brazil, Colombia, Ecuador, Guyana, Peru, Suriname, and Venezuela are generally thought to be the states that contain part of the Amazon rainforest. The forest itself is defined to some extent as the watershed of the Amazon River, leading to some disagreement about where its actual boundaries lie.

5 Norman Myers, Russell A. Mittermeier, Cristina G. Da Foseca, A. B. Gustavo, and Jennifer Kent, 'Biodiversity Hotspots for Conservation Priorities' *Nature* 403 (24 February 2000), pp. 853–8.

6 World Resources Institute, *World Resources 1992–1993* (New York: Oxford University Press, 1992), p. 128.

7 Mohammed Dore and Jorge Noguiera, 'The Amazon Rain Forest, Sustainable Development and the Biodiversity Convention: A Political Economy Perspective,' *Ambio* 23(8) (December 1994), pp. 492.

8 Bunyard, pp. 81–4.

9 Bunyard, pp. 81–4.

10 Andrew Hurrell, 'Brazil and the International Politics of Amazonian Deforestation,' in Andrew Hurrell and Benedict Kingsbury, eds, *The International Politics of the Environment: Actors, Interests, and Institutions* (Oxford: Clarendon Press, 1992), pp. 399–400.

11 Peter H. Raven and Jeffrey A. McNeely, 'Biological Extinction: Its Scope and Meaning for Us,' in Lakshman D. Guruswamy and Jeffrey A. McNeely, *Protection of Global Biodiversity: Converging Strategies* (Durham, NC: Duke University Press, 1998), p. 15.

12 Raven and McNeely, p. 20.

13 Rachel McCleary, 'Development Strategies in Conflict: Brazil and the Future

of the Amazon,' *Pew Case Studies in International Affairs 501* (Washington, DC: Institute for the Study of Diplomacy, 1990), p. 6.

14 Norman Myers, 'The Anatomy of Environmental Action: The Case of Tropical Deforestation,' in Andrew Hurrell and Benedict Kingsbury, eds, *The International Politics of the Environment: Actors, Interests, and Institutions* (Oxford: Clarendon Press, 1992), p. 432.

15 McCleary, p. 7.

16 McCleary, p. 6.

17 Myers, p. 432.

18 Laura Murphy, Richard Bilsborrow and Francisco Pinchon, 'Poverty and Prosperity Among Migrant Settlers in the Amazon Rainforest Frontier of Ecuador,' *Journal of Development Studies* 34(2) (December 1997), pp. 35–66.

19 McCleary, p. 10.

20 McCleary, p. 11.

21 Margaret E. Keck and Kathryn Sikkink, *Activists Beyond Borders: Advocacy Networks in International Politics* (Ithaca, NY: Cornell University Press, 1998), pp. 137–40.

22 McCleary, p. 10.

23 McCleary, p. 8.

24 McCleary, p. 9.

25 Andrew Hurrell, 'The Politics of Amazonian Deforestation,' *Journal of Latin American Studies* 23 (1991), p. 203.

26 Myers, p. 444.

27 Myers, p. 445.

28 McCleary, p. 7.

29 Alex Shoumatoff, *The World Is Burning* (Boston: Little, Brown & Company, 1990), p. 85.

30 Myers, p. 443.

31 Dore and Nogueira, p. 496; McCleary, p. 6.

32 Myers, p. 434.

33 Graciela Chichilnisky, 'Sustainable Development and North-South Trade,' in Lakshman D. Guruswamy and Jeffrey A. McNeely, eds, *Protection of Global Biodiversity: Converging Strategies* (Durham, NC: Duke University Press, 1998), p. 105.

34 Dore and Nogueira, p. 494.

35 Charles Arden-Clarke, 'South–North Terms of Trade, Environmental Protection and Sustainable Development,' *International Environmental Affairs* 4(2) (Spring 1992), p. 123.

36 Alex Shoumatoff, *The World Is Burning* (Boston: Little, Brown & Co., 1990), p. 84.

37 Dore and Noguiera, p. 493.

38 A. Sarkar, 'Debt-Relief for Environment: Experience and Issues,' *Journal of Environment and Development* 3(1), p. 124.

39 Moritz Kraemer and Jorg Hartmann, 'Policy Responses to Tropical Deforestation: Are Debt-for-Nature Swaps Appropriate?' *Journal of*

Environment and Development 2(2), pp. 41–65.

40 Hurrell, p. 203.

41 International Tropical Timber Agreement (1994), Article 1 (d).

42 ITTA (1994), Article 21(1).

43 Cited in Edith Brown Weiss, 'The Five International Treaties: A Living History,' in Edith Brown Weiss and Harold Jacobson, eds, *Engaging Countries* (Cambridge, MA: MIT Press, 1998), p. 124.

44 CBD 1992, Article 7 (a through d).

45 CBD 1992, Article 6(a).

46 CBD 1992, Article 15.

47 Cartagena Biosafety Protocol to the Convention on Biological Diversity (2000), Articles 7 through 9.

48 Biosafety Protocol Article 15(1).

49 Robert B. Horsch and Robert Fraley, 'Biotechnology Can Help Reduce the Loss of Biodiversity,' in Guruswamy and McNeely, pp. 49–65.

50 Thomas Lovejoy, 'Aid Debtor Nation's Ecology,' *New York Times*, 4 October 1984, p. 31.

51 Cord Jacobeit, 'Nonstate Actors Leading the Way: Debt-for-Nature Swaps,' in Robert O. Keohane and Marc A. Levy, eds, *Institutions for Environmental Aid* (Cambridge, MA: MIT Press, 1997), p. 137.

52 Jakobeit, pp. 128.

53 Jakobeit, pp. 136–7.

54 Jakobeit, p. 140.

55 United States Congress, House of Representatives, 105th Congress, 'Tropical Forest Conservation Act of 1998,' *Report* 105–443.

56 Janeen Klinger, 'Debt-for-Nature Swaps and the Limits to International Cooperation on Behalf of the Environment,' *Environmental Politics* 3(2), p. 241.

57 B. Thapa, 'Debt-for-Nature Swaps: An Overview,' *International Journal of Sustainable Development and World Ecology* 5(4), p. 260.

58 Rhona Mahoney, 'Debt-for-Nature Swaps: Who Really Benefits?' *The Ecologist* 22(3), pp. 97–102.

59 A. G. Bruner, R. E. Gullison, R. E. Rice and G. A. B. da Fonseca 'Effectiveness of Parks in Protecting Tropical Diversity,' *Science* 291 (5 January 2001), pp. 125–7.

60 Sarkar, pp. 123–36.

61 Kraemer and Hartmann, pp. 41–65.

62 Thapa, p. 260.

63 Roque Sevilla, 'Banks, Debt, and Development – II,' *International Environmental Affairs* 2(2) (1990), pp. 150–2.

64 Diana Page, 'Debt-for-Nature Swaps: Experience Gained, Lessons Learned,' *International Environmental Affairs* 1(4) (1989), p. 286.

65 'Indigenous People's Knowledge: Pharmaceuticals and Their Business,' *Nuestra Amazonia* (July 1996), p. 7.

66 Andrew Kimbrell, 'High Tech Piracy,' *UTNE Reader* (March/April 1996), p. 85.

67   Christopher J. Hunter, 'Sustainable Bioprospecting: Using Private Contracts and International Legal Principles and Policies to Conserve Medicinal Materials,' *Boston College Environmental Affairs Law Review* 25 (1997), p. 130.

68   C. Joyce, *Earthly Goods: Medicine Hunting in the Rainforest* (Boston: Little, Brown, & Co., 1994).

69   Michele Zebich-Knos, 'Preserving Biodiversity in Costa Rica: The Case of the Merck-INBio Agreement,' *Journal of Environment and Development* 6(2) (June 1997), pp. 180–6.

70   International Development Research Centre, 'Shaman Pharmaceuticals: Socially Responsible Drug Development,' 25 October 1996, http://idrc.ca/books/reports/1996/30-02e.html (date visited: 4 June 2001).

71   Shaman Pharmaceuticals Inc., *Quarterly Report* (SEC form 10-Q), 15 May 2001.

72   Ricard Bonalume Neto, 'MITs Amazon Outpost,' *Nature* 365 (9 September 1993), p. 101.

73   Anthony Sisky, Project Coordinator, MIT, e-mail message received 6 June 2001.

74   S. Watson, 'Are Licensing Agreements Key to Technology Transfer?' *Legal Intelligencer*, 14 June 1994, pp. 13ff.

75   Joseph Henry Vogel, *The Successful Use of Economic Instruments to Foster Sustainable Use of Biodiversity* (Quito: Facultad Latinoamericana de Ciencias Sociales, 1996), p. 3.

76   Douglas Southgate, *Alternatives for Habitat Protection* (Washington, DC: Interamerican Development Bank, 1997), p. 36.

77   Kimbrell, p. 85. It should be noted, however, that Eli Lilly did not specifically have a bioprospecting agreement with Madagascar.

78   Shaman Botanicals, 'Shaman: About Us,' http://www.shamanbotanicals.-com/aumaster.html (date visited: 2 June 2001).

79   Katy Moran, 'Compensating Forest-dwelling Communities for Drug Discovery: The World of the Healing Forest Conservancy,' *Unasylva* 47 (1996), p. 42.

80   Christopher Locke, 'Forest Pharmers Go Bioprospecting,' *Red Herring* (12 April 2001), http://www.redherringcom/index/asp?/layout+story&doc_id=175001897&channel+10000001 (date visited: 4 June 2001).

81   Jennifer Pepall, 'Putting a Price on Indigenous Knowledge,' 7 July 1998 (International Development Research Centre), http://www.idrc.ca/books/reports/1996/30-01e.html (date visited: 4 June 2001).

82   Southgate, p. 7.

83   Megan Epler Wood, 'Global Solutions: An Ecotourism Society,' in Tensie Whelan, ed., *Nature Tourism: Managing for the Environment* (Washington, DC: Island Press, 1991), p. 201.

84   Martha Honey, *Ecotourism and Sustainable Development* (Washington, DC, and Covelo, CA: Island Press, 1999), p. 18.

85   Abigail Rome, 'Amazon Adventure,' *E* 10(2) (March 1999), p. 48.

86   Jennifer Bogo and Tracey C. Rembert, 'Close to Nature.' *E* 10(6) (November

1999), p. 46.

87 Honey, pp. 32–59.

88 Tensie Whelan, 'Ecotourism and Its Role in Sustainable Development,' in Tensie Whelan, ed., *Nature Tourism: Managing for the Environment* (Washington, DC: Island Press, 1991), p. 11.

89 Southgate, p. 1.

90 Ray Ashton, 'The Natural Alternative: Planning for Success in Latin American Ecotourism Projects,' *Latin Finance* 67 (May 1995), p. 16.

91 Alwyn Gentry, Charles Peters, and Robert Mendelsohn, 'Valuation of the Amazonian Rainforest,' *Nature* 339 (29 June 1989), pp. 655–6.

92 UN Environment Programme, 'Partnerships for Sustainable Development: The Role of Business and Industry,' (London: Flashprint Enterprises, Ltd., for UNEP and the Prince of Wales Business Leaders Forum, 1994), pp. 13–16.

93 Conservation International, 'Rainforest Buttons Get Wider Distribution,' *Press Release* (14 March 1995), http://conservation.org/WEB/NEWS/pressrel/95-0314.html (date visited: 4 June 2001).

94 UNEP, p. 14.

95 R. David Simpson, 'The Price of Biodiversity,' *Issues in Science and Technology* 15(3), p. 68.

96 Southgate, p. 25.

97 Simpson, pp. 65–70; Christopher B. Barrett and Travis J. Lybbert, 'Is Bioprospecting a Viable Strategy for Conserving Tropical Ecosystems,' *Ecological Economics* 34 (2000), pp. 293–300.

98 GEF Secretariat, 'Biodiversity Projects,' 2000, http://gefweb.org (date visited: 4 June 2001).

99 GEF Secretariat, 'Biodiversity and Amazon,' http://gefweb.org (date visited: 4 June 2001).

100 Thelma Krug, 'Space Technology and Environmental Monitoring in Amazonia,' *Journal of International Affairs* 51(2) (Spring 1998), pp. 655–75.

101 Krug, pp. 655–75.

102 Jacobeit, p. 127.

CHAPTER 9

1 Speech delivered 26 October 1983, as quoted in Robert B. Stewart, 'Negotiations on Acid Rain,' in Jurgen Schmandt, Judith Clarkson, and Hilliard Roderick, eds, *Acid Rain and Friendly Neighbors: The Policy Dispute Between Canada and the United States*. Revised edition (Durham, NC: Duke University Press, 1988), p. 73.

2 John McCormick, *Acid Earth: The Politics of Acid Pollution* (London: Earthscan Publications, 1997), p. 8.

3 Marc A. Levy, 'European Acid Rain: The Power of Tote-Board Diplomacy,' in Peter M. Haas, Robert O. Keohane, and Marc A. Levy, *Institutions for the Earth: Sources of Effective International Environmental Protection* (Cambridge,

MA, and London: The MIT Press, 1993), p. 78.

4 Svante Odén, 'The Acidification of Air and Precipitation and Its Consequences in the Natural Environment' *Ecology Committee Bulletin* 1 (Stockholm: Swedish National Research Council, 1968).

5 Levy, p. 80.

6 Gregory S. Wetstone and Armin Rosencranz, *Acid Rain in Europe and North
   America: National Responses to an International Problem: A Study for the German
   Marshall Fund of the United States* (Washington, DC: The Environmental Law
   Institute, 1983), p. 9.

7 Organization for Economic Cooperation and Development, *The OECD
   Programme on Long-Range Transport of Air Pollutants: Summary Report* (OECD,
   1977).

8 Levy, pp. 81–2.

9 Convention on Long-Range Transboundary Air Pollution (1979), Articles 2
   and 6.

10 LRTAP, Articles 7 and 8.

11 Levy, pp. 91–4.

12 Helen M. ApSimon and Rachel F. Warren, 'Transboundary Air Pollution in
    Europe,' *Energy Policy* 24(7) (1996), pp. 631–40.

13 Protocol to LRTAP Concerning the Control of Emissions of Nitrogen Oxides
    or Their Transboundary Fluxes (1988), Article 2.

14 Protocol to LRTAP Concerning the Control of Emissions of Volatile Organic
    Compounds or Their Transboundary Fluxes (1991), Article 2.

15 Protocol to LRTAP on Further Reductions of Sulphur Emissions (1994),
    Article 2, Annex I; see also Barbara Connolly, 'Asymmetrical Rivalry in
    Common Pool Resources and European Responses to Acid Rain,' in J.
    Samuel Barkin and George E. Shambaugh, eds, *Anarchy and the Environment:
    The International Relations of Common Pool Resources* (Albany, NY: SUNY
    Press, 1999), p. 129.

16 Protocol to LRTAP on Heavy Metals (1998) and Protocol to LRTAP on
    Persistent Organic Pollutants (1998).

17 Don Munton, 'Acid Rain and Transboundary Air Quality in Canadian-
    American Relations,' *American Review of Canadian Studies*, Autumn 1997, pp.
    328–9.

18 Robert B. Stewart, 'Negotiations on Acid Rain,' in Schmandt, Clarkson, and
    Hilliard, pp. 64–82.

19 Lois Ember, 'US, Canada Still Far Apart on Acid Rain Accord,' *Chemical and
    Engineering News*, 8 February 1988, p. 15.

20 Kim J. DeRidder, 'The Nature and Effects of Acid Rain: A Comparison of
    Assessments,' in Schmandt, Clarkson, and Roderick, p. 62.

21 Vicki L. Golich and Terry Forrest Young, 'United States-Canadian Negotia-
    tions for Acid Rain Controls,' *Pew Case Studies in International Affairs*, Case
    452, 1993, pp. 21, 24.

22 Agreement Between the Government of Canada and the Government of the
    United States on Air Quality (known colloquially as the U.S.-Canada Air

Quality Agreement), 1991, Article IV(2).

23 Article III(2)(b).

24 Annex I, Paragraph 1(A)(B).

25 Annex I, Paragraph 2(A)(B).

26 http://sedac.ceisin.org/charlotte (date visited: 13 August 1999).

27 http://www.unece.org/env/protocol/94s_s.htm (date visited: 6 June 2001).

28 http://www.unece.org/env/protocol/98hm_s.htm and http://www.unece.org/env/protocol/98hm_h1.htm (date visited: 5 June 2001).

29 Stewart, p. 67.

30 Sheila Jasanoff, 'Cross-National Differences in Policy Implementation,' *Evaluation Review* 15(1) (February 1991), pp. 103–19.

31 Roderick W. Shaw, 'Acid Rain Negotiations in North America and Europe: A Study in Contrast,' in Gunner Sjöstet, ed., *International Environmental Negotiation* (Newbury Park, London; and Delhi: Sage Publications, 1993), p. 88.

32 Sheila Jasanoff, 'American Exceptionalism and the Political Acknowledgment of Risk,' *Daedalus* 119(4) (Fall 1990), pp. 63–78.

33 Jurgen Schmandt, Judith Clarkson, and Hilliard Roderick, 'Introduction,' in Schmandt, Clarkson, and Roderick, p. 5.

34 Oran Young, 'Science and Social Institutions: Lessons for International Resource Regimes,' in Steinar Andresen and Willy Ostreng, eds, *International Resource Management: The Role of Science and Politics* (London and New York: Bellhaven Press, 1989), p. 10.

35 Detlef Sprinz and Tapani Vaahtoranta, 'The Interest-based Explanation of International Environmental Policy,' *International Organization* 41(1) (Winter 1994), pp. 77–105.

36 Golich and Young, p. 11–12.

37 Interestingly, they point to Britain's distrust of scientific findings as a possible cause of its reluctance on this issue. Sprinz and Vaahtoranta, p. 100.

38 Golich and Young, p. 12.

39 Elizabeth R. DeSombre, *Domestic Sources of International Environmental Policy: Industry, Environmentalists, and US Power* (Cambridge, MA: The MIT Press, 2000).

40 Levy, p. 76.

41 Levy, p. 93.

42 Connolly, p. 129.

43 Levy, p. 76, for example.

CHAPTER 10

1 Also relevant to note in this case is that it was the industry actors themselves hoping to be regulated, to prevent the tragedy of the commons.

BIBLIOGRAPHY

Adler, Emanuel, and Peter M. Haas (1992) 'Conclusion: Epistemic Communities, World Order, and the Creation of a Reflective Research Program.' *International Organization* 46(1) (Winter): 367–90.

Agreement Between the Government of Canada and the Government of the United States on Air Quality ('The U.S.–Canada Air Quality Agreement') (1991).

Allenby, Braden R. (1999) *Industrial Ecology: Policy Framework and Implementation.* Upper Saddle River, NJ: Prentice-Hall.

Alliance for Responsible CFC Policy (1986) *A Search for Alternatives to the Current Commercial Fluorocarbons.* Arlington, VA: Alliance for Responsible CFC Policy.

Andresen, Steinar (1989) 'Science and Politics in the International Management of Whales.' *Marine Policy* 13 (April): 99–117.

ApSimon, Helen M., and Rachel F. Warren (1996) 'Transboundary Air Pollution in Europe.' *Energy Policy* 24(7) (July): 631–40.

Arden-Clarke, Charles (1992) 'South-North Terms of Trade, Environmental Protection and Sustainable Development.' *International Environmental Affairs* 4(2) (Spring): 122–38.

Arnt, Ricardo (1993) 'The Inside out, the Outside In: Pros and Cons of Foreign Influence on Brazilian Environmentalism.' In *Green Globe Yearbook 1992,* edited by Helge O. Bergesen, Magnar Norderhaug, and Georg Parmann. Oxford: Oxford University Press, pp. 15–23.

Ashton, Ray (1995) 'The Natural Alternative: Planning for Success in Latin American Ecotourism Projects.' *Latin Finance* 67 (May): 16.

Axelrod, Robert (1984) *The Evolution of Cooperation.* New York: Basic Books.

Baram, Michael S. (1994) 'Multinational Corporations, Private Codes, and Technology Transfer for Sustainable Development.' *Environmental Law* 24(1) (Winter): 33–66.

Barbera, Anthony J., and Virgina D. McConnell (1990) 'The Impact of Environmental Regulations on Industry Productivity: Direct and Indirect Effects.' *Journal of Environmental Economics and Management* 18: 56–65.

Barkin, J. Samuel, and Elizabeth R. DeSombre (2000) 'Unilateralism and Multilateralism in International Fisheries Management.' *Global Governance* 6(3) (July–September): 339–60

Barkin, J. Samuel, and George E. Shambaugh (1999) 'Hypotheses on the

International Politics of Common Pool Resources.' In *Anarchy and the Environment: The International Relations of Common Pool Resources*, edited by J. Samuel Barkin and George E. Shambaugh. Albany, NY: SUNY Press, pp. 1–25.

Barrett, Christopher B., and Travis J. Lybbert (2000) 'Is Bioprospecting a Viable Strategy for Conserving Tropical Ecosystems?' *Ecological Economics* 34: 293–300.

Begley, Ronald, Allison Lucas, and Michael Roberts (1996) 'Producers Set for CFC Phaseout.' *Chemical Week* 157(23)(13 December): 40.

Benedick, Richard Elliot (1998) *Ozone Diplomacy: New Directions in Safeguarding the Planet*, enlarged edition. Cambridge, MA: Harvard University Press.

Berejekian, Jeffrey (1997) 'The Gains Debate: Framing State Choice.' *American Political Science Review* 91(4) (December): 789–805.

Betsill, Michele M. (2000) 'Linking the Local and Global in Climate Change Policies.' Paper prepared for delivery at the Annual Meeting of the American Political Science Association, September.

Bin Mohd, Rusli, and Jan G. Laarman (1994) 'The Struggle for Influence: US Nongovernmental Organizations and Tropical Forests.' *Journal of Forestry* 92(6) (June): 32–6.

Birnie, Patricia (1985) *International Regulation of Whaling: From Conservation of Whaling to Conservation of Whales and Regulation of Whale Watching*, vols. I and II. New York: Oceana Publications.

Birnie, Patricia (1985) 'The Role of Developing Countries in Nudging the International Whaling Commission from Regulating Whaling to Encouraging Nonconsumptive Uses of Whales.' *Ecology Law Quarterly* 12: 937–75.

Birnie, Patricia, and Alan E. Boyle (1992) *International Law and the Environment*. Oxford: Clarendon Press.

Bodansky, Daniel (1991) 'Scientific Uncertainty and the Precautionary Principle.' *Environment* 33(7) (September): 4–5, 43.

Boettcher III, William A. (1995) 'Context, Methods, Numbers, and Words: Prospect Theory in International Relations.' *Journal of Conflict Resolution* 39(3) (September): 561–83.

Bogo, Jennifer, and Tracey C. Rembert (1999) 'Close to Nature.' *E* 10(6) (November): 46.

Brack, Duncan (1996) *International Trade and the Montreal Protocol*. London: Earthscan Publications.

Bramble, Barbara J., and Gareth Porter (1992) 'Non-Governmental Organizations and the Making of U.S. International Policy.' In *The International Politics of the Environment*, edited by Andrew Hurrell and Benedict Kingsbury. Oxford: Clarendon Press, 313–53.

Brand, Paul (1999) 'Hot Question for Air Conditioner: Recharge or Convert?' *Minneapolis Star Tribune* (31 July): 1M.

Breen, Tim (2001) 'Climate Change II: Voluntary Greenhouse Gas Reductions "Significant" – UNEP.' *Greenwire* (2 July)

Breitmeier, Helmut and Volker Rittberger (1998) 'Environmental NGOs in an Emerging Global Civil Society.' No. 32. Tübingen: Center for International

Relations/Peace and Conflict Studies, Institute for Political Science, University of Tübingen.

Breyer, Stephen J. (1993) *Breaking the Vicious Circle: Toward Effective Risk Regulation*. Cambridge, MA: Harvard University Press.

Brickman, Ronald, Sheila Jasanoff, and Thomas Ilgen (1985) *Controlling Chemicals: The Politics of Regulation in Europe and the United States*. Ithaca, NY, and London: Cornell University Press.

Brown, Lester R. (1977) 'Redefining National Security.' *Worldwatch Paper 14*. Washington, DC: Worldwatch Institute.

Brown, Paul (1993) 'Playing Football with the Whales.' *Guardian*, 1 May, p. 26.

Brown, Paul (1994) 'Foreign Focus: Whaling Scandal: Soviet Union Illegally Killed Great Whales.' *Guardian*, 12 February, p. 12ff.

Brühl, Tanja (1998) 'NGOs and Formation of International Environmental Regimes: Explaining Their Inclusion.' Paper presented at the Third Pan-European International Relations Conference, September, Vienna, Austria.

Bruner, A. G., R. E. Gullison, R. E. Rice, and G. A. B. da Fonseca (2001) 'Effectiveness of Parks in Protecting Tropical Diversity.' *Science* 291 (5 January): 125–7.

Brunnee, Jutta and Stephen J. Toope (1997) 'Environmental Security and Freshwater Resources: Ecosystem Regime Building.' *American Journal of International Law* 91(1) (January): 26–59.

Bruno, Kenny (1992) 'The Corporate Capture of the Earth Summit.' *Multinational Monitor* 13 (July–August): 15–20.

Bulloch, J., and A. Darwish (1993) *Water Wars: Coming Conflicts in the Middle East*. London: Victor Gollancz.

Bunyard, Peter (1999) 'Eradicating the Amazon Rainforests Will Wreak Havoc on Climate.' *The Ecologist* 29(2) (March–April): 81–5.

Burns, William (2001) 'From the Harpoon to the Heat: Climate Change and the International Whaling Commission in the 21st Century.' *Georgetown International Law Review* 13(2): 335–59.

Butler, Nick (2000) 'Companies in International Relations.' *Survival* 42(1) (Spring): 149–64.

Butterworth, D.S. (1992) 'Science and Sentimentality.' *Nature* 357 (18 June): 532–4.

Butts, Kent Hughes (1994) 'Why the Military Is Good for the Environment.' In *Green Security or Militarized Environment*, edited by Jyrki Käkönen. Aldershot: Dartmouth Publishing Company, pp. 83–109.

Buzan, Barry (1991) *People, States, and Fear. An Agenda for International Security Studies in the Post-Cold War Era*. 2nd ed. Boulder, CO: Lynne Rienner Publishers.

Cairncross, Frances (1990) 'Cleaning Up.' *The Economist*, 8 September, p. S1ff.

Cairncross, Frances (1991) *Costing the Earth*. Boston: Harvard Business School Press.

Caldwell, Lynton Keith (1996) *International Environmental Policy*. 3rd ed. Durham, NC, and London: Duke University Press.

'Call Me Smiley' (1994) *New York Times Magazine*, 13 March, p. 14.

Carius, Alexander, and Kerstin Imbusch (1999) 'Environment and Security in International Politics – An Introduction.' In *Environmental Change and Security: A European Perspective*, edited by Alexander Carius and Kurt M. Lietzmann. Berlin and New York: Springer, pp. 7–30.

Carroll, John E. (1989) 'The Acid Challenge to Security.' *Bulletin of the Atomic Scientists* 45(8) (October): 32–4.

Cartagena Biosafety Protocol to the Convention on Biological Diversity (2000).

CBS News (2000) 'Water Fight in the Mideast.' Broadcast 2 July; also available at http://cbsnews.cbs.com/now/story/0,1597,211735-412,00.shtml, date visited: 3 July 2000.

Chadwick, Alex (2001) 'The Treasured Islands of Palmyra,' *National Geographic* 199(3) (March) 46–56.

Charnovitz, Steve (1997) 'Two Centuries of Participation: NGOs and International Governance.' *Michigan Journal of International Law* 18 (Winter): 183–286.

Chayes, Abram, and Antonia Chayes (1995) *The New Sovereignty: Compliance with International Regulatory Agreements*. Cambridge, MA: Harvard University Press.

'Chemical Production: Holed Up' (1995) *The Economist*, 9 December, p. 63.

Chichilnisky, Graciela (1998) 'Sustainable Development and North-South Trade.' In *Protection of Global Biodiversity: Converging Strategies*, edited by Lakshman D. Guruswamy and Jeffrey A. McNeely, Durham, NC, and London: Duke University Press, pp. 101–17.

Choucri, Nazli (1991) 'The Global Environment and Multinational Corporations.' *Technology Review* 94(3) (April): 52–9.

'Citizens' Groups: The Non-Governmental Order – Will NGOs Democratise, or Merely Disrupt, Global Governance?' (1999) *The Economist*, 11 December, p. 20.

Clapp, Jennifer (1996) 'Multinational Corporations and Environmental Hazards in the Asia-Pacific Region.' Paper prepared for the International Studies Association Annual Meeting, San Diego, April.

Clapp, Jennifer (1997) 'The Illegal CFC Trade: An Unexpected Wrinkle in the Ozone Protection Regime.' *International Environmental Affairs* 9(4): 261ff.

Clark, Colin W. and R. Lamberson (1992) 'An Economic History and Analysis of Pelagic Whaling.' *Marine Policy* 6(2)(April): 107–9.

Clark, John (1990) *Democratizing Development: The Role of Voluntary Organizations*. West Hartford, CT: Kumarian Press.

Connole, Patrick (1999) 'Ford Exits Anti-Kyoto Climate Change Group.' *Reuters News Service*, 7 December.

Connolly, Barbara (1999) 'Asymmetrical Rivalry in Common Pool Resources and European Responses to Acid Rain.' In *Anarchy and the Environment: The International Relations of Common Pool Resources*, edited by J. Samuel Barkin and George E. Shambaugh. Albany, NY: SUNY Press, pp. 122–54.

Conservation International (1995) 'Rainforest Buttons Get Wider Distribution.' Press Release, 14 March. http://conservation.org/WEB/NEWS/pressrel/95-0314.htm, date visited: 4 June 2001.

Convention on Biological Diversity (1992).

Convention on Long-Range Transboundary Air Pollution (1979).

Convention on the Law of the Non-Navigational Uses of International Watercourses (1997).

Convention on the Protection of the Marine Environment of the Baltic Sea Area (1992).

Copenhagen Amendments to the Montreal Protocol (1992).

Cox, Susan Jane Buck (1985) 'No Tragedy on the Commons.' *Environmental Ethics* 7 (Spring): 49–61.

Dabelko, Geoffrey D. and David D. Dabelko (1995) 'Environmental Security: Issues of Conflict and Redefinition.' *Environmental Change and Security Project Report* 1 (Spring): 6.

Dalby, Simon (1994) 'The Politics of Environmental Security.' In *Green Security or Militarized Environment*, edited by Jyrki Käkönen. Aldershot, England: Dartmouth Publishing Company, pp. 25–53.

Daniels, Lee (2000) 'Texaco Buys 20 Percent Stake in Energy Conversion Company.' *Reuters News Service*, 7 June.

Dasgupta, Chandrashekhar (1994) 'The Climate Change Negotiations.' In *Negotiating Climate Change*, edited by Irving Mintzer and J. A. Leonard. Cambridge: Cambridge University Press, pp. 138–9.

Day, David (1987) *The Whale War*. San Francisco: Sierra Club Books.

De Aragão, Murillo, and Stephen Bunker (1998) 'Brazil: Regional Inequalities and Ecological Diversity in a Federal System.' In *Engaging Countries: Strengthening Compliance with International Environmental Accords*, edited by Edith Brown Weiss and Harold K. Jacobson. Cambridge, MA: MIT Press, pp. 475–509.

De Oliveira, Miguel Darcy and Rajesh Tandon (1994) 'An Emerging Global Civil Society.' In *Citizens: Strengthening Global Civil Society*, edited by Miguel Darcy de Oliveira and Rajesh Tandon. Washington, DC: Civicus: World Alliance for Citizen Participation, pp. 1–17.

DeRidder, Kim J. (1988) 'The Nature and Effects of Acid Rain: A Comparison of Assessments.' In *Acid Rain and Friendly Neighbors: The Policy Dispute Between Canada and the United States*, edited by Jurgen Schmandt, Judith Clarkson, and Hilliard Roderick. Durham, NC: Duke University Press, pp. 31–63.

Dernbach, John C. (1998) 'Sustainable Development as a Framework for National Governance.' *Case Western Reserve Law Review* 49(1) (Fall): 93.

DeSimone, Livio D and Frank Popoff (1997) *Eco-Efficiency: The Business Link to Sustainable Development*. Cambridge, MA: MIT Press.

DeSombre, Elizabeth R. (1998) 'International Environmental Policy.' In *Environmental Management in Practice: Analysis, Implementation, and Policy*, edited by B. Nath, L. Hens, P. Compton, and D. Devust. New York: Routledge Press, pp. 361–77.

DeSombre, Elizabeth R. (2000) 'Developing Country Influence in Global Environmental Negotiations.' *Environmental Politics* 9(3) (Autumn): 23–42.

DeSombre, Elizabeth R. (2000) *Domestic Sources of International Environmental Policy: Industry, Environmentalists, and US Power*. Cambridge, MA: MIT Press.

DeSombre, Elizabeth R. (2000) 'Flags of Convenience and the Enforcement of

International Environmental, Safety, and Labor Regulations at Sea.' *International Politics* 37(2) (June): 213–32.

DeSombre, Elizabeth R. (2001) 'United Nations Conference on the Human Environment.' In *Oxford Encyclopedia of Global Change*, edited by Andrew Goudie. New York and Oxford: Oxford University Press

DeSombre, Elizabeth R. (2001) 'United Nations Conference on Environment and Development.' In *Oxford Encyclopedia of Global Change*, edited by Andrew Goudie. New York and Oxford: Oxford University Press.

DeSombre, Elizabeth and Joanne Kauffman (1996) 'The Montreal Protocol Multilateral Fund: Partial Success Story.' In *Institutions for Environmental Aid*, edited by Robert O. Keohane and Marc A. Levy. Cambridge, MA: The MIT Press, pp. 89–126.

Deudney, Daniel (1990) 'The Case Against Linking Environmental Degradation and National Security.' *Millennium* 19(3): 461–76.

Deudney, Daniel (1991) 'Environment and Security: Muddled Thinking.' *Bulletin of the Atomic Scientists* 47(3) (April): 22–8.

Deudney, Daniel H. (1999) 'Bringing Nature Back In: Geopolitical Theory from the Greeks to the Global Era.' In *Contested Grounds: Security and Conflict in the New Environmental Politics*, edited by Daniel H. Deudney and Richard A. Matthew, Albany, NY: SUNY Press, pp. 25–57.

Dewar, Helen (1997) 'Senate Advises Against Emissions Treaty That Lets Developing Nations Pollute.' *Washington Post*, 26 July, p. A11.

Diebert, Ronald J. (1996) 'From Deep Black to Green? Demystifying the Military Monitoring of the Environment.' *Environmental Change and Security Project Report*. Issue 2. (Spring) Woodrow Wilson Center.

Dobkowski, Michael N. and Isidor Wallimann, eds (1998) *The Coming Age of Scarcity: Preventing Mass Death and Genocide in the Twenty-first Century*. Syracuse, NY: Syracuse University Press.

Donovan, G. P. (1989) 'Forty-second Annual Meeting of the International Whaling Commission.' *Polar Record* 24 (June): 631–63.

Dore, Mohammed H. I. and Jorge M. Nogueira (1994) 'The Amazon Rain Forest, Sustainable Development, and the Biodiversity Convention: A Political Economy Perspective.' *Ambio* 23(8) (December): 491–6.

Douglas, David (1996) 'Environmental Eviction.' *The Christian Century* 113(26) (11 September): 839–41.

Douglas H. (2001) 'Pursuing the Minke,' *National Geographic* 199(4) (April): 58–71.

Douglas, Mary and Aaron Wildavsky (1982) *Risk and Culture: An Essay on the Selection of Technical and Environmental Dangers*. Berkeley, Los Angeles, and London: University of California Press.

Dyer, Hugh C. (1996) 'Environmental Security as a Universal Value: Implications for International Theory.' In *The Environment and International Relations*, edited by John Vogler and Mark F. Imber. London and New York: Routledge, pp. 22–40.

Eccleston, Bernard (1996) 'Does North-South Collaboration Enhance NGO

Influence on Deforestation Policies in Malaysia and Indonesia?' In *NGOs and Environmental Policies: Asia and Africa*, edited by David Potter. Portland, OR: Frank Cass, pp. 66–89.

Eckert, Paul (2001) 'Update – EU Says China to Back Climate Pact Without US.' *Reuters News Service*, 10 April.

Elliot, G. (1979) 'Failure of the International Whaling Commission 1946–1966.' *Marine Policy* 3: 149–55.

Ellis, Richard (1999) *Men and Whales*. New York: Lyons Press.

Ember, Lois (1988) 'US, Canada Still Far Apart on Acid Rain Accord.' *Chemical and Engineering News*, 8 February, p. 15.

Fagan, Lauren (2000) 'Water a Vexed Issue for Israel, Palestinians.' *Reuters*, 6 July.

Fairman, David (1996) 'The Global Environmental Facility: Haunted by the Shadow of the Future.' In *Institutions for Environmental Aid: Pitfalls and Promise*, edited by Robert O. Keohane and Marc A. Levy. Cambridge, MA, and London: The MIT Press, pp. 55–87.

Fernandes, Ruben Cesar (1994) 'Threads of Planetary Citizenship.' In *Citizens: Strengthening Global Civil Society*, edited by Miguel Darcy de Oliveira and Rajesh Tandon. Washington, DC: Civicus: World Alliance for Citizen Participation, 319–46.

Finger, Matthias (1991) 'The Military, the Nation-State and the Environment.' *The Ecologist* 21(5) (September–October): 220–5.

Finger, Matthias (1994) 'NGOs and Transformation: Beyond Social Movement Theory.' In *Environmental NGOs in World Politics: Linking the Local and the Global*, edited by Thomas Princen and Matthias Finger. London and New York: Routledge, pp. 48–66.

Finger, Matthias and James Kilcoyne (1997) 'Why Transnational Corporations Are Organizing to "Save the Global Environment."' *The Ecologist* 27(4) (July–August): 138–42.

Flatt, Victor B. (1994) 'Book Reviews: Should the Circle Be Unbroken? A Review of the Hon. Stephen Breyer's "Breaking the Vicious Circle."' *Environmental Law* 24(4) (Fall): 1707–28.

'Focus – Interview: Wildlife Protection in West and Central Africa.' (1991) *Greenwire*, 11 June.

Foley, Grover (1999) 'The Looming Environmental Refugee Crisis.' *The Ecologist* 29(2) (March–April): 96–7.

Foster, Kenneth R., Paolo Vecchia and Michael H. Repacholi (2000) 'Science and the Precautionary Principle,' *Science* 288 (12 May): 979–81.

Fox, Jonathan A. and L. David Brown (1998) 'Introduction.' In *The Struggle for Accountability: The World Bank, NGOs, and Grassroots Movements*, edited by Jonathan Fox and L. David Brown. Cambridge, MA: MIT Press.

Framework Convention on Climate Change (1992).

Framework Convention on Climate Change, Conference of the Parties (1997) 'Methodological Issues Related to a Protocol Or Another Legal Instrument: Draft Decision Submitted by the Committee of the Whole.' FCCC/CP/1997/

L.5, 8 December.

Framework Convention on Climate Change, Conference of the Parties (1998) 'Actions Taken by the Conference of the Parties.' 4th Session, Annex 60, FCCC/CP/1997/7/Add.1, (1997).

Francis, Daniel (1990) *A History of World Whaling*. Toronto: Viking.

Friends of the Earth (1990) *Funding Change: Developing Countries and the Montreal Protocol*.

Fritz, Jan-Stefan (1998) 'Earthwatch Twenty-five Years On: Between Science and International Environmental Governance.' *International Environmental Affairs* 10(3) (Summer): 173–96.

Garcia-Johnson, Ronie (2000) *Exporting Environmentalism: US Multinational Chemical Corporations in Brazil and Mexico*. Cambridge, MA: MIT Press.

Gardner, Timothy (2000) 'Global Warming Business Group Cools Its Message.' *Reuters News Service*, 9 November.

Gelbspan, Ross (1997) *The Heat Is On: The High Stakes Battle over Earth's Threatened Climate*. Reading, MA: Addison-Wesley.

Gentry, Alwyn H., Charles M. Peters, and Robert O. Mendelsohn (1989) 'Valuation of an Amazonian Rainforest.' *Nature* 339(6227) (29 June): 655–6.

Gibbs, W. Wayt (1995) 'The Treaty That Worked – Almost.' *Scientific American* 273 (September): 18.

Gleick, Peter H. (1989) 'The Implications of Global Climatic Changes for International Security.' *Climatic Change* 15: 309–25.

Global Commons Institute (1996) 'Draft Proposals for a Climate Change Protocol Based on Contraction and Convergence.' Section 2.14. (September) http://www.gci.org.uk/contconv/protweb.html. Date visited: 26 June 2001.

Global Environment Facility Secretariat (n.d.) 'Biodiversity and Amazon.' http://gefweb.org. Date visited: 4 June 2001.

Global Environment Facility Secretariat (2000) 'Biodiversity Projects.' http://gefweb.org. Date visited: 4 June 2001.

Goleman, Daniel (1994) 'Hidden Rules Often Distort Ideas of Risk.' *New York Times*, 1 February, p. C1.

Golich, Vicki L., and Terry Forrest Young (1993) 'United States–Canadian Negotiations for Acid Rain Control.' Case 452. *Pew Case Studies in International Affairs*. Institute for the Study of Diplomacy, Pew Case Studies Center, Georgetown University.

Greene, Owen. 'The System for Implementation Review in the Ozone Regime.' In *The Implementation and Effectiveness of International Environmental Commitments*, edited by David G. Victor, Kal Raustiala, and Eugene B. Skolnikoff Cambridge, MA: The MIT Press, pp. 97–8.

Greer, Jed and Kenny Bruno (1996) *Greenwash: The Reality Behind Corporate Environmentalism*. Penang, Malaysia: Third World Network / New York: Apex Press.

Griffin, Dale, and Amos Tversky (1992) 'The Weighing of Evidence and the Determinants of Confidence.' *Cognitive Psychology* 24: 411–35.

Grubb, Michael, Matthias Koch, Abby Munson, Francis Sullivan, and Koy

Thomson (1993) *The Earth Summit Agreements: A Guide and Assessment.* London: Earthscan Publications.

Haas, Peter M. (1992) 'Banning Chlorofluorocarbons: Epistemic Community Efforts to Protect Stratospheric Ozone.' *International Organization* 46(1) (Winter): 187–224.

Haas, Peter M. (1992) 'Introduction: Epistemic Communities and International Policy Coordination.' *International Organization* 46(1) (Winter): 1–35.

Haas, Peter M., Robert O. Keohane, and Marc A. Levy (1995) 'The Effectiveness of International Environmental Institutions.' In *Institutions for the Earth: Sources of Effective International Environmental Protection,* edited by Peter M. Haas, Robert O. Keohane, and Marc A. Levy. Cambridge, MA: MIT Press, pp. 3–24.

Hardin, Garrett (1968) 'The Tragedy of the Commons.' *Science* 162: 1243–8.

Hart, Jeffrey A. (1976) 'The Anglo-Icelandic Cod War of 1972–1973: A Case Study of a Fishery Dispute.' Research Series, No. 20, Institute of International Studies, University of California, Berkeley.

Hart, Stuart L. and Gautam Ahuja (1996) 'Does It Pay to Be Green? An Empirical Examination of the Relationship Between Emission Reduction and Firm Performance.' *Business Strategy and Environment* 5: 30–7.

Heath, Chip, Richard P. Larrick and George Wu. (1999) 'Goals as Reference Points.' *Cognitive Psychology* 38: 79–109.

Heiman, Michael K. (1997) 'Science by the People: Grassroots Environmental Monitoring and the Debate over Scientific Expertise.' *Journal of Planning Education and Research* 6: 291–303.

Heinzerling, Lisa (1995) 'Political Science.' *University of Chicago Law Review* 62 (Winter): 449ff.

Henkin, Louis (1979) *How Nations Behave: Law and Foreign Policy,* 2nd ed. New York: Columbia University Press for the Council on Foreign Relations.

Hileman, Better (1997) 'Ozone Treaty: Successful But Pitfalls Remain.' *Chemical and Engineering News,* 15 September, p. 24.

Hillel, Daniel J. (1994) *Rivers of Eden: The Struggle for Water and the Quest for Peace in the Middle East.* Oxford: Oxford University Press.

Homer-Dixon, Thomas (1991) 'On the Threshold: Environmental Changes as Causes of Acute Conflict.' *International Security* 16(2) (Fall): 76–116.

Homer-Dixon, Thomas F. (1994) 'Environmental Scarcities and Violent Conflict: Evidence from Cases.' *International Security* 19(1) (Summer): 5–40.

Homer-Dixon, Thomas F. (1996) 'The Project on Environment, Population, and Security: Key Findings of Research.' *Environmental Change and Security Project Report.* Woodrow Wilson Center 2 (Spring): 45–57.

Homer-Dixon, Thomas (1998) 'Environmental Scarcity and Mass Violence.' In *The Geopolitics Reader,* edited by Gearóid O'Tuathail, Simon Dalby, and Paul Routledge. London: Routledge.

Honey, Martha (1999) *Ecotourism and Sustainable Development.* Washington, DC, and Covelo, CA: Island Press.

Horsch, Robert B., and Robert T. Fraley (1998) 'Biotechnology Can Help Reduce the Loss of Biodiversity.' In *Protection of Global Biodiversity: Converging*

Strategies, edited by Lakshman D. Guruswamy and Jeffrey A. McNeely. Durham, NC, and London: Duke University Press, pp. 49–65.

Hundewadt, Erik (1995) 'The Role of Voluntary Associations (NGOs) in a Democratic Society.' In *The Role of Non-Governmental Organizations in the New European Order*, edited by Jurgen Schramm. Germany: Nomos Verlagsgesellschaft, pp. 7–12.

Hunter, Christopher J. (1997) 'Sustainable Bioprospecting: Using Private Contracts and International Legal Principles and Policies to Conserve Raw Medicinal Materials.' *Boston College Environmental Affairs Law Review* 25(1) (Fall): 129–74.

Hunter, Robert (1979) *Warriors of the Rainbow: A Chronicle of the Greenpeace Movement*. New York: Holt, Reinhart & Winston.

Hurrell, Andrew (1991) 'The Politics of Amazonian Deforestation.' *Journal of Latin American Studies* 23: 197–215.

Hurrell, Andrew (1992) 'Brazil and the International Politics of Amazonian Deforestation.' In *The International Politics of the Environment: Actors, Interests, and Institutions*, edited by Andrew Hurrell and Benedict Kingsbury. Oxford: Clarendon Press, pp. 399–429.

'Iceland Rejoins IWC, But Exempt from Whaling Ban' (2001) *Reuters News Service*, 4 July.

'Indigenous People's Knowledge: Pharmaceuticals and Their Business' (1996) *Nuestra Amazonia* (July): 7.

Intergovernmental Panel on Climate Change. 'About IPCC.' http://www.ipcc.ch/about/about.htm. Date visited: 24 June 2001.

Intergovernmental Panel on Climate Change (2001) 'Summary for Policymakers: A Report of Working Group I of the Intergovernmental Panel on Climate Change.' Available at http://www.ipcc.ch. Date visited: 24 June 2001.

International Convention for the Prevention of Pollution from Ships (1973).

International Convention for the Regulation of Whaling (1946).

International Development Research Centre (1996) 'Shaman Pharmaceuticals: Socially Responsible Drug Development.' 25 October. http://idrc.ca/books/reports/1996/30–02e.html. Date visited: 4 June 2001.

'International – Primates: Congo Civil War Endangering Great Apes' (2000) *Greenwire*, 5 June.

International Tropical Timber Agreement (1994).

International Whaling Commission (1993) *Verbatim Record*. Cambridge: IWC.

International Whaling Commission (1996) 'Chairman's Report of the 47th Annual Meeting.' Cambridge: IWC.

'International Whaling Commission: 50th Annual Meeting: Opening Statement by the United Kingdom Delegation' (1998) IWC/50/OS/UK. Cambridge: IWC.

Jacobson, Harold K. and Edith Brown Weiss (1998) 'A Framework for Analysis.' In *Engaging Countries: Strengthening Compliance with International Environmental Accords*, edited by Edith Brown Weiss and Harold K. Jacobson, Cambridge, MA: MIT Press.

Jakobeit, Cord (1997) 'Nonstate Actors Leading the Way: Debt-for-Nature

Swaps.' In *Institutions for Environmental Aid: Pitfalls and Promise*, edited by Robert O. Keohane and Marc A. Levy. Cambridge, MA: MIT Press, 127–66.

Jamieson, Dale (1996) 'Scientific Uncertainty and the Political Process.' *Annals of the American Academy of Political and Social Sciences* 545 (May): 35–43.

Jasanoff, Sheila (1990) 'American Exceptionalism and the Political Acknow-ledgment of Risk.' *Daedalus* 119(4) (Fall): 63–78.

Jasanoff, Sheila (1991) 'Cross-National Differences in Policy Implementation.' *Evaluation Review* 15(1) (February): 103–19.

Jasanoff, Sheila (1992) 'Pluralism and Convergence in International Science Policy.' In *Science and Sustainability: Selected Papers on IIASA's 20th Anniversary*. Laxenburg, Austria: The International Institute for Applied Systems Analysis, pp. 157–80.

Jasanoff, Sheila (1997) 'NGOs and the Environment: From Knowledge to Action.' *Third World Quarterly* 18(3): 579–94.

Jervis, Robert (1976) *Perception and Misperception in International Politics*. Princeton: Princeton University Press.

Jervis, Robert (1992) 'Political Implications of Loss Aversion.' *Political Psychology*. 13: 187–204.

Joffé, George (1993) 'The Issue of Water in the Middle East and North Africa.' In *Resource Politics, Freshwater, and Regional Relations*, edited by Caroline Thomas and Darryl Howlett. Buckingham: Open University Press, 73–80.

Joyce, Christopher (1994). *Earthly Goods: Medicine-Hunting in the Rainforest*. Boston: Little, Brown & Company.

Kahneman, Daniel and Amos Tversky (1979) 'Prospect Theory: An Analysis of Decision Under Risk.' *Econometrica* 47(2)(March): 263–92.

Kaplan, Robert D. (1994) 'The Coming Anarchy.' *Atlantic Monthly* 273(2) (February): 44–76.

Kates, Robert W. (1962) 'Hazard and Choice Perception in Flood Plain Management.' *Research Paper 78*. Department of Geography, University of Chicago.

Keck, Margaret E., and Kathryn Sikkink (1998) *Activists Beyond Borders: Advocacy Networks in International Politics*. Ithaca, NY, and London: Cornell University Press.

Keohane, Robert O. (1985) *After Hegemony: Cooperating and Discord in the World Political Economy*. Princeton: Princeton University Press.

Keohane, Robert O. and Joseph S. Nye (1977) *Power and Interdependence: World Politics in Transition*. Boston and Toronto: Little, Brown, and Company.

Keohane, Robert O. and Elinor Ostrom (1995) 'Introduction.' In *Local Commons and Global Interdependence*, edited by Robert O. Keohane and Elinor Ostrom. London: Sage Publications, pp. 1–26.

Kerr, Richard A. (1986) 'Antarctic Ozone Hole Is Still Deepening.' *Science* 232 (June): 1602.

Kerr, Richard A. (2001) 'Rising Global Temperature, Rising Uncertainty.' *Science* 292 (April): 192–4.

Kimbell, Andrew (1996) 'High-Tech Piracy.' *Utne Reader* (March–April): 84–6.

King, Michael D. and David D. Herring (2000) 'Monitoring Earth's Vital Signs.' *Scientific American* 282(4) (April): 92–7.

Kirby, Alex (2000) 'Whaling Ban Set to End.' *BBC News*, 11 June. http://news.bbc.co.uk/hi/english/sci/tech/newsid_782999/782697.stm. Date visited: 12 June 2000.

Klinger, Janeen (1994) 'Debt-for-Nature Swaps and the Limits to International Cooperation on Behalf of the Environment.' *Environmental Politics* 3(2) (Summer): 229–46.

Kliot, Nurit (1994) *Water Resources and Conflict in the Middle East.* London: Routledge.

Kobrin, Stephen J. (1987) 'Testing the Bargaining Hypothesis in the Manufacturing Sector in Developing Countries.' *International Organization* 41(4) (Autumn): 609–38.

Kowert, Paul A. and Margaret G. Hermann (1997) 'Who Takes Risks? Daring and Caution in Foreign Policy Making.' *Journal of Conflict Resolution* 41(5) (October): 611–37.

Kraemer, Moritz and Jörg Hartmann (1993) 'Policy Responses to Tropical Deforestation: Are Debt-for-Nature Swaps Appropriate?' *Journal of Environment and Development* 2(2) (Summer): 41–65.

Krasner, Stephen D. (1982) 'Structural Causes and Regime Consequences: Regimes as Intervening Variables'. In *International Regimes*, edited by Stephen D. Krasner. Ithaca, NY, and London: Cornell University Press, pp. 1–21.

Krug, Thelma (1998) 'Space Technology and Environmental Monitoring in Brazil.' *Journal of International Affairs* 51(2) (Spring): 655–75.

Kyoto Protocol to the Framework Convention on Climate Change (1997).

Landers, Frederick Pool, Jr. (1997) 'The Black Market Trade in Chlorofluorocarbons: The Montreal Protocol Makes Banned Refrigerants a Hot Commodity.' *Georgia Journal of International and Comparative Law* 26 (Spring): 478–9.

Lee, Shin-wha (1997) 'Not a One-Time Event: Environmental Change, Ethnic Rivalry, and Violent Conflict in the Third World.' *Journal of Environment and Development* 6(4) (December): 365–96.

Leonard, H. Jeffrey (1988) *Pollution and the Struggle for World Product: Multinational Corporations, Environment, and International Comparative Advantage.* Cambridge: Cambridge University Press.

Levene, Abigail (2001) 'Greenpeace Boards "Wrong" Oil Rig in Bush Protest,' *Reuters News Service*, 18 June.

Levinson, Arik (1996) 'Environmental Regulations and Industry Location: International and Domestic Evidence.' In *Fair Trade and Harmonization: Prerequisites for Free Trade? Vol. 1: Economic Analysis*, edited by Jagdish Bhagwati and Robert E. Hudec. Cambridge, MA, and London: MIT Press, pp. 429–57.

Levy, Jack S. (1996) 'Loss Aversion, Framing, and Bargaining: The Implications of Prospect Theory for International Conflict.' *International Political Science Review* 17(2): 179–95.

Levy, Marc A. (1986) 'Leviathan's Leviathan: Power, Interests, and Institutional

Change in the International Whaling Commission.' Unpublished paper, Harvard University, June.

Levy, Marc. A. (1993) 'European Acid Rain: The Power of Tote-Board Diplomacy.' In *Institutions for the Earth: Sources of Effective International Environmental Protection*, edited by Peter M. Haas, Robert O. Keohane, and Marc A. Levy. Cambridge, MA, and London: MIT Press, pp. 74–132.

Levy, Marc A. (1995) 'Is the Environment a National Security Issue?' *International Security* 20(2) (Fall): 35–62.

Levy, Marc A. (1995) 'Time for a Third Wave of Environment and Security Scholarship?' *Environmental Change and Security Project Report*. Woodrow Wilson Center. 1 (Spring): 44–6.

Lichtenstein, Slovic, B. Fischhoff, M. Layman and B. Combs (1978) 'Judged Frequency of Lethal Events.' *Journal of Experimental Psychology: Human Learning and Memory* 4: 551–78.

Liftin, Karen (1993) 'Ecoregimes: Playing Tug of War with the Nation-State.' In *The State and Social Power in Global Environmental Politics*, edited by Ronnie D. Lipschutz and Ken Conca. New York: Columbia University Press, pp. 94–117.

Liftin, Karen T. (1994) *Ozone Discourses: Science and Politics in Global Environmental Cooperation*. New York: Columbia University Press.

Lindström, Per (1995) 'The Role of NGOs as Seen by the United Nations and Its Member States.' In *The Role of Non-Governmental Organizations in the New European Order*, edited by Jurgen Schramm. Germany: Nomos Verlagsgesellschaft, pp. 43–8.

Lipschutz, Ronnie D. and John P. Holdren (1990) 'Crossing Borders: Resource Flows, the Global Environment, and International Security.' *Bulletin of Peace Proposals* 21(2): 121–33.

List, Martin and Volker Rittberger (1992) 'Regime Theory and International Environmental Management.' In *The International Politics of the Environment*, edited by Andrew Hurrell and Benedict Kingsbury. Oxford: Clarendon Press, pp. 85–109.

Locke, Catherine, W. Neil Adger, and P. Mick Kelly (2000) 'Changing Places: Migration's Social and Environmental Consequences.' *Environment* 42(7) (September): 24–35.

Locke, Christopher (2001) 'Forest Pharmers Go Bioprospecting.' *Red Herring* (12 April) http://www.redherringcom/index/asp?/layout+story&doc_id=175001897&channel+10000001. Date visited: 4 June 2001.

London Amendments to the Montreal Protocol (1990).

Lopes, Lola L. (1992) 'Risk Perception and the Perceived Public.' In *The Social Response to Environmental Risk*, edited by Daniel W. Bromley and Kathleen Segerson. Boston, Dordrecht, and London: Kluwer Academic Publishers, pp. 57–74.

Lovejoy, Thomas (1984) 'Aid Debtor Nation's Ecology.' *New York Times*, 4 October, p. 31.

Macnow, Alan (1984) 'A Whaling Moratorium Opposed by IWC's Own Scientists.' Letter to the Editor, *New York Times*, 29 September, p. 22.

Mahony, Rhona (1992) 'Debt-for-Nature Swaps: Who Really Benefits?' *The Ecologist* 22(3) (May-June): 97–102.

Makhijani, Arun and Kevin R. Gurney (1995) *Mending the Ozone Hole: Science, Technology, and Policy*. Cambridge, MA, and London: The MIT Press.

Mandel, Robert (1984) 'Transnational Resource Conflict: The Politics of Whaling.' *International Studies Quarterly* (March): 99–127.

Martin, Gene S. Jr., and James W. Brennan (1989) 'Enforcing the International Convention for the Regulation of Whaling: The Pelly and Packwood-Magnuson Amendments.' *Denver Journal of International Law and Policy* 17(2): 293–315.

Mathews, Jessica Tuchman (1989) 'Redefining Security.' *Foreign Affairs* 68(2) (Spring): 162–77.

Matthew, Richard A. (1999) 'Scarcity and Security: A Common-Pool Resource Perspective.' In *Anarchy and the Environment: The International Relations of Common Pool Resources*, edited by J. Samuel Barkin and George E. Shambaugh. Albany, NY: SUNY Press, pp. 155–75.

McCleary, Rachel (1990) 'Development Strategies in Conflict: Brazil and the Future of the Amazon.' *Pew Case Studies in International Affairs*. Washington, DC: Carnegie Council on Ethics and International Affairs.

McCormick, John (1997) *Acid Earth: The Politics of Acid Pollution*. 3rd ed. London: Earthscan Publications.

McCormick, John (1999) 'The Role of Environmental NGOs in International Regimes.' In *The Global Environment: Institutions, Law, and Policy*, edited by Norman J. Vig and Regina S. Axelrod. Washington, DC: CQ Press, pp. 52–71.

McDermott, Rose (1998) *Risk-Taking in International Politics: Prospect Theory in American Foreign Policy*. Ann Arbor: University of Michigan Press.

Mclaughlin, Daniel (2000) 'Whaling Watchdog Aims to Regain Control over Seas.' *Reuters, Planet Ark*, 13 June.

Michaels, Patrick (1993) 'Environmental Rules Should Be Based on Science.' *Insight on the News*, 12 April, p. 21–2.

Miles, Edward L., Arild Underdal, Steinar Andresen, Jørgen Wettestad, Jon Birger Skjaerseth, and Elaine M. Carlin (2001) *Explaining Regime Effectiveness: Confronting Theory with Evidence*. Cambridge, MA: MIT Press.

Miller, Alan S. (1989) 'Incentives for CFC Substitutes: Lessons for Other Greenhouse Gases.' In *Coping with Climate Change: Proceedings of the Second North American Conference on Preparing for Climate Change*, edited by John C. Topping. Washington, DC: Climate Institute.

Mintzer, Irving M. and J. Amber Leonard (1994) *Negotiating Climate Change*. Cambridge: Cambridge University Press.

Mitchell, Ronald (1992) 'Membership, Compliance, and Non-Compliance in the International Convention for the Regulation of Whaling 1946–Present.' Paper for presentation at Harvard University, International Environmental Institutions Research Seminar, October. Cited with permission.

Mitchell, Ronald (1994) *Intentional Oil Pollution at Sea: Environmental Policies and Treaty Compliance*. Cambridge, MA: MIT Press.

Mitrić, Joan McQueeny (2000) 'Who's Going to Clean up Serbia?' *Washington Post*, 9 July, p. B1.

Molina, M. J. and F. S. Rowland (1974) 'Stratospheric Sink for Chlorofluoromethanes: Chlorine Atom-catalyzed Destruction of Ozone.' *Nature* 249: 810–12.

Montreal Protocol (as amended) (1997).

Montzka, S. A., J. H. Butler, J. W. Elkins, T. M. Thompson, A. D. Clarke, and L. T. Locke (1999) 'Present and Future Trends in the Atmospheric Burden on Ozone-depleting Halogens.' *Nature* 398 (22 April): 690–3.

Moran, Katy (1996) 'Compensating Forest-dwelling Communities for Drug Discovery: The World of the Healing Forest Conservancy.' *Unasylva* 47: 42.

Morgenthau, Hans J. (1967) *Politics Among Nations: The Struggle for Power and Peace*. 4th ed. New York: Alfred A. Knopf.

Morris, Jim (1996) 'Lost at Sea: Accident Underscores Potential Hazards of Foreign Vessels.' *Houston Chronicle*, 16 December, p. 12.

Munton, Don (1997) 'Acid Rain and Transboundary Air Quality in Canadian–American Relations.' *American Review of Canadian Studies* (Autumn): 327–55.

Murphy, Laura, Richard Bilsborrow and Francisco Pichon (1997) 'Poverty and Prosperity Among Migrant Settlers in the Amazon Rainforest Frontier of Ecuador.' *Journal of Development Studies* 34(2)(December): 35–66.

Myers, Norman (1987) 'Linking Environment and Security.' *Bulletin of the Atomic Scientists* 43 (June): 46–7.

Myers, Norman (1992) 'The Anatomy of Environmental Action: The Case of Tropical Deforestation.' In *The International Politics of the Environment: Actors, Interests, and Institutions*, edited by Andrew Hurrell and Benedict Kingsbury. Oxford: Clarendon Press.

Myers, Norman (1993) *Ultimate Security: The Environmental Basis of Political Stability*. New York and London: WW Norton & Company.

Myers, Norman, Russell A. Mittermeier, Cristina G., Da Foseca, A. B. Gustavo, and Jennifer Kent (2000) 'Biodiversity Hotspots for Conservation Priorities.' *Nature* 403 (24 February): 853–8.

Na, Seong-lin and Hyun Song Shin (1998) 'International Environmental Agreements Under Uncertainty.' *Oxford Economic Papers* 50(2) (April): 173–85.

Neto, Ricardo Bonalume (1993) 'MIT's Amazon Outpost.' *Nature* 365(6442) (9 September): 101.

'New Era for the IWC.' (1991) *Greenpeace Magazine*. (October–November–December): 5.

Odén, Svante (1968) 'The Acidification of Air and Precipitation and Its Consequences in the Natural Environment.' *Ecology Committee Bulletin*. Stockholm: Swedish National Research Council.

Offe, Claus (1984) *Contradictions of the Welfare State*, edited by John Keane. Cambridge, MA: MIT Press.

Olson, Mancur, Jr. (1965) *The Logic of Collective Action: Public Goods and the Theory of Groups*. Cambridge, MA: Harvard University Press.

Organization for Economic Cooperation and Development (1977) *The OECD*

Programme on Long-Range Transport of Air Pollutants: Summary Report. Paris: OECD.

Organization for Economic Cooperation and Development (1985) *Environmental Policy and Technical Change*. Paris: OECD.

Oye, Kenneth A. (1986) 'Explaining Cooperation Under Anarchy: Hypotheses and Strategies.' In *Cooperation Under Anarchy*, edited by Kenneth A. Oye. Princeton: Princeton University Press, pp. 18–20.

Oye, Kenneth and James H. Maxwell (1995) 'Self-Interest and Environmental Management.' In *Local Commons and Global Interdependence: Heterogeneity and Cooperation in Two Domains*, edited by Robert O. Keohane and Elinor Ostrom. Newbury Park, CA: Sage, pp. 191–221.

'Ozone Depletion at Record Level, UN Agency Says' (2000) *Reuters News Service*, 9 October.

Ozone Secretariat (1993) *Handbook for the Montreal Protocol on Substances That Deplete the Ozone Layer*. 3rd ed. Nairobi: United Nations Environment Program.

Ozone Secretariat (n.d.) 'Press Backgrounder.' http://www.unep.org.ozone/ PressBack. Date visited: 19 June 2001.

Page, Diana (1989) 'Debt-for-Nature Swaps: Experience Gained, Lessons Learned.' *International Environmental Affairs* 1(4): 275–89.

Palmer, Geoffrey (1992) 'New Ways to Make International Environmental Law.' *American Journal of International Law* 86 (April): 274–6.

'Panama Increases Lead as Merchant Fleet Reaches Record Tonnage' (n.d.) *Lloyds Register News Release* http://www.lr.org/news/pr/41wfs.html. Date visited: 21 July 1998.

Parson, Edward A. (1993) 'Protecting the Ozone Layer.' In *Institutions for the Earth*, edited by Peter M. Haas, Robert O. Keohane, and Marc A. Levy. Cambridge, MA: MIT Press.

Paskett, Curtis J. (1998) 'Refugees and Land Use: The Need for Change in a Growing Problem.' *Journal of Soil and Water Conservation* 53(1) (Spring): 57–8.

Paterson, Matthew (1996) *Global Warming and Global Politics*. London and New York: Routledge.

Paterson, Matthew (2000) *Understanding Global Environmental Politics: Domination, Accumulation, Resistance*. London: Macmillan.

Payne, Rodger A. (1996) 'Nonprofit Environmental Organizations in World Politics: Domestic Structure and Transnational Relations.' *Policy Studies Review* 14(1–2) (Spring-Summer): 171–82.

Pearce, Fred (2000) 'A Cool Trick.' *New Scientist* 8 (April): 18.

Pearson, Charles S. (1985) *Down to Business: Multinational Corporations, the Environment, and Development*. Washington, DC: World Resources Institute.

Pepall, Jennifer (1998) 'Putting a Price on Indigenous Knowledge.' International Development Research Centre. 7 July. http://www.idrc.ca/books/reports/1996/ 30-01e.html. Date visited: 4 June 2001.

Percival, Val, and Thomas F. Homer-Dixon (1998) 'Environmental Scarcity and Violent Conflict: The Case of South Africa.' *Journal of Peace Research* 35(3) (May): 279–98.

Peterson, M. J. (1992) 'Whalers, Cetologists, Environmentalists, and the International Management of Whaling.' *International Organization* 46(1) (Winter): 147–86.

Porter, Michael E. (1990) *The Competitive Advantage of Nations*. New York: Free Press.

Porter, Michael E. (1991) 'America's Green Strategy.' *Scientific American* 264(4) (April): 168.

Potter, David (ed.) (1996) *NGOs and Environmental Policies: Asia and Africa*. London and Portland, Oregon: Frank Cass.

Potter, David (1996) 'Democratisation and the Environment: NGOs and Deforestation Policies in India (Karnataka) and Indonesia (North Sumatra).' In *NGOs and Environmental Policies: Asia and Africa*, edited by David Potter. London and Portland, Oregon: Frank Cass, pp. 9–38.

Price, Marie (1994) 'Ecopolitics and Environmental Nongovernmental Organizations in Latin America.' *The Geographical Review* 84(1) (January): 42–58.

Princen, Thomas and Matthias Finger (1994) 'Introduction,' in Thomas Princen and Matthias Finger, *Environmental NGOs in World Politics: Linking the Local and the Global*. New York: Routledge, pp. 1–25.

Protocol to LRTAP Concerning the Control of Emissions of Nitrogen Oxides or their Transboundary Fluxes (1988).

Protocol to LRTAP Concerning the Control of Emissions of Volatile Organic Compounds or Their Transboundary Fluxes (1991).

Protocol to LRTAP on Further Reductions of Sulphur Emissions (1994).

Protocol to LRTAP on Heavy Metals (1998).

Protocol to LRTAP on Persistent Organic Pollutants (1998).

Raustiala, Kal (1997) 'States, NGOs, and International Environmental Institutions.' *International Studies Quarterly* 41: 719–40.

Raven, Peter H. and Jeffrey A. McNeely (1998) 'Biological Extinction: Its Scope and Meaning for Us.' In *Protection of Global Biodiversity: Converging Strategies*, edited by Lakshman D. Guruswamy and Jeffrey A. McNeely. Durham, NC: Duke University Press, pp. 13–32.

Rawls, John (1971) *A Theory of Justice*. Cambridge, MA: Bellknap Press of Harvard University Press.

Reaney, Patricia (2000) 'Deep Ocean Current Linked to Global Climate Change.' *Reuters News Service*, 3 August.

Renner, Michael (1997) 'Transforming Security.' In *State of the World 1997*, edited by Lester R. Brown *et al.* New York and London: WW Norton and Company, pp. 115–31.

Renner, Michael (1989) 'National Security: The Economic and Environmental Dimensions.' *Worldwatch Paper 89*. Washington, DC: Worldwatch Institute.

Renner, Michael (1991) 'Assessing the Military's War on the Environment.' In *The State of the World 1991*, edited by Lester R. Brown *et al.* New York and London: WW Norton & Company, pp. 132–52.

Richardson, Tim, Jiri Dusik, and Pavla Jindrova (1998) 'Parallel Public Participation: An Answer to Inertia in Decision-Making.' *Environmental Impact*

Assessment Review 18: 201–16.

Ridgeway, Collette (1996) 'Privately Protected Places.' *Cato Policy Report* 18(2) (March–April). http://www.cato.org/pubs/policy_report/pr-xviii2-ridge-way.html. Date visited: 24 August 2000.

Rifkin, Jeremy (1991) *Biosphere Politics*. New York: Crown Publishers, Inc.

Rio Declaration on Environment and Development (1992).

Ripley, Randall B. and Grace A. Franklin (1980) *Congress, the Bureaucracy, and Public Policy*, revised edition. Homewood, IL: The Dorsey Press.

Risse-Kappan, Thomas (1994) 'Ideas Do Not Float Freely: Transnational Coalitions, Domestic Structures, and the End of the Cold War.' *International Organization* 48(2) (Spring): 185–214.

Rittberger, Volker and Michael Zürn (1991) 'Regime Theory: Findings from the Study of "East–West" Regimes.' *Cooperation and Conflict* 26: 171–2.

Rome, Abigail (1999) 'Amazon Adventure.' *E* 10(2)(March): 48.

Rosen, Yereth (1992) 'USSR Leaves Radioactive Legacy.' *Christian Science Monitor*, 26 August, p. 8 .

Rowlands, Ian H. (1995) *The Politics of Global Atmospheric Change*. Manchester and London: Manchester University Press.

Saab, Saleem S. (1998) 'Move over Drugs, There's Something Cooler on the Black Market – Freon.' *Dickenson Journal of International Law* 16 (Spring): 634.

Sands, P. J. (1991) 'The Role of Non-Governmental Organizations in Enforcing International Environmental Law.' In *Control over Compliance with International Obligations*, edited by William E. Butler. Dordrecht: Martinus Nijhoff Publishers.

Sands, Philippe (1995) *Principles of International Environmental Law*, vol. 1. Manchester and New York: Manchester University Press.

Sarkar, Amin U. (1994) 'Debt Relief for Environment: Experience and Issues.' *Journal of Environment and Development* 3(1) (Summer): 123–36.

Schmandt, Jurgen, Hilliard Roderick, and Judith Clarkson (1988) 'Introduction to Part One.' In *Acid Rain and Friendly Neighbors: The Policy Dispute Between Canada and the United States*. Revised edition, edited by Jurgen Schmandt, Judith Clarkson, and Hilliard Roderick. Durham, NC: Duke University Press, pp. 3–6.

Schmandt, Jurgen, Hilliard Roderick, and Andrew Morriss (1988) 'Acid Rain Is Different.' In *Acid Rain and Friendly Neighbors: The Policy Dispute Between Canada and the United States*. Revised edition, edited by Jurgen Schmandt, Judith Clarkson, and Hilliard Roderick. Durham, NC: Duke University Press, pp. 7–30.

Schmidheiny, Stephan and Federico J.L. Zorraquín (1996) *Financing Change: The Financial Community, Eco-Efficiency, and Sustainable Development*. Cambridge, MA: MIT Press.

Schneider, Greg (2001) 'Taking No Chances: Disaster-conscious Firms Treat Global Warming as a Reality.' *Washington Post*, 26 June, p. E01.

Schrijver, Nico (1997) *Sovereignty over Natural Resources: Balancing Rights and Duties*. Cambridge: Cambridge University Press.

Sebenius, James K. (1992) 'Challenging Conventional Explanations of International Cooperation: Negotiation Analysis and the Case of Epistemic Communities.' *International Organization* 46(1): 323–65.

Secretariat of the Multilateral Fund. 'General Information.' http://www.unmfs.org/genera.htm. Date visited: 5 June 2001.

Sevilla, Roque (1990) 'Banks, Debt, and Development – II.' *International Environmental Affairs* 2(2): 150–2.

Shaman Botanicals (2000) 'Shaman: About Us.' http://www.shamanbotanicals.com/aumaster.htm. Date visited: 2 June 2001.

Shaman Pharmaceuticals, Inc. (2001) *Quarterly Report* (SEC form 10-Q). 15 May.

Shaw, Martin (1992) 'Global Society and Global Responsibility: The Theoretical, Historical, and Political Limits of "International Society".' *Millennium* 21(3): 421–34.

Shaw, Roderick W. (1993) 'Acid Rain Negotiations in North America and Europe: A Study in Contrast.' In *International Environmental Negotiations*, edited by Gunnar Sjöstedt. Newbury Park, CA: Sage Publications, pp. 84–109.

Sheff, David (1997) 'The Chilling Effect.' *Outdoor Magazine* (August): 91.

'Shell to Provide Solar Power for Chinese Homes' (2001) *Reuters News Service*, 3 July.

Sherman, K. (1992) 'Large Marine Ecosystems.' In *Encyclopedia of Earth System Science*, vol. 2. New York: Academic Press, pp. 653–73.

Shoumatoff, Alex (1990) *The World Is Burning*. Boston: Little, Brown & Company.

Simpson, R. David (1999) 'The Price of Biodiversity.' *Issues in Science and Technology* 15(3): 65–70.

'Sinking CO' (2001) *Environment* 43(2) (March): 6.

Sinnar, Shirin (1995–6) 'Mixed Blessing: The Growing Influence of NGOs,' *Harvard International Review* (Winter) 54ff.

Slovic, Paul (1991) 'Beyond Numbers: A Broader Perspective on Risk Perception and Risk Communication.' In *Acceptable Evidence: Science and Values in Risk Management*, edited by Deborah G. Mayo and Rachelle D. Hollander. New York and Oxford: Oxford University Press, pp. 48–65.

Slovic, Paul, Baruch Fischhoff, and Sarah Lichtenstein (1979) 'Rating the Risks.' *Environment* 21(3) (April): 14–20, 36–9.

Smart, Bruce (1992) *Beyond Compliance: A New Industry View of the Environment*. Washington, DC: World Resources Institute.

Snidal, Duncan (1985) 'The Limits of Hegemonic Stability Theory.' *International Organization* 30(4): 579–615.

Snidal, Duncan (1995) 'The Politics of Scope: Endogenous Actors, Heterogeneity, and Institutions.' In *Local Commons and Global Interdependence*, edited by Robert O. Keohane and Elinor Ostrom. London: Sage.

Soroos, Marvin S. (1991) 'The Atmosphere as an International Common Property Resource.' In *Global Policy Studies*, edited by S. S. Nagel. London: Macmillan.

Soroos, Marvin S. (1994) 'Global Change, Environmental Security, and the Prisoner's Dilemma.' *Journal of Peace Research* 31(3): 317–32.

Southgate, Douglas (1997) *Alternatives for Habitat Protection and Rural Income*

Generation. Washington, DC: Inter-American Development Bank.

Spencer, Leslie (1991) 'The Not So Peaceful World of Greenpeace.' *Forbes*, 11 November, p. 174ff.

Spiro, Peter J. (1994) 'New Global Communities: Nongovernmental Organizations in International Decision-making Institutions.' *Washington Quarterly* 18(1): 45–56.

Sprinz, Detlef and Tapani Vaahtoranta (1994) 'The Interest-based Explanation of International Environmental Policy.' *International Organization* 41(1) (Winter): 77–105.

Stein, Arthur A. (1982) 'Coordination and Collaboration: Regimes in an Anarchic World.' In *International Regimes*, edited by Stephen D. Krasner. Ithaca, NY, and London: Cornell University Press, pp. 115–40.

Stewart, Robert B. (1988) 'Negotiations on Acid Rain.' In *Acid Rain and Friendly Neighbors: The Policy Dispute Between Canada and the United States*, revised edition, edited by Jurgen Schmandt, Judith Clarkson, and Hilliard Roderick. Durham, NC: Duke University Press, pp. 64–82.

Stoett, Peter J. (1995) *Atoms, Whales, and Rivers: Global Environmental Security and International Organization*. New York: Nova Science Publishers.

Susskind, Lawrence E. (1994) *Environmental Diplomacy: Negotiating More Effective Global Agreements*. New York and Oxford: Oxford University Press.

Territo, Michele (2000) 'Note and Comment: The Precautionary Principle in Marine Fisheries Conservation and the US Sustainable Fisheries Act of 1996.' *Vermont Law Review* 24 (Summer): 1351ff.

Tesh, Sylvia Noble (2000) *Uncertain Hazards: Environmental Activists and Scientific Proof*. Ithaca, NY, and London: Cornell University Press.

'Texaco Quits Anti-Kyoto Climate Change Group' (2001) *Reuters News Service*, 2 March.

Thapa, Brijesh (1998) 'Debt-for-Nature Swaps: An Overview.' *International Journal of Sustainable Development and World Ecology* 5(4): 249–62.

Thomas, Alan (1996) 'NGO Advocacy, Democracy, and Policy Development.' In *NGOs and Environmental Policies: Asia and Africa*, edited by David Potter. Portland, OR: Frank Cass, pp. 38–65.

Thomas, Caroline and Darryl Howlett (1993) 'The Freshwater Issue in International Relations.' In *Resource Politics: Freshwater and Regional Relations*, edited by Caroline Thomas and Darryl Howlett. Buckingham: Open University Press, pp. 9–11.

Tolba, Mostafa Kamal (1994) 'Middle East Water Issues: Action and Political Will.' In *International Waters of the Middle East*, edited by Asit K. Biswas. Oxford: Oxford University Press, pp. 1–4.

Tønnessen, J. N. and A. O. Johnsen (1982) *The History of Modern Whaling*. Berkeley: University of California Press.

Touraine, Alain (1988) *Return of the Actor: Social Theory in Postindustrial Society*. Minneapolis: University of Minnesota Press.

Tufts Climate Initiative (n.d.) 'Who We Are,' http://www.tufts.edu/tie/tci/WhoWeAre.html (date visited: 4 July 2001).

Tversky, Amos and Daniel Kahneman (1982) 'Judgments of and by Representativeness.' In *Judgment Under Uncertainty: Heuristics and Biases*, edited by Daniel Kahneman, Paul Slovic, and Amos Tversky. Cambridge: Cambridge University Press, pp. 84–98.

Tversky, Amos and Daniel Kahneman (1991) 'Loss Aversion in Riskless Choice.' *Quarterly Journal of Economics* 106(4) (November): 1039–61.

Ullman, Richard H. (1983) 'Redefining Security.' *International Security* 8(1) (Summer): 129–53.

Underdal, Arild (1997) 'Patterns of Effectiveness: Examining Evidence from Thirteen International Regimes.' Paper presented at the International Studies Association Annual Convention, Toronto, March.

Union of International Associations (1993) *The Yearbook of International Organizations 1993–4*. Vol. 1. Munich: K. S. Saur.

United Nations Environment Programme (1994) 'Partnerships for Sustainable Development: The Role of Business and Industry.' London: Flashprint Enterprises, for UNEP and the Prince of Wales Business Leaders Forum.

United States General Accounting Office (1988) 'Water Pollution: Stronger Enforcement Needed to Improve Compliance at Federal Facilities.' Washington, DC: GAO. GAO/RCED-89-144.

Van Beers, Cees and J. C. J. M. van der Bergh (1999) 'An Empirical Multi-Country Analysis of the Impact of Environmental Regulations on Foreign Trade Flows.' *Kyklos* 50(1): 29–46.

VanderZwaag, David (1999) 'The Precautionary Principle in Environmental Law and Policy: Elusive Rhetoric and First Embrace,' *Journal of Environmental Law and Practice* 8(3) (October): 355–75.

Victor, David G. (1998) ' "Learning by Doing" in the Nonbinding International Regime to Manage Trade in Hazardous Chemicals and Pesticides.' In *The Implementation and Effectiveness of International Environmental Commitments*, edited by David G. Victor, Kal Raustiala, and Eugene B. Skolnikoff. Cambridge, MA: MIT Press, pp. 221–81.

Victor, David G. (1998) 'The Montreal Protocol's Non-Compliance Procedure.' In *The Implementation and Effectiveness of International Environmental Commitments*, edited by David G. Victor, Kal Raustiala, and Eugene B. Skolnikoff. Cambridge, MA: MIT Press, p. 147.

Victor, David G. (1998) 'The Operation and Effectiveness of the Montreal Protocol's Non-Compliance Procedure.' In *The Implementation and Effectiveness of International Environmental Commitments*, edited by David G. Victor, Kal Raustiala, and Eugene B. Skolnikoff. Cambridge, MA: MIT Press, pp. 137–76.

Victor, David G. (2001) *The Collapse of the Kyoto Protocol and the Struggle to Slow Global Warming*. Princeton: Princeton University Press.

Victor, David, Kal Raustiala, and Eugene B. Skolnikoff (1998) *The Implementation and Effectiveness of International Environmental Commitments*. Cambridge, MA: MIT Press.

Vidal, John (1995) 'As the World Runs Dry ... Next, Wars over Water?' *World Press Review* 42(11) (November): 8ff.

Vienna Convention for the Protection of the Ozone Layer (1985).

Vogel, David (1993) 'Representing Diffuse Interests in Environmental Policy-making.' In *Do Institutions Matter? Government Capabilities in the United States and Abroad*, edited by David Vogel. Washington, DC: The Brookings Institution, pp. 237–71.

Vogel, Joseph Henry (1996) *The Successful Use of Economic Instruments to Foster Sustainable Use of Biodiversity*. Quito: Facultad Latinoamericana de Ciencias Sociales.

Von Neumann, John and Oskar Morgenstern (1947) *Theory of Games and Economic Behavior*, 2nd ed. Princeton: Princeton University Press.

Waltz, Kenneth N. (1959) *Man, the State, and War: A Theoretical Analysis*. New York: Columbia University Press.

Wapner, Paul (1995) 'Politics Beyond the State: Environmental Activism and World Civic Politics.' *World Politics* 47(3) (April): 311–40.

Wapner, Paul (1996) *Environmental Activism and World Civic Politics*. Albany, NY: SUNY Press.

Wapner, Paul (1998) 'Reorienting State Sovereignty: Rights and Responsibilities in the Environmental Age.' In *The Greening of Sovereignty in World Politics*, edited by Karen T. Liftin. Cambridge, MA: MIT Press, pp. 275–97.

Warrick, Joby (1998) 'Kyoto Pact Includes a Pentagon Exemption; Armed Forces Permitted to Pollute During Some Overseas Missions.' *Washington Post*, 1 January, p. A10.

Watson, Robert T., F. Sherwood Rowland, and John Gille (1988) *Ozone Trends Panel: Executive Summary*. Washington, DC: NASA.

Watson, S. (1994) 'Are Licensing Agreements Key to Technology Transfer?' *Legal Intelligencer*, 14 June, p. 13ff.

Webb, Jason (1998) 'Scientists Clearing up Clouds' Effects on Climate.' *Reuters News Service*, 10 November.

Weiss, Edith Brown (1998) 'The Five International Treaties: A Living History.' In *Engaging Countries: Strengthening Compliance with International Environmental Accords*, edited by Edith Brown Weiss and Harold K. Jacobson. Cambridge, MA: MIT Press.

Wendt, Alexander (1999) *Social Theory of International Politics*. Cambridge: Cambridge University Press.

Westing, Arthur H. (1984) 'Environmental Warfare: An Overview.' In *Environmental Warfare: A Technical, Legal, and Policy Appraisal*, edited by Arthur H. Westing. Philadelphia and London: Taylor & Francis, pp. 3–12.

Wetstone, Gregory S. and Armin Rosencranz (1983) *Acid Rain in Europe and North America: National Responses to an International Problem: A Study for the German Marshall Fund of the United States*. Washington, DC: The Environmental Law Institute.

Whelan, Tensie (1991) 'Ecotourism and Its Role in Sustainable Development.' In *Nature Tourism: Managing for the Environment*, edited by Tensie Whelan. Washington, DC: Island Press, pp. 3–22.

White, Robert M. (1993) 'Introduction: Environmental Regulation and Changing

Science and Technology.' In *Keeping Pace with Science and Engineering: Case Studies in Environmental Regulation*, edited by Myron F. Uman. Washington, DC: National Academy Press, pp. 1–7.

Wiener, Jonathan Baert (1999) 'On the Political Economy of Global Regulation.' *Georgetown Law Journal* 87 (February): 749–94.

Willetts, Peter (ed.) (1996) *The Conscience of the World: The Influence of Non-Governmental Organisations in the UN System*. Washington, DC: The Brookings Institution.

Williams, Wendy (2000) 'Toxins on the Firing Range.' *Scientific American* 282(6) (June): 18–19.

Wood, Megan Epler (1991) 'Global Solutions: An Ecotourism Society.' In *Nature Tourism: Managing for the Environment*, edited by Tensie Whelan. Washington, DC: Island Press, pp. 200–6.

World Resources Institute (1992) *World Resources: A Report by the World Resources Institute and the International Institute for Environment and Development 1992–1993*. New York: Basic Books.

'Worldview – Whaling: Soviet Kills Could Affect Sanctuary Decision.' (1994) *Greenwire*, 22 February.

Yohe, Gary W. (1979) 'The Backward Incidence of Pollution Control – Some Comparative Statics in General Equilibrium.' *Journal of Environmental Economics and Management* 6: 187–98.

Young, Oran R. (1989) 'Science and Social Institutions: Lessons for International Resource Regimes.' In *International Resource Management: The Role of Science and Politics*, edited by Steinar Andresen and Willy Ostreng. London and New York: Bellhaven Press, pp. 7–24.

Young, Oran R. (1999) *Governance in World Affairs*. Ithaca, NY: Cornell University Press.

Young, Oran R. and Marc A. Levy (with the assistance of Gail Osherenko) (1999) 'The Effectiveness of International Environmental Regimes.' In *The Effectiveness of International Environmental Regimes*, edited by Oran R. Young. Cambridge, MA: MIT Press, pp. 1–24.

Zebich-Knos, Michele (1997) 'Preserving Biodiversity in Costa Rica: The Case of the Merck-INBio Agreement.' *Journal of Environment and Development* 6(2) (June): 180–6.

Zimmerman, William, Elena Nikitina, and James Clem (1998) 'The Soviet Union and the Russian Federation: A Natural Experiment in Environmental Compliance.' In *Engaging Countries: Strengthening Compliance with International Environmental Accords*, edited by Edith Brown Weiss and Harold K. Jacobson. Cambridge, MA: MIT Press.

INDEX